Evolution of
United States Budgeting

Evolution of United States Budgeting

Revised and Expanded Edition

Annette E. Meyer

Westport, Connecticut
London

HJ
2051
.M49
2002

Library of Congress Cataloging-in-Publication Data

Meyer, Annette E.
    Evolution of United States budgeting / Annette E. Meyer—Rev. and expanded ed.
        p.   cm.
    Previously published: New York : Greenwood Press, 1989.
    Includes bibliographical references and index.
    ISBN 0–275–96861–8 (alk. paper)—ISBN 0–275–97526–6 (pbk. : alk. paper)
    1. Budget—United States.   I. Title.
  HJ2051.M49   2002
  352.4'8'0973—dc21   2001036305

British Library Cataloguing in Publication Data is available.

Library of Congress Catalog Card Number: 2001036305
ISBN: 0–275–96861–8
       0–275–97526–6 (pbk.)

First published in 2002

Praeger Publishers, 88 Post Road West, Westport, CT 06881
An imprint of Greenwood Publishing Group, Inc.
www.praeger.com

Printed in the United States of America

 2/24/03 JT

The paper used in this book complies with the
Permanent Paper Standard issued by the National
Information Standards Organization (Z39.48–1984).

10 9 8 7 6 5 4 3 2 1

2/26/03 LK

Contents

Tables

Acronyms

ACB	Agricultural Credit Bank
ACH	Automated Clearing House System
AEA	American Economics Association
AFDC	Aid to Families with Dependent Children
AICPA	American Institute of Certified Public Accountants
BEA	Budget Enforcement Act
BPD	Bureau of the Public Debt
BRD	Budget Review Division
CBA	Congressional Budget Act
CBMS	Central Budget Management System
CBO	Congressional Budget Office
CEA	Council of Economic Advisers
CED	Committee for Economic Development
CFO	Chief Financial Officers
CPI	Consumer Price Index
DI	Disability Insurance
ECB	European Central Bank
EMU	European Economic and Monetary Union
EOP	Executive Office of the President
EPA	Environmental Protection Agency
EU	European Union

FAMC	Federal Agricultural Mortgage Corporation
FASAB	Federal Accounting Standards Advisory Board
FCB	Farm Credit Banks
FCS	Farm Credit System
FDIC	Federal Deposit Insurance Corporation
FFB	Federal Financing Bank
FHA	Federal Housing Administration
FHLB	Federal Home Loan Banks
FHLMC	Federal Home Loan Mortgage Company
FNMA	Federal National Mortgage Association
FRB	Federal Reserve Board
FRS	Federal Reserve System
FY	fiscal year
GAAP	generally accepted accounting principles
GAO	General Accounting Office
GDP	gross domestic product
GNP	gross national product
G-R-H	Gramm-Rudman-Hollings Act
GSEs	Government Sponsored Enterprises
HHS	Health and Human Services
HUD	Department of Housing and Urban Development
IMF	International Monetary Fund
IRS	Internal Revenue Service
MBSs	Mortgage-backed Securities
NBER	National Bureau of Economic Research
NIPA	National Income and Product Accounts
NPR	National Performance Review
OASI	Old Age Survivors Insurance
OECD	Organization for Economic Cooperation and Development
OMB	Office of Management and Budget
OPEC	Organization of Petroleum Exporting Countries
PAYGO	pay-as-you-go
SEC	Securities and Exchange Commission
SLMA	Student Loan Marketing Association
SNA	System of National Accounts

SSA	Social Security Administration
SSI	Supplemental Security Income
USDA	U.S. Department of Agriculture
VA	Veterans Administration
WTO	World Trade Organization

Introduction

More than any other single document, the federal budget reflects the national objectives, and the priorities for them assigned by the citizens of the United States. It places dollar signs before numbers that add up to trillions for items ranging from national defense, to Head Start, to the federal debt. Many individuals are involved in the determination of the figures in both the legislative and executive branches of government but, fundamentally, the document should express the will of the people. To make that possible, citizens, as taxpayers, should be able to have access to the budget, should be able to understand its overall means and goals, and, through the voting process or otherwise, should be able to contribute to setting the priorities for its composition.

This book is dedicated to working toward an improved and a more comprehensive budget than the present one. In the years since the first edition of *Evolution of United States Budgeting* (1989) there have been major changes in the structure and the process of budgeting. The present work covers entirely new ground in many aspects of domestic and international fiscal and financial policy. Part I, "Foundations of U.S. Budget Policies," provides information on practical and ideal considerations for government expenditures and taxes in Chapter 1, and for debt, money, and credit in Chapter 2. Part II, "An Overview of the Budget Process," presents the three phases of the annual budget cycle, from the making of the executive budget in Chapter 3, to congressional decision making on the president's proposal in Chapter 4, to the actual spending and control measures in Chapter 5. The budget contents, its format, financing, and general trends in government expenditures and taxes over time are discussed and tabled in Part III, "Budget Content and Presentation." Special topics appear in Part IV, "Budget Reporting and Control," which include some vital issues with respect to spending limits, capital budgeting, Social Security, and the Government Sponsored Enterprises (GSEs). In Part V, "The U.S. Budget in an International Setting," Chapter 11 deals with international finance and the huge global financial markets, including their recent crises. Chapter 12 contains a medley of topics pertinent to private and public purposes. The major reasons why individuals require national and supranational government are specified, along with examination of the subjects of information technology, voting procedures, and world trade. The Epilogue, "Mega-economics and the Federal Budget," would place the United States' budget within the context of the world.

Part I

Foundations of U.S. Budget Policies

Chapter 1

Fiscal Institutions and Concepts

The constitutional origins of fiscal policy—government spending, taxing, and debt management—are contained in Article I, sections 8–10. The Sixteenth Amendment provided for the present income tax, and subsequent statutes built a complex body of rules, exceptions, and limitations for both the spending and taxing sides of the national budget. This chapter commences with background information on spending and economic policy. The following sections describe the types of spending, debt management, and the degree of success of the automatic stabilizers in achieving short-run stability. The final sections on spending deal with the use of spending caps, or limitations on spending and the recent revival of interest in fiscal federalism. In the second part of the chapter, taxation in its various forms is the theme, along with the manner in which it harmonizes with economic policy. The chapter closes with economists' recommendations for attaining optimal taxation including efficiency and equity in the U.S. system.

SPENDING AND ECONOMIC POLICY

In the introduction to Book IV, "Of Systems of Political Oeconomy," of *An Inquiry into the Nature and Causes of the Wealth of Nations* by Adam Smith, he begins:

Political oeconomy, considered as a branch of the science of a statesman or legislator, proposes two distinct objects: first to provide a plentiful revenue or subsistence for the people, or more properly to enable them to care for themselves; and secondly, to supply the state or commonwealth with a revenue sufficient for the public services. It proposes to enrich both the people and the sovereign. (Smith 1776/1976: 449)

At the first government business meeting on 27 June 1921, after the passage of the Budget and Accounting Act of 1921, President Warren G. Harding expressed his determination to have economy and efficiency in governmental administration. The Director of the Budget, Charles G. Dawes, added that he would not only prepare the budget, but would attempt to reduce expenditures out of monies appropriated by the Congress for fiscal year (FY) 1922. He stressed that congressional appropriations were "ceilings and every effort would be made to spend less than the maximum specified" (Meyer 1978: 12).

World War II and its aftermath changed the budget outlook as new legislation changed the focus of congressional concerns for the national economy. Herbert Stein discusses the planning for peacetime prosperity after World War II in his work, *Presidential Economics* (1994). He mentions several interest groups working toward the same goal, including the Twentieth Century Fund, the American Economic Association (AEA), and the Committee for Economic Development (CED). There were three macroeconomic developments that consolidated the general consensus on the major issues involved, according to Stein.

The first was the Employment Act of 1946, which had originally contained the term "full employment." It was removed to allow greater flexibility, and the bill referred to "maximum employment, production and purchasing power" instead. In addition, there were passages about controlling the rise in the level of the deficit that were deleted. Leon Keyserling mentions how both of these omissions were reinstated when the Full Employment and Balanced Growth Act of 1978, or the Humphrey-Hawkins Act, was enacted. It called for annual numerical goals for the reduction of unemployment, and established the aim of reducing the federal deficit and eventually achieving a balanced budget (Keyserling: 1979b: 2–5).

Although the 1946 Act was brief and most general in its coverage, it had lasting impact through its establishment of the Council of Economic Advisers in the executive branch of government. Keyserling was one of the first members and its second chairman after Edwin Nourse.

The second development, writes Stein, was an outgrowth of the Keynesian viewpoint of functional finance. Economists claimed that in order to attain full employment after defense expenditures had dropped, nondefense expenditures must rise to compensate for it. With the appropriate size deficit in the government's budget, full employment would be achieved.

After the war, continues Stein, the scenery shifted because monetary factors were working more strongly than had been anticipated by fiscal-minded Keynesian analysts. Households and businesses were anxious to spend on real assets after the wartime restrictions had been lifted. In 1947, the CED published a statement, "Taxes and the Budget: A Program for Stability in a Free Society," rejecting the theory of functional finance because of its large forecasting errors and its political bias that would lead to increased government spending and inflation. Functional finance, originally proposed by Abba Lerner, uses any policy instrument to maintain aggregate demand and prevent inflation or deflation, regardless of the state of the budget.

Furthermore, the CED renounced the budget-balancing concepts as being destabilizing because they call for tax increases in recession and tax cuts in prosperity periods. In their place, the statement recommended a policy of balancing the budget or running a small surplus in the budget at high employment. Thus, if the economy was below high employment, the budget would automatically attain a deficit, and if the economy was overheated a surplus would appear. In this manner, the economy would tend to stabilize itself. There were two additional provisions: (1) any new expenditures of continued duration should be matched with tax increases, and (2) if the CED balanced budget concept was not entirely successful in its goal, monetary policy should be used to correct the problem.

The last development, claims Stein, represents an awakening to the possibilities of monetary policy. Milton Friedman and Anna Schwartz' major work, *A Monetary History of the United States, 1867–1960* (1963), had not been published at this time. The Federal Reserve System (FRS), during World War II and up to the Korean War, had been maintaining the price of government securities by pegging interest rates (Stein 1994: 82–83). Therefore, it was not at liberty to use monetary policy to fight inflation. On the other hand, the Treasury did not want to give up the ability to finance the debt cheaply (Meulendyke 1989: 32). However, in March 1951, an "accord" was reached that permitted the Federal Reserve to follow an independent monetary policy. The Federal Open Market Committee (FOMC) no longer pegged interest rates after 1953, and developed open market operations (or buying and selling of government securities) as its primary tool of monetary policy. The operations involved contracting and expanding the money supply by changing the amount of reserve assets held by the banking system.

Herbert Stein suggests that in the 1960s there were four national economic problems to be considered:

1. A rising level of unemployment.

2. An increased concern about our 3 percent rate of economic growth as compared to faster growing nations such as France, Germany, and Japan.

3. A greater interest in social concerns including the environment and a leaning toward government action to determine the proper pattern of national output. John Kenneth Galbraith had said in *The Affluent Society* (1958) that the value system of the U.S. citizen had deteriorated. The book outsold Adam Smith's *An Inquiry into the Nature and Causes of the Wealth of Nations*. A disciple of Thorstein Veblen and the Institutionalist School of Economics, Galbraith recommended that government intervene to correct the social imbalance created by advertising and manipulation of consumer wants for new goods (Ekelund and Hébert 1990: 476).

4. A growing concern that the existence of poor people in the United States was a
   national problem.

The four economic problems enunciated by Stein had been present prior
to the 1960s. In the first edition of Paul A. Samuelson's *Economics: An
Introductory Analysis*, he closes the chapter on "Individual and Family
Income" by observing that

Among the most important economic problems is the continued growth of the
average level of real income. Equally important both for politics and economics is
the question of the degree to which income is unequally distributed around the
average. (Samuelson 1948: 84)

By writing this paragraph, Samuelson recognized growth of real income
and inequality in its growth as national concerns. In another chapter on
"Fiscal Policy and Full Employment Without Inflation," he argues that public spending and tax policies, or fiscal policy, should be used to minimize
the swings of the business cycle and to help maintain a progressively high
employment economy with relatively stable prices. However, the analysis
is modified by the statement at the beginning of the chapter, "The reader
is warned that the subject matter of this chapter is still in a controversial
stage" (Samuelson 1948: 409–410).

The third of Herbert Stein's national economic problems on the need for
government action to correct the observed value systems has, as its origin,
the more specific accusations of Thorstein Veblen in his *Theory of the
Leisure Class* (1899). He indicated, using the phrase "conspicuous consumption," that many consumers place value on items simply because they
are more expensive (Samuelson 1948: 476).

During the 1960s, the heaviest pressure was placed on the two goals of
increasing the rate of economic growth and achieving full employment.
Keynesian fiscal policy recommended the expansion of demand to reach
these goals. At first, the tool used was rapid growth of the money supply,
but then it shifted to the opposite: tighter money to raise interest rates in
order to attract capital from abroad and reduce the large deficit in the
balance of payments. The monetary policy was coupled with an expansionary fiscal policy in the form of greater government expenditures. In
early 1964, the largest tax cut in U.S. history was enacted. It was claimed
that it was weaker in performance than it could have been if reliance had
been placed on raising expenditures. Economists who agreed with this
viewpoint soon got what they wanted when Vietnam War expenditures and
the Great Society spending programs began at the end of the 1960s.

However, the economy was overheated and inflation developed as the
effects of the tax cut and the excess spending of the war and the Great
Society programs continued. As the *Economic Report of the President* of

1999 comments, when the excess spending was brought to a halt, unemployment rose from its 4 percent level in the mid-1960s but inflation was not curbed. The new condition was described as "stagflation" and was soon aggravated by the oil price shocks dealt by the Organization of the Petroleum Exporting Countries (OPEC) in the 1970s. In the 1980s, inflation was high again, and supply-side policies in place of the prior Keynesian treatments were invoked. Marginal tax rates were reduced in the expectation that it would stimulate investment and work effort. At the same time as the expansionary fiscal policy was applied, the Federal Reserve adopted strict anti-inflationary measures. The budget deficit grew. During the expansion of 1982–1990, federal budget deficits were huge, while inflation and unemployment stayed high. The combination of tight monetary policy and expansionary fiscal policy led to "high interest rates, an appreciating dollar, and a large current accounts deficit" (Council of Economic Advisers 1999: 23).

TYPES OF SPENDING

Fiscal policy, in the modern context, is composed of government taxes and expenditures used to achieve the nation's macroeconomic goals, such as full employment and price-level stability. The budget process is the main mechanism for expressing and implementing the chosen fiscal policy. In the private sector, Alan J. Auerbach remarks on fiscal policy since the 1970s in terms of tax legislation and expenditure policy. Since 1974, collections from income and payroll taxes have risen to 80 percent of federal revenues. Expenditures, writes Auerbach, have become more important for entitlement programs, such as Social Security, Medicare, Medicaid, and less important for discretionary spending since that date.

Tax policy has included the Economic Recovery Tax Act (ERTA) of 1981, the Tax Equity and Fiscal Responsibility Act (TEFRA) of 1982, the Tax Reform Act of 1986, the Deficit Redemption Act of 1984, the Omnibus Reconciliation Act (OBRA93) of 1993 and 1990 (OBRA90), and the Taxpayer Relief Act of 1997.

Revenue as a share of gross domestic product (GDP) had increased to 20.5 percent in 1998 from 18.3 percent in 1974, but almost all of the rise in revenues had occurred since 1994. The biggest drop in tax revenues over the period was a result of ERTA in 1981. The largest increases in tax revenues, though of smaller magnitude than the 1981 Act, resulted from TEFRA, the Deficit Reduction Act of 1984, OBRA90, and OBRA93. As the outcome of the various changes in tax policy, the federal income tax was less progressive with a maximum statutory rate of 39.6 percent in 2000 as compared to 70 percent, the top marginal tax rate prior to 1981.

Expenditure policy, Auerbach continues, is less clear as the composition of expenditures changed markedly over the period. Most expenditure changes after 1981 were downward with the largest policy reductions occurring in 1986, 1991, 1993, and 1997. In 1985, the Balanced Budget and Emergency Deficit Control Act, known as the Gramm-Rudman-Hollings (G-R-H) Act, called for setting up deficit targets and automatic spending cuts if those targets were not met. The Budget Enforcement Act (BEA) of 1990 established limits on discretionary spending in place of the former system and provided that if entitlement spending increased or taxes were reduced, these new events must be offset by appropriate action elsewhere in the budget. In 1993 and 1997, new discretionary spending limits were indicated as an extension of the BEA of 1990 (Auerbach 2000: 9–23).

In commenting on the Auerbach paper, Barry Bosworth discusses the modifications in government outlays. Three components of changes in government outlays from estimate to actual outlay are: legislative actions, changes in economic projections, and changes in technical reestimates. Recently, most of the differences in budget projections from 1996 to 1999 were due to revisions in the economic outlook and technical changes. The most surprising change was the unexpected rise in personal income tax receipts, the biggest sum coming from capital gains taxes (Bosworth 2000: 25–27).

Government outlays were of particular concern to C. Eugene Steuerle, who directs attention to entitlement programs in his remarks. Economic growth was strong in the period after World War II until 1974. There was a shift in domestic policy actions from defense expenditures of about 14 percent of GDP in 1953 to 5.5 percent in 1974, and about 3 percent in 1998, but not all spending diminished. Before 1982, domestic expenditures increased or taxes were reduced with every major budget act. After that, and until 1997, major legislation revealed the net of the two factors moving in the opposite direction.

The composition of expenditures changed drastically as the larger portion was now for the entitlement programs as opposed to discretionary spending. Some entitlement programs were and are scheduled to grow faster than GDP indefinitely. The main issue centers around designing entitlement programs, according to Steuerle, independently of the taxes and taxpayers who would finance them. Earlier spending increases were meant to be temporary to suit particular needs at that point of time. Entitlement programs are permanent and designed to grow regardless of the state of the economy. In addition to the appearance of future deficits because of the growth of entitlement spending, fiscal policy needs to take account of the importance of human capital as well as the market for saving and investing. Large withdrawals from the labor force by retirees or large injections into the labor force from immigration flows can have important effects on the economic structure (Steuerle 2000: 29–32).

DEBT MANAGEMENT

Gary Gensler, Undersecretary of Domestic Finance at the Treasury Department, expressed satisfaction with the state of Treasury financing as a result of the budget surplus. The federal deficit, stated Gensler, was at its highest during the past seven years and reached $290 billion in FY 1992. Since then, there have been continuous declines in the deficit until 1998 when the budget balance changed to a surplus of $69 billion. By 1999, the unified budget surplus almost doubled to $123 billion.

Treasury financing, therefore, has diminished its share in the capital markets. It is now less than 25 percent when it had been 33 percent of outstanding debt in the U.S. market in 1993. The stock of publicly held debt outstanding amounts to $3.6 trillion, or two-thirds as much as it had been expected to reach by 1999. Gensler views the reduced Treasury debt as a benefit to the economy but it means, also, new concerns for Treasury debt management. The main goals of the Treasury with respect to the debt are sufficient availability of cash balances, achieving lowest-cost financing methods, and encouraging capital markets.

The recent operations of the Treasury with respect to the declining debt have consisted of refunding maturing debt with smaller amounts of new debt, and reducing the number of coupon issuances. Under consideration is the possibility of reducing the frequency of auctions. One of the several problems, writes Gensler, has to do with the maturity pattern of the debt. Issuing long-term financing at the present level would mean lengthening the average maturity of the debt and increasing interest cost to the taxpayer. To meet these and other problems, the Treasury has a adopted a new rule that permits it to reopen benchmark securities within one year of issuance. The Treasury is in the process of adopting a second rule that would permit it to buy back Treasury debt before it matures. These two options will help to provide more flexibility in managing the maturity structure of the debt and absorbing excess cash as needed.

Gensler remarks that the role of Treasury securities in global capital markets will diminish. Markets are changing their reliance on Treasury yields; they are looking to eurodollar futures, high grade corporates, and other new issues, rather than working with Treasury securities only. The benefits to the economy from reducing the nation's debt outweigh the challenges to financial markets presented by the reduction in federal debt (Gensler 2000: 83–85). The fact that the debt held by the public is diminishing does not mean the gross national debt will decline. In FY 1998, the first year of the unified budget surplus since 1969, there was a deficit in the federal funds group of $92 billion, but the trust fund surplus was $161.2 billion. Together, the two fund groups summed to a surplus of $69.2 billion. Social Security runs the largest surpluses. Other trust funds, such as

Hazardous Substance Superfund, were in deficit in 1998. Medicare Hospital Insurance, Part A, has had a cash deficit since 1992. When it does, the fund redeems some of its securities' holdings to pay current claims (General Accounting Office, hereafter GAO 1999b: 21). However, all the trust funds are required by law to invest their surpluses, when they have them, in government securities. Therefore, debt holdings by the public may decline as existing issues are redeemed, but the gross federal debt continues to grow as the trust funds invest their surpluses in government securities.

The main effect of the federal debt on the budget is the amount of interest payments. In particular, the effect is through net interest payments that include interest on the debt held by the public, plus or minus some other sources that amount to a fraction of the publicly held debt but reduce its total slightly. Gross interest is net interest plus interest paid to the government accounts including the trust funds. The interest payments to the government accounts wash out because one government account does the paying while the other does the receiving. It makes a difference, though, to the trust fund surplus, which rises because of the additional revenue and, in turn, means additional investment in government debt securities. Net interest was 9 percent of total federal outlays in FY 1980, and 15 percent in 1995. Since that time, it has remained about the same, representing the third largest outlay category in the federal budget.

Interest outlays depend on interest rates and the size of the debt. An increase in borrowing raises interest rates, which increase interest costs in the budget. In the past, the government responded by increased borrowing to finance the larger interest payments. A larger public debt was the outcome. It is expected that the move from budget deficit to budget surplus will stem this trend and lead to lower debt levels and lower interest payments (GAO 1999b: 22–28).

The information so far may indicate that the trend for debt held by the public is declining, but debt held by the government accounts is estimated to rise. Trust fund balances rose by nine times their initial sum of approximately $0.2 trillion in 1982 to $1.9 trillion in 1999. Practically all the balances of the funds are invested in government securities and earn interest. Interest earned by trust funds is reported as part of receipts from the federal funds or, an intragovernmental transaction. Nevertheless, the earnings are used to purchase more government securities. In FY 1999, interest payments to the trust funds totaled $120.4 billion. Interest payments on debt held by the public including foreign holdings is reported as $234.9 billion in FY 1999 (*Analytical Perspectives* 2000: 280, 345–346).

SHORT-RUN SPENDING STABILITY

The success of fiscal policy in a short-run setting is frequently investigated by noting the reaction of the automatic stabilizers when there is a shock to the economic system. Darrel Cohen and Glenn Follette comment upon the role of automatic stabilizers, particularly that of the income tax and unemployment insurance benefits in a model in which perfect stabilization would be the entire elimination of the change in consumption after an income shock. The conclusions of the study, after using the Federal Reserve Board's FRB/US quarterly econometric model, are that the automatic fiscal stabilizers play a limited role in offsetting any aggregate demand shocks to real GDP. The multiplier tends to be reduced by up to 10 percent. However, the stabilizers are of little use when the shock comes from the aggregate supply side (Cohen and Follette 2000: 35–36).

Oliver Blanchard's (2000) comments on the stabilizers lead to a discussion of the Ricardian equivalence theorem and the usefulness of the stabilizers with respect to both demand and supply-side shocks. He remarks that the standard discussion of the automatic stabilizers begins with the Ricardian equivalence theorem, which says that the timing of taxes does not matter because taxes to support spending will have to be paid whether now or in the future. Blanchard continues by listing some reasons why Ricardian equivalence may fail:

1. If current taxpayers are not alive at the future date to pay the adjusted taxes.
2. People are shortsighted and do not think about the future.
3. If borrowing is not possible, people will change their consumption now if taxes are changed now.
4. If taxes are primarily proportional in nature, they will tend to affect consumption.

Blanchard claims that fiscal policy affects U.S. output, according to all the macroeconomic models, FRB/US included. But, the outcome is dependent on the elimination of the Ricardian equivalence principle as it applies to the consumption function. Nevertheless, he accepts the outcome on the basis of specific evidence. The first relates to the assumption that Ricardian equivalence implies that exogenous shifts in public saving should be completely offset by a shift in private saving. He argues that the historical evidence from 1970 to 1999 confirms the relationship. However, the relationship appears to lead to higher growth which improves the budget, and again leads to expectation of higher growth and, therefore, a rise in wealth and a decline in private saving. The second item of evidence relates to research work done with Roberto Perotti in 1999. Results demonstrate that a change in taxes affects taxes for about 18 months and, in addition, has an effect on output that mounts up before disappearing. Fiscal policy is found to affect output with a multiplier of unity. The question of whether the automatic stabilizers have a similar impact is independent of this outcome.

Additional findings are reported using cross-sectional data across OECD (Organization for Economic Cooperation and Development) countries and using the FRB/US model. Blanchard draws two conclusions from these studies: (1) the larger the automatic stabilizers, the more output will be stabilized by either demand or supply shocks; (2) with supply shocks, output is prevented from moving by the automatic stabilizers. The outcome in terms of the gap demonstrates that it is reduced by the automatic stabilizers when the shock comes from the demand side but it is increased when the shock comes from the supply side.

On the basis of the findings, Blanchard suggests that automatic stabilizers should be thought about in terms of reactions to supply shocks. A proportional tax on the price of oil is an example. An adverse supply shock will increase taxes because of the rise in the price of oil. Investigators should look for more general automatic stabilizers for the supply side; consider increasing the amount of automatic stabilizers beyond the present tax and transfer system, and study the possibility of automatic tax credits for investment (Blanchard 2000: 69–74).

SPENDING LIMITATIONS

Rudolph Penner spoke at the conference sponsored by the FRB of New York in April 2000 on "The Near-Term Outlook for Fiscal Policy." Penner began by admitting confusion concerning the topic for two reasons: the implications of methods used this year (2000) to enact appropriations, and contradictions between his knowledge of macroeconomics and financial markets and the current good economic and stock market news. Then, he added, we have the "best fiscal situation since the 1920's," which were fine up until the last year (Penner 2000).

Penner proceeds to describe some of the details of the budget process. Discretionary spending for 2000, as decided in 1997, was higher than the existing caps would allow. Congress decided to use methods that would make it appear that the caps were observed and that the Social Security trust fund surplus was approximately equal to the unified budget surplus. In order to attain this goal, outlays were moved ahead into 1999 and/or delayed to 2001 while receipts were moved ahead from 2001 to 2000. The Office of Management and Budget (OMB) had prepared more than one set of outlay estimates and the Congressional Budget Office (CBO) was advised to choose the lower outlay estimates totaling $23 billion and to take advantage of emergency provisions that eliminate spending from the caps. Under this cover, says Penner, the 2000 census was declared an emergency, although in each decade they have been performed routinely since 1789. In 1999, emergency outlays will total $19 billion, but some emergencies occurring in 2000 will change outlays in 2001.

According to Penner, there will be an increase of 8 percent in discretionary spending from 1999 to 2000 but you will not see this fact reported in the budget documents. Actually, *Historical Tables* (2001: 143) reports that discretionary outlays totaled $572 billion in 1999 and $614.8 billion in 2000, an increase of more than 7 percent. There were further adjustments made to improve the surplus in January and February 2000. The adjustments were due to the new arrangements initiated during the appropriations process and to the reclassification of some agricultural outlays from discretionary to mandatory expenditures. On paper, therefore, there are spending caps but, in actual fact, they are nonexistent. Penner explains that there has been a violation of the spending caps' rule and the pay-as-you-go (PAYGO) rule, which states that entitlement increases and tax cuts must be compensated by other entitlement cuts of other tax increases for 10 years in the Senate and for five years in the House. A more restrictive rule was introduced to replace the one which insisted that none of the Social Security Trust fund contents be spent. Even that one appears not to have been observed as of the CBO July 2000 estimates, continues Penner.

Budget projections are very sensitive to economic and technical assumptions. Because of these assumptions, estimates of the budget balance can change by as much as $100 billion while changes in policy measures seldom alter the balance by more than half that figure. In other words, trying to follow a rule of balancing the unified budget is an impractical guide for a long-run constraint on budgeting.

As Penner was aware of the above factors, he was surprised when a budget surplus appeared in 1998. It was the result of an unexpected slowdown in Medicare cost growth and an equally unexpected growth in the ratio of revenue to GDP. In 1995, the revenue ratio was 18.8 percent and, by 1999, it reached 20.6 percent. Penner relates much of the increase in revenues to the rising stock market and capital gains taxes. Taxpayers with an adjusted gross income over $200,000, representing 1.5 percent of total returns, contributed 37.2 percent to tax revenues in 1997, while they had contributed 29.5 percent in 1995. As for the amount of debt outstanding for the next decade, Rudolph Penner believes it will be less than the current 41 percent debt-to-GDP ratio but more than the 6 percent projected by the CBO in July 2000 for FY 2009. If the debt should come down to the low of 24 percent that existed in 1974, people might start worrying again about a shortage of public debt. The event could happen as foreigners and state and local governments currently hold U.S. debt of approximately 20 percent of GDP, and the Federal Reserve could want to retain as much as 6 percent of GDP (Penner 2000: 77–80).

DECENTRALIZATION OR FISCAL FEDERALISM

Fiscal federalism is a branch of public finance; it is concerned with the vertical structure of the public sector. Nations, whether industrialized or striving to be so, are currently attracted to keeping more power at the lower levels of government. The concept of decentralization has emerged in the transition economies as a way to escape the rigidity of central planning. In the United States, it is believed that state and local governments might be more responsive to the needs and wants of citizens and might do so more efficiently and effectively than the central government. Wallace C. Oates comments in an "Essay on Federalism," which appeared in the *Journal of Economic Literature* (1999), that the traditional theory of fiscal federalism can be traced to Richard Musgrave's classic work, *The Theory of Public Finance: A Study in Public Economy* (1959) and the later work of Wallace C. Oates in *Fiscal Federalism* (1972). Musgrave adds the prior contributions to the field by James M. Buchanan in 1950 and J. A. Maxwell in 1946 (Musgrave 1959: 182; Oates 1999: 1120–1149).

In an article entitled "Reconsidering the Fiscal Role of Government," which appeared in the May 1997 issue of the *American Economic Review*, Richard Musgrave writes that the call for decentralization or devolution has become popular. He observes that the call reflects the idea that the federal share of total government spending should be reduced; but Musgrave does not agree, as he indicates that the present level of 71 percent of the total, including grants, does not sound like excessive spending to him. Although the idea of leaving decisions about public services to the locals may be appealing, the fact is, according to Musgrave, many public services have benefit regions that differ from their political description and/or overlap with other regions. Central supervision or provision may be necessary.

An associated problem is that basic services may not be affordable to a given jurisdiction and, therefore, grants may be necessary. In the past, additional funds were furnished by grants that were needs-based, either matching or selective. Today, the tendency is to use block grants, which reduce federal oversight along with the chances of obtaining the appropriate level of services, particularly in the event of recession. Musgrave cites the decentralization of welfare as a representative case of the problem. It leads to greater reliance on state and local financing from unsatisfactory, inequitable sources, such as the property and sales taxes, and away from the progressive income tax. If distribution is a priority in the fiscal system, it should be guided at the federal level. Musgrave argues, on these grounds, that the logic of decentralization is biased against progressive taxation. The proponents of devolution claim that intragovernmental competition is furthered by the adoption of decentralization. The reasoning is faulty, writes Musgrave, because each jurisdiction will try to attract business and capital by lowering taxes rather than increasing or improving services. The only way to avoid the smaller tax base and possible lowered service level is to choose tax coordination instead of competition (Musgrave 1997: 156–159).

Wallace Oates explains his viewpoint on fiscal federalism differently, but agrees essentially on the difficulty of dealing with overlapping jurisdictions for provision and regulation of the good or service with public characteristics. Oates claims that the theory of fiscal federalism indicates that the level of government providing public goods and services most efficiently should be responsible for doing so.

In a textbook written with Peggy B. Musgrave, entitled *Public Finance in Theory and Practice* (1989), Richard Musgrave indicates the nature of the supply problem. It is the mixed or quasi-public good or service which raises the most discussion when it comes to the question of supply. These goods may be to some extent nonrival, such as adding another student to a small class in public finance, and/or they may be to some extent nonexcludable, such as attempting to charge a community resident or pedestrian for a concert offered in the park. But, besides these features, the good or service has private characteristics. An individual can consume them alone and benefit: education. An individual can consume them and subtract from the availability of the good to someone else: a hospital bed. An individual may benefit from the good or service whether he/she pays for it or not: immunization shots for smallpox or a larger number of educated persons in the surrounding neighborhood. These examples are chosen to highlight some of the particular dilemmas involved in supplying education and health care. The fact that these two vital budget items are quasi-public in nature does not reveal who should provide them or who should produce them, or in what quantity.

Some criteria for decision makers to consider are: the relative priority of the public good characteristic, the level of quality desired, the relative costs of production in public and private sectors, consideration of government contract methods of provision, and the most recent suggestion, the maintenance of substantial competition whether production is carried on in the private or the public arena (Meyer 1989a: 7–8; Musgrave 1959: 3–57; Rosen 1999: 61–81; Rutherford 1992: 375).

Macroeconomic stabilization and income redistribution, however, are necessarily provided by the central government, according to Oates, because lower levels of government have no control over monetary or exchange rates or over reactions to fiscal measures adopted by the central government. In addition, movements of individuals from one jurisdiction to another can prevent the success of any income redistribution plan. These guidelines have been extended at times by Edward Gramlich in 1987 and Mark Pauly in 1973, to show that some macroeconomic efforts can be made at lower levels of government (Oates 1999: 1122). One of the more difficult problems of fiscal federalism is deciding the extent to which a good or service has public characteristics and the extent to which one or more levels of government should provide or regulate its provision. A pure public good is nonrival in consumption, or the cost of one more person consuming the good is zero, and it is nonexcludable or no one can be prevented from consuming the good whether the person pays or not. Either of these pre-requisites can be violated even by what is most often cited as a pure public good, national defense. For one thing, there is a spatial parameter involved where there is, eventually, an additional mile or kilometer that entails the enlargement of the national defense system. Also, the introduction of new technologies may change the shape and level of the cost curve. Nevertheless, there is general agreement that the central government is the most efficient level of government for its provision.

According to Jacob Oser and Stanley L. Brue, the major contributions in public expenditure theory are Knut Wicksell, Eric Lindahl, Richard Mus-grave, and Paul Samuelson. In "The Pure Theory of Public Expenditures," which appeared in the *Review of Economics and Statistics* in November 1957, Samuelson made the mathematical statement in which a public good appears in the utility functions of two or more persons (Oser and Brue 1988: 451). Robert B. Ekelund and Robert F. Hébert have said, alterna-tively, that a public good may be distinguished from a private good in that a person's individual consumption of the public good does not reduce its simultaneous consumption by all others (Ekelund and Hébert 1990: 633).

The other side of fiscal federalism is the sharing of tax revenues among the different levels of government. The central government may extend grants to lower levels of government on the basis of assuring the desired amount of public services or, it may be offered if the subgovernment can match the grant in all or in part, or it may be given outright. There is the option, also, of different levels of government financing their public expen-ditures by different types of taxes (e.g., income or sales tax, or their sharing of revenues from the same taxes) (Oates 1999: 1125–1130; Rosen 1999: 480–481; Rutherford 1992: 173).

TAXING AND ECONOMIC POLICY

Modern tax policy has its roots in both theoretical and practical consid-erations for revenue choices. In the theoretical roots are questions, initially, of efficiency and equity. On the practical side, the questions relate to sim-plicity and fairness.

Taxation's main purpose is to collect funds for the maintenance of the government and for the outlays that the citzenry chooses for it to make. Problems arise concerning the distribution of that taxation among the pop-ulation and the efficiency with which it is collected and spent. The first problem may be referred to as one of vertical and horizontal equity in taxation while efficiency refers to the cost of collection as well as any in-fluence on the economic behavior of the taxpayer. More recently, time has become an important element in taxation debates so that discussion has included the concepts of economic stability and economic growth.

In a survey of tax policy, J. A. Kay reviews the changing climate of deliberations on taxation. He recalls that economic policy consisted of public finance for hundreds of years. Defense, police, and the law of contracts were the public goods provided by the government. Their enforcement and the funds necessary for their provision, taxes, were to be obtained as unobtrusively and cheaply as possible.

Goods, such as education, health, and income maintenance, are at least as important in the United States today, and are considerably more important in France, Germany, Japan, and the United Kingdom. There has been an alteration in the outlook on how to finance these activities, the taxes to be considered, and how the matters should be decided. Relevant questions concern selection of the tax base, the rate structure, objectives other than revenue, relationships among the levels of government, effects on income distribution, resource allocation and individual welfare and, finally, administration and enforcement (Kay 1990: 18–20).

The optimal tax system's criteria were described by James Alm in an article in the *National Tax Journal* (1996). There are three main criteria, according to Alm, which can be phrased as follows. Choose that tax package that affords the greatest tax yield while maintaining taxpayer equity and the most efficient responses on the part of the agents affected. Simplicity is not given a separate dictum as it is assumed an inherent part of the three criteria (Alm 1996: 125).

However, international concerns are significant to any deliberations on large-scale tax reform. In an open economy such as the United States, unforeseen happenings may more than offset any domestic advantages of the tax changes. As for arguments that basic tax reform could improve international competitiveness, there does not seem to be evidence of the possibility. Fundamental tax reform entails two additional concerns: incentives introduced and removed by the change should be compared and there should be an examination of the distribution of income before and after the change (Hines 1996: 465–493). One of the most significant acts of tax legislation of the 1980s was the Economic Recovery Tax Act (ERTA) of 1981. ERTA reduced tax rates and the maximum tax rate on income dropped from 70 to 50 percent while the maximum tax rate on capital gains dropped from 28 to 20 percent. The Act provided for bracket indexation for inflation beginning in 1985. In addition, it introduced the accelerated cost recovery system (ACRS), which shortened service lives and increased allowable depreciation in early years. Although a liberal investment tax credit system was included in the Act, it was spread unevenly among assets. ERTA was designed to stimulate work effort and investment incentives in an economy that suddenly moved into recession in 1982. Budget deficits increased as Congress faced a substantial drop in revenues. The same year, Congress enacted the Tax Equity and Fiscal Responsibility Act (TEFRA) of 1982, in order to raise tax revenues. TEFRA slowed down the recovery cost system, made incentives more neutral among investors, and reduced the possible benefits gained through the investment tax credit. It did not change the general direction of the earlier ERTA and it did not recapture all the needed revenue to close the deficit gap.

Both ERTA and TEFRA were designed to lower the level and variations in tax rates on corporate capital income via indexing and lower marginal tax rates. Similar concerns were apparent in the Tax Reform Act (TRA) of 1986, which lowered corporate and individual income tax rates to a maximum of 34 and 28 percent, respectively, eliminated the investment tax credit, slowed depreciation schedules, made capital gains subject to tax as ordinary income, and shifted a good deal of the tax burden from the individual to the corporate income tax over the next five years.

TYPES OF TAXATION

The main objectives of the major tax reform of 1986, as explained by Charles E. McLure in the report *Treasury I Tax Reform for Fairness, Simplicity and Economic Growth* were (1) fairness in the sense of vertical and horizontal equity, (2) noninterference with market resource allocation, (3) simplification of tax forms and preferences, and (4) inclusion of more economic incentives (McLure 1985: 1–3).

In their work for comprehensive tax reform, the Treasury study committee worked on four possible changes from the present progressive income tax based system: a pure flat tax, a modified flat tax, a general sales tax/value added tax, and a retail sales tax. Treasury I proposed a modified flat tax (Meyer 1991a: 34).

There are many criteria for evaluating an broad-based tax, but essentially, they may be reduced to five major ones:

1. *Efficiency*—minimum interference in individual decision making and minimum cost of collection.
2. *Equity*—fairness in terms of vertical and horizontal equity as well as with respect to tax burden and incidence.
3. *Flexibility*—responsiveness of the system to demand or supply-side shocks and ability to achieve sustained economic growth.
4. *Simplicity*—ease with which the taxpayer can understand and comply combined with administrative facility.
5. *Transparency*—taxpayer is aware of his/her personal share in the cost of government services and the general purposes of the levy (Meyer 1991a: 34–35).

In the late 1980s, tax reformers began to reevaluate the issues of tax base, structure, and rates. In most cases, the present tax system was reviewed first and then compared to other systems.

Comprehensive income taxation was initially associated with Henry

Simons (1988), who described income as the addition of an individual's consumption and change in net worth during a specific time period. Although there were others who introduced similar definitions, including Robert Murray Haig in the United States, Simons used it as the basis for an agenda for reform (Pechman 1987: 11). In the early 1940s, Simons worked for the CED to develop a tax reform program for the post–World War II period. Simons' major proposals were to tax realized capital gains presented as ordinary income, allow full deduction for realized capital losses, repeal the tax exemptions for interest on state and local securities, and include imputed rent for owner-occupied houses in the tax base. Some of the proposals were included in the CED's policy statement, "A Postwar Federal Tax Plan for High Employment" in 1944.

After World War II, there were politicians, economists, and tax lawyers who argued for tax reform. Wilbur T. Mills, chairman of the House Ways and Means Committee, invited many tax experts to prepare papers for a "Tax Revision Compendium" of three volumes. In the late 1960s, Stanley Surrey introduced the term "tax expenditures" or private subsidies, gained through special provisions of the tax law. The Congressional Budget Act of 1974 required a "tax expenditures budget" annually as part of the budget process. Another contribution to the ongoing tax reform debate was that of J. Pechman. He estimated the value of the personal income tax base under the Haig-Simons definition of income and the rate reductions possible with that base. After the initial publication of estimates in 1955, they were updated periodically.

In the 1990s, a new group of tax reformers preferred the adoption of a consumption tax in place of the income tax. In the 1930s, the consumption tax had been associated with Irving Fisher in the United States, and in the 1950s with Nicholas Kaldor in Great Britain. There are many proponents of the new tax base who currently argue for it on the basis of the need for a comprehensive tax base regardless of the tax chosen.

In spite of good intentions, the trend after the war was toward increasing existing tax preferences and generating new ones. For that reason alone, Joseph Pechman remarks, the passage of the Tax Reform Act of 1986 was an impressive event. Pechman suggests several reasons, in addition to undermined confidence in the tax system due to growing use of tax shelters, for the passage of the 1986 act. Some of them include the influence of new supply-siders in promoting lower tax rates, the insistence of the Treasury and its supporters on relying on economic and not tax considerations, the support of the president, and important members of each House who supported base broadening and reducing tax rates (Pechman 1987: 15).

Income as the tax base has the advantage of many years of use, whereas no industrial country has ever implemented a personal tax on consumption. The concept of a consumption tax can be traced to Thomas Hobbes and John Stuart Mill. During the 1980s, there were numerous advocates of the consumption tax including some income tax advocates who were willing to accept it, provided gifts and bequests were made part of the consumption base (Pechman 1987: 13–14). The tax maintains its appeal primarily on the grounds that it is neutral toward saving. However, gaps in economic knowledge concerning incidence, interdependence, interaction of finance and other taxes hinder general consensus on the optimal tax base.

Other problems with respect to the choice of a consumption-based tax relate to preventing bogus international transactions which seek to defer or evade a tax on consumed income, the necessity for renegotiation of international tax treaties and related matters in order to replace the existing income tax. A major issue would be questions about distribution that can be answered only after the corporate income tax is attributed to individuals. However, the incidence of the tax remains highly controversial.

OPTIMAL TAXATION

Optimal taxation theory does not have much relevance to the income tax reforms of the 1980s. If consumption is the base, then Pigou's rule that a higher rate of tax should be imposed on products with inelastic demand, and Ramsey's extension of it by the use of rates that would reduce all outputs by the same fraction, requires detailed information for application (Musgrave 1987: 50). Joel Slemrod mentions the emphasis on production efficiency or "a level playing field" outlook adopted by the reform movements of the 1980s. The plan was to reduce disparities in capital income tax rates for capital investment across industries. The problem had been that some capital goods, such as housing, are not taxed, so that taxing other goods uniformly is not optimal. Perhaps the most serious omission of optimal taxation theory, says Slemrod, is its failure to consider the technology of collecting taxes. These resource costs occur in the operation of the tax system and include administrative and compliance costs. Other concerns should be the choice of tax instruments, the optimal design of enforcement policy, and the tax treatment of financial strategies (Slemrod 1996: 355–391; Slemrod and Bakija 1996: 180–187).

A textbook approach to the current income tax and alternatives is offered by Stephen J. Rice in his 1992 edition of *Introduction to Taxation*. He advises that income as the tax base can be analyzed in two classification systems: (1) in terms of its uses (current consumption and future consumption or saving) or (2) in terms of its sources (rendering personal services or from ownership of property). As Congress has chosen total income as the tax base, both the portion to be saved and the portion to be consumed are taxed. Congress made the choice because the Constitution had not permitted any direct taxation, claims Rice. In order to have an income tax, the Sixteenth Amendment, ratified on 3 February 1913, was passed without a definition of income. However, taxing total income results in an inherent bias toward present consumption and away from future consumption. The reason is because the portion saved and any interest earned on it reduces the possibility of future consumption by more than double the tax burden it would have been on current consumption. According to Rice, a consumption tax in its place would be unbiased; but the tax rate would need to increase in order to maintain the same amount of revenue. If the arrangement were made, current and future consumption possibilities are reduced by the same percentage and there is no incentive to move toward saving or consuming on the basis of the tax (Rice 1992: 3–4).

Because of the inherent bias toward present consumption and away from saving, Congress realized that the tax discourages capital accumulation and passed legislation to relieve the problem. The foregoing are the reasons, in large part, for provisions for profit sharing and pension plans, accelerated depreciation schemes, and the reduced tax rates on long-term capital gains. To make up for the lack of a definition of income in the Sixteenth Amendment, the Internal Revenue Code, section 61(a) attempted to surmount the omission by naming specific inclusions and exclusions from income. Its definition of gross income refers to all income from any source, which includes but is not limited to a list of 15 items ranging from compensation for services to income from an interest in an estate or trust.

Without an explicit legal definition of income, continues Rice, it has been up to the judicial system to define income through specific cases that come before the Supreme Court from time to time. For example, the Court found in 1920 that an increase in wealth is taxable whether it is an asset found or received in exchange for labor services, as realization has occurred. In the same year, however, if the asset, once acquired, increases in value but is not exchanged, the increase in wealth is not taxable. Finally, implemented in 1962, income realization and liability for tax can occur if a taxpayer gains on the exchange of an asset during a period whether or not he receives cash.

There are many inclusions and exclusions which have evolved via various sections of the Internal Revenue Code rather than through the judicial system. Consumption in kind is an important one. Additional examples include home repairs, net rental value of living in your own home, and consumption value from use of household durables (Rice 1992: 3-5–3-24).

In conclusion, what is taxed under present law is not income, consumption, or wages, but rather the realized portion of economic income. On the subject of tax reform, Joel Slemrod and Jon Bakija have sought to compare the benefits of various plans by reducing their inquiries to three issues:

1. Does it have a single or multiple rate?
2. Is the tax base clean?
3. Does it rely on income or a consumption base?

Slemrod and Bakija proceed to evaluate some of the existing proposals. Representative Archer's suggestion to replace the present income tax with a consumption tax with a clean base and a single rate is not satisfactory because the value added tax version of it would tend to shift the burden to most of us and away from wealthy Americans. The options remaining for comprehensive tax reform are the flat tax and the graduated flat tax. The problem with either of these choices is that they are untested, may involve some regressivity, and the transition period is too complicated to predict. Moreover, Slemrod and Bakija suspect that most Americans will consider the tax to be on labor income rather than all income. They argue there is no easy solution but, Slemrod and Bakija admit, the income tax can be fixed up enough so that tax rates could be lowered (Slemrod and Bakija 1996: 250–251).

A number of economists at the Brookings Institution tend toward the same finding by indicating the failures of the present system but noting that many of the accusations against it have not been substantiated. In "The Rocky Road to Tax Reform" in *Setting National Priorities: The 2000 Election and Beyond* (1999), Henry J. Aaron, William Gale, and James Sly discuss the fundamental goals of a tax system, simplicity and fairness. They add that taxes should encourage market efficiency and economic prosperity and raise enough revenues to cover the necessary level of government spending while maintaining freedom and privacy. Objections to these goals have been raised by Milton Friedman (1993), and by Gary S. Becker and Casey B. Mulligan (1998). These economists take the viewpoint that less government with a less efficient, unfair, or complicated tax system is to be preferred to more government with an efficient tax system. Although the goals of an optimum tax system may be stated in general, the article continues, there is much disagreement in defining the goals specifically and how to achieve them. The U.S. tax system taxes wages, income, wealth, and consumption, but its major revenues derive from the personal income tax. The tax base of an income tax should be on all net additions to individual spending power during the tax period; however, in practice, some income under the definition is taxed more than once, some is not taxed at all, and some receipts that are not income are taxed. In 1999, there were six statutory tax rates: 15, 28, 31, 36, and 39.6 percent, that increase with income. The income bracket for each of these rates and for personal exemptions and the standard deductions are adjusted each year to reflect changes in the price level.

The personal income tax has a graduated tax rate schedule and, because it has a narrow tax base, higher tax rates are needed to raise a given amount of revenue. The narrow tax base results from the many credits, deferrals, deductions, exclusions, and exemptions that are part of the income tax laws. In 1996, taxable income was 68 percent of adjusted gross income and 48 percent of personal income in the national income accounts. In spite of the many charges made against the income tax on economic grounds, there is little evidence that it discourages economic growth or work effort, or lowers the level of saving in the economy.

Nevertheless, Aaron, Gale, and Sly complain that taxes have become an enormous chore for the taxpayer to calculate and file, in view of their complexity and time-consuming aspects. They tend to distort individual economic decision making and necessitate higher marginal tax rates than would be necessary without the many special provisions. Aaron, Gale, and Sly recommend incremental reform as the solution instead of a complete replacement of the system by one or a combination of the several other tax schemes that have been proposed (Aaron, Gale, and Sly 1999: 211–266).

Herbert Stein has written about the increasing need for revenues in *Tax Policy in the Twenty-First Century* (1997). The reason for it, writes Stein, is primarily expenditures rising relative to the national income and secondarily because of the coming rise in (1) the costs of an aging population, (2) growing interest burdens as debt to national income and to gross national product rise, and (3) political pressure for greater egalitarianism. The need for taxes to rise, claims Stein, will be difficult administratively, politically, and in terms of economic consequences. He presents a "law of increasing marginal costs" to prove his case. If a 25 percent rate is raised to 26, it hurts much less than if a 50 percent rate is raised to 51 because the percentage change in after-tax incomes is greater in the second case. Stein mentions other reasons for rising taxes such as international resource mobility and international integration of business. For business, double taxation hurts more as tax rates rise while, for government, international competition sets the limit for rate increases. Domestic structural changes will compound the problem as, for example, in advancing economies, a rising share of total income comes from capital. Capital, more than labor income, has both measurement and timing problems. To minimize the problems, Stein suggests either broadening the base of the income tax and/ or introducing a broad-based consumption or expenditure tax, perhaps a value added tax. The political feasibility of a reform of this type is doubtful and, furthermore, public opinion does not appear favorable to a move away from income taxes.

The performance of the economy as it grows is an important element in these considerations. Stein notes that his simple calculations of U.S. performance for 40 years before 1929, and for 40 years after World War II reveal that productivity per capita GNP, and total GNP have grown as fast in the first period of low taxes and small budgets as in the later period of high taxes and large budgets. A study done at Groningen University in the Netherlands for Japan, Western European countries, and the United States, covering a period of 25 years after World War II and 50 years preceding the war, found the later period of large budgets and high taxes demonstrated greater growth than the earlier period. The point is, claims Stein, that "growth works out a lot of other problems." They should serve as warnings and give us the opportunity to design policy with the given information (Stein 1997: 289–295).

EFFICIENCY AND EQUITY

In the same year, 1997, the CBO's attention was drawn not to the revenue issue but toward efficiency and equity in taxation. The CBO focused on the complexity of the income tax and its interference with household and business decision making, and its discouraging effect on saving, investment, and work effort. Recent proposals, which were studied for improvements to the current system with these factors in mind, were the Gibbons value added tax, the Armey-Shelby flat tax, the Unlimited Savings Allowance tax, and the Gephardt 10 percent tax which calls for a broader-based income tax.

An important issue in the transition from one tax to another, according to the CBO report, is the fact that there would be sharp losses for some individuals and windfalls for others unless an interim complex adjustment process were used to counteract this outcome. As for the effect on investment, saving, and labor supply as a result of the switch from the income-based tax to the consumption-based tax, outcomes vary according to assumptions and the period of time selected. Researchers agree that in the move to a consumption-based tax, "comprehensive tax reform would lower the marginal product of capital (the amount of output produced by the last unit of capital invested) and would lift the after-tax return from saving" (Congressional Budget Office, hereafter CBO 1997: xi). Other rates of return including the interest rate on corporate debt and the market rate for securities cannot be determined.

With respect to resource allocation, the CBO predicts a change in the composition of output which might be higher in total, and a change in the manner in which it is produced. Many current tax inequalities would be removed by fundamental tax reform. "The current income tax system favors financing through debt over equity, encourages retaining earnings over disbursing dividends, taxes noncorporate businesses and owner-occupied housing at lower rates than corporate businesses, and treats equipment and intangible capital more generously than other forms of capital (CBO 1997: xi).

Other advantages of changing to the consumption-based tax are the reduction of the effective tax rate on capital income, and removal of many tax preferences such as itemized deductions, inclusions and credits for mortgage interest, state and local income and property taxes, and charitable contributions. As for the economic efficiency of the tax change, generally, it would depend on weighing the gains of the winners against the loss of the losers. The revamped tax system, whether accomplished through more comprehensive income tax or consumption tax arrangements, may be more or less efficient and/or improve social welfare only to the extent of consumers' sensitivity in terms of changing their spending and working patterns (CBO 1997: ix–xii).

CONCLUDING COMMENTS

The problem with fiscal policy, taxing or spending, is that it is not independent of how, when, or where it is financed. If money is printed or borrowed, if it is spent now or later, or if it is sought internally or externally, results will be substantially different. The arguments concerning the effectiveness of the automatic stabilizers might be significantly altered by such considerations. As for the use of limits on spending, whether "caps" or the PAYGO rule, Congress will manage to find a way around almost any rule if that will suit their political purposes and their constituencies.

Fiscal federalism is another matter, a more complicated matter. The arguments for decentralization are strong from the individual's point of view and weak from the collective point of view. Individuals prefer power close to home and resent paying taxes for benefits not entirely retained in their jurisdiction; but there are those who, through lack of opportunity, ability, or income, cannot obtain the education or health services, for example, that they need. When these factors are combined with the inherent complexity of finding the most efficient way to furnish and regulate the production of these services, the issue appears overwhelming.

The problem of taxation, in general, is not one that will go away. Nobody wants to pay taxes but revenue must be raised to provide for the ever-increasing quantity and quality of services demanded, and their administration. Whether the income-based tax is the "optimal" tax or not is a moot question. It has been around for a long time and most people accept it. However, the complexity, the inequity, and the resulting inefficiency of the present income tax system is unworthy of any nation. If the Sixteenth Amendment is faulty in not defining income, which contributed to the problem, perhaps a presidential commission could recommend a clear-cut and simple description of its content. At least there would be a basic model on which to add, subtract, or amend over time. Efficiency and equity in income taxation or any other taxation cannot be achieved until the starting point is unmistakably indicated.

Chapter 2

Financial Institutions and Concepts

The federal budget is essentially a fiscal document in the sense that it expresses the government's policies for taxing and spending to achieve the nation's economic goals such as high employment and price-level stability. However, the budget cannot be implemented or the goals attained without the finances to make it happen. Therefore, this chapter begins with basic information on the operations of the Federal Reserve System (FRS) and the most significant financial act in decades, the Gramm-Leach-Bliley Act (GLBA) of 1999. Background on money and monetary policy, inflation, debt, and debt management are provided. More controversial issues arise in the sections on private debt and public debt, interest rates, and federal credit programs including the Treasury agency known as the Federal Financing Bank (FFB). The chapter concludes with discussion of two issues of substantial magnitude and impact on the private economy: contingent liabilities and federal participation in credit markets. A list of federal budget documents is furnished.

THE FEDERAL RESERVE SYSTEM AND THE GRAMM-LEACH-BLILEY ACT OF 1999

The FRS is an enormous organization that carries out many functions including monetary policy. There is no comparable organizational structure within any other central bank in the world. The system is responsible for monetary policy now, but that was not its original purpose. The Federal Reserve Act of 1913 was designed to provide facilities for discounting commercial paper, to improve the supervision of banking, and to provide for seasonal currency needs (Famighetti 1999: 117–118; Melton 1985: 4–5). The system's responsibilities over the years have increased to encompass encouraging high levels of employment, maintaining the purchasing power of the dollar, seeking overall economic stability and growth, and attaining a reasonable balance of payments position. In addition to these duties, the FRS acts as "lender of last resort" to individual banks who may apply to it when they are temporarily short of reserves. The accommodation was one of the more important functions of the system with the discount rate as the cost of borrowing for the purpose. More recently, the federal funds rate, the rate at which member banks can borrow from each other, has assumed as great an importance at least in ordinary times. William J. Melton writes in his book *Inside the Fed* (1985) that the New York Fed kept a huge steamer trunk on casters solely for the purpose of holding bank collateral—mostly in the form of commercial loan notes—which must be deposited with the FRS in advance of the loan.

Melton mentions another duty of the FRS, which has been of particular concern currently: bank supervision. Nationally chartered banks, he reports, are regulated by the Comptroller of the Currency; state-chartered banks that are not members of the FRS are regulated by the state banking commissions, while state-chartered banks which belong to the FRS and bank holding companies are regulated by the FRS itself. The FRS has residual authority for regulating the operation of foreign banks in the United States. Adding to the number of supervisory agencies for banks are those for thrift institutions with state or national charters, money market mutual funds, and the U.S. branches of foreign banks with state or national charters. Supervisory agencies have been expanded to include the Federal Home Loan Bank Board and the Securities and Exchange Commission (SEC). With the passage of the Monetary Control Act of 1980, the Fed's information resources increased and monetary statistics improved as they now reported data from nonmember banks. The Act established the Thrift Institutions Advisory Council to study the needs and problems of thrift institutions, also. The Council is composed of agents from credit unions, savings and loan associations, and mutual savings banks. The Financial Modernization Act of 1999 installed a reorganized regulatory structure which reduced the supervisory role of the FRS.

For the purposes of the federal budget, another vital responsibility of the FRS is its role as fiscal agent for the Treasury. Not only does it handle all payments to and from the government, but it is in charge of Treasury securities auctions and it monitors conditions in the government securities market. At the foreign desk of the Federal Reserve Bank in New York, the bank acts as the Treasury's agent and, on its own, for the purpose of intervening in foreign exchange markets.

The FRS is composed of 12 regional Federal Reserve Banks, privately owned and with special charters. Their shareholders are the commercial banks in the same regions that are members of the FRS. The hub of the system is the seven-member Board of Governors housed in Washington,

D.C. However, with the passage of the Banking Act of 1935, which provided for centralized control over monetary policy by the Federal Reserve, authority for the policy was shared between the Board of Governors and the Federal Open Market Committee (FOMC). The FOMC is responsible for the key instrument of monetary policy, open market operations, or the buying and selling of government securities to influence the availability and cost of money and credit. The other two instruments are reserve requirements and the discount rate. Changes in the discount rate, the rate at which depository institutions can borrow from the FRS at their discretion, are recommended by individual banks subject to approval by the Board of Governors. Reserve requirements, or the amounts that a bank must hold in cash or at a reserve bank as a proportion of its total deposits, are set by the Board of Governors by type of account. However, the changes in the reserve ratio, as it is called, must operate within the guidelines of legislation passed by Congress.

The FOMC consists of seven members of the Board of Governors and five of the regional bank presidents. One of these, the president of the New York Federal Reserve Bank, is a permanent member. The remaining four places are filled by rotation of the eleven other bank presidents. With the new arrangement of power given to the Board of Governors and the FOMC, the privately owned district banks lost authority with respect to monetary policy (Famighetti 1999: 118; Melton 1985: 5–9).

Of the recent banking legislation, there has been one that has extended and made the day-to-day operations of the FRS more complex. The major recent reform is the Gramm-Leach-Bliley Act (GLBA) or the Financial Modernization Act (Public Law 106–102), which became law on 12 November 1999. It repealed parts of the Banking Act of 1933, those sections known as Glass-Steagall and parts of the Bank Holding Act of 1956. With the new Act, single holding companies no longer must separate banking and securities activities as required by Glass-Steagall, or separate commercial banking from insurance activities as required by the 1956 Act. In effect, holding companies were returned to the status they had before the great depression (Barth, Brumbaugh, and Wilcox 2000: 191–204). The new law provides that bank holding companies must engage solely in activities that are financial in nature, must have satisfactory ratings in the Community Reinvestment Act (CRA), and must be well managed and capitalized. For decisions as to what activities are financial in nature, the law authorizes the Federal Reserve and the Treasury Department to make the determination. It grants them, also, the option to expand merchant banking power in five years (Federal Reserve Bank of Atlanta 2000: 2).

The GLBA allows many more activities to be undertaken by the subsidiaries of U.S. banks and new institutions than formerly. Financial holding companies can engage in many types of banking, securities, and insurance affairs, even beyond those undertakings they were permitted over 60 years ago. Nevertheless, they do not have the larger scope of the European "universal" model, which permits commercial banks to own and be owned by nonfinancial companies. On many details the GLBA is not clear, so there will likely be some delay in effecting these changes as courts and regulators interpret the new law. State regulators are forbidden to override any financial practices that the GLBA permits, except for certain insurance activities. Savings and loan and other thrift holding companies are able to operate banking, securities, and insurance activities.

A preliminary list of financial activities that may be undertaken is defined by the GLBA. The list consists of "underwriting and dealing in securities; sponsoring and distributing all types of mutual funds; insurance underwriting and agency activities; merchant banking; and holding insurance company portfolio investments" (Barth, Brumbaugh, and Wilcox 2000: 193). The regulatory structure under the new system is complex and the Federal Reserve will not serve as primary bank regulator except for approximately 15 percent of banks that are state-chartered federal member banks. The FRS determines what activities a financial holding company may conduct by limiting that financial or semifinancial activity to those which will not affect the safety or soundness of banks. However, the Treasury Department contributes to the decision as to which new operations are financial in nature.

"Functional regulation," or the concept that like activities should be supervised by the same regulator, is the guideline of the GLBA. Banking regulators of the federal or state governments regulate bank operations, securities regulators of the federal and state governments regulate securities operations, and insurance regulators of state governments regulate insurance operations. Some bank activities that deal with securities are exempted from regulation by the SEC. However, the SEC and the FRS must consult to set up definitions and rules for new financial products. The GLBA provides for some standards with respect to consumer privacy in telemarketing and other issues, also. Privacy and banking companies will continue to be a significant issue.

In other countries, banks have greater powers than in the United States, even after the passage of the GLBA. Most of the countries in the European Union, for example, permit commercial firms to own banks, or the other way around. Before the Bank Holding Act of 1956, it was true in the United States, also. Bank holding companies are found in France, Italy, the Netherlands, and the United States while other countries either do not have them at all or use them infrequently.

The role of banking has changed in terms of its importance in the field of finance. In the 1960s, nearly 75 percent of the total assets of all financial intermediaries were held by banks. At the present time, 25 percent of total assets are held by banks in the United States. If one adds insurance companies, securities firms, and investment companies to the banks, the figure rises to over 65 percent of the assets of all financial intermediaries. If all these companies combine under the provisions of the GLBA, banking companies may regain some of their former market share (Barth, Brumbaugh, and Wilcox 2000: 192–194).

MONEY AND MONETARY POLICY

Henry Kaufman, one of Wall Street's leading critics of monetary policy, has expressed his viewpoint in *On Money and Markets: A Wall Street Memoir*. In the book's foreword by Paul A. Volcker, former Chairman of the Federal Reserve, he comments on the statements of Henry Kaufman. "He, rightly in my judgment, calls attention to the weaknesses and uncertainties in so-called modern risk management and trading techniques rooted more in mathematical constructs than in clear understanding of the characteristics of financial markets and of human nature, now as always prone to excesses of exuberance and despair" (Kaufman 2000: vi).

The Keynesian vision is interpreted by Henry Kaufman at the outset of the work. Kaufman indicates that it was not until after World War II that John Maynard Keynes' book, *The General Theory of Employment, Interest and Money* (1936), gained a following. Although fiscal and monetary policy were dealt with in the book, the lasting impression was that the economic well-being of the nation depended on fiscal measures. Keynes' view was dominant until the late 1970s when the monetarists' outlook gained in stature until today, when monetarism is in the forefront. Milton Friedman has been the primary exponent of monetarism and the work he coauthored with Anna J. Schwartz, *A Monetary History of the United States, 1867–1960* (1963), has become the major work in the history of the field. While the Keynesian view was to cure the depression of the 1930s with the use of fiscal intervention and stimulation, the monetarists argued that the depression was caused by the failure of the FRS to increase the money supply. Generally speaking, monetarists prescribe a steady growth of the money supply over time, writes Kaufman, and in this way, the economy will find its own full-employment equilibrium without involuntary unemployment. Keynesians claim that there are markets, particularly labor markets, where prices and/or wages tend to be unchanging so that these markets will not clear and disequilibrium may exist for long periods of time if government does not intervene.

Kaufman, after giving this account of the two camps of modern macroeconomic thought, states that as a practicing economist, he does not subscribe to either point of view. His main objection is the failure of both theories to lead to accurate forecasts for a year or so into the future. There is no consistent time relationship between changes in either monetary or fiscal policy and the behavior of the economy. Kaufman recalls the debate between Walter Heller, former chairman of the CEA, and Milton Friedman,

foremost proponent of the monetarist school, in the often-cited session on
the topic of which policy matters most: fiscal or monetary. From his own
experience, Kaufman concludes that both policies matter but credit matters
more. He suggests that the link between money and credit is much looser
than economic theorists proclaim (Kaufman 2000: 187–190).

In contrast to Kaufman's approach is the earlier view of William C.
Melton, who spent four years at the Federal Reserve Bank of New York
and wrote *Inside the Fed* in 1985. Since the 1930s, policy makers had been
concerned with credit, terms of lending, and interest rates, but in the 1970s,
the new direction was toward monetary aggregates. In October of 1979,
the FRS decided to drop numerical targets for the federal funds rate as a
way to control money growth and to turn instead to an operating procedure based on the supply of bank reserves. The move did not entail total
control of reserves, but used a growth path of nonborrowed reserves such
that pressure on banks to borrow from the discount window changed automatically. It was believed that the result of the action would be to change
interest rates and, hence, affect money demand. The basis for the procedure
was the annual growth targets for the monetary aggregates, particularly
M1, the transactions aggregate. Reserve requirements included in M1 are
relatively high compared to the other monetary aggregates, so as long as
the relationship between cash, the zero reserve requirement, and demand
deposits (the two components of M1) remain the same, the path of required
reserves would closely trail that of M1.

It was the practice of the FRS, according to Melton, to compute the path
of nonborrowed reserves by subtracting from total reserves a constant
amount of borrowed reserves. Ordinarily, the amount was established by
using that level of discount window borrowing that occurred in the previous period to the FOMC meeting. Thus, the link ran from the monetary
target to the nonborrowed reserves path to interest rates as banks hesitated
to borrow from the Fed. In turn, interest rates were being used indirectly
to control money growth (Melton 1985: 51–57).

Henry Kaufman, as an outsider and in a later period of time, is not
confident about the methods of the Fed in controlling the money supply.
He remarks that defining the money supply has been a continuing problem
for the FRS. It has redefined the monetary aggregates several times since
the 1960s, and the new definitions have included ones for M1, M1A, M1B,
M3, M4, M5, M1+, L, M1B-shifted. It is Kaufman's opinion that the new
definitions simply reflected how changes in the financial markets were affecting the relationship between the growth of money and the economy.
Financial market development was placing greater emphasis on credit than
on money, or as Kaufman restates the proposition, "the Fed had lost control over the debt-creation process" (Kaufman 2000: 193). Kaufman considers that the loss of control began in the 1960s when the Fed instituted
the policy of creating debt via the process of automation. The removal of

Regulation Q ceilings for interest rates on larger-denominated certificates of deposit gave banks a reason to purchase assets and to bid for liabilities. Loan commitments grew in sharp spurts through the 1970s. Other challenges that faced the Fed in the 1980s and 1990s were the large budget deficits and huge national debt, the growth of nonbank financial institutions, the development of securitization or the technique of changing non-marketable credit instruments such as mortgages into marketable ones, and the introduction of derivatives. All of these financial market innovations tend to foster lower standards for granting credit (Kaufman 2000: 193–204). As a result, the increase in the size and complexity of the credit market reduced the ability of the central bank to affect individual economic decisions through standard monetary policy actions. Benjamin Friedman discussed the reasons for this change in July 1999 at a "Conference on Social Science and the Future" at Oxford, England, in his talk entitled "The Future of Monetary Policy: The Central Bank as an Army with Only a Signal Corps?" He explains that first, there is the rise in money substitutes such as "smart" cards and the decline in the demand for bank money. Second, there is a sharp rise in the use of nonbank credit cards. Third, there is the increase in private clearing mechanisms which would probably lead to a drop in the use of reserves of the central bank as a way of settling interbank deposits.

In spite of the several claims that the Fed does not have as much control over the money supply as might be desirable, there are others who argue that the problem is rather whether the Fed should adopt a monetary rule instead of using its discretionary powers. In this camp is William Poole of the Federal Reserve Bank of St. Louis. He writes that a monetary rule means the central bank must be open in its actions and necessarily accountable for them. The rule, of course, may be changed over time as more knowledge concerning its effects become known. In following the rule, there could be continuous improvement in the operation of monetary policy over the long run (Poole 1999: 3–12). Several monetary policy rules are investigated and tested in econometric models as reported in the National Bureau of Economic Research (NBER) volume entitled *Monetary Policy Rules* (1999), edited by John B. Taylor. Discussion of the Taylor rule (1993), which identifies changes in the central bank's interest rate as a function of variations in the price level and real output, is included.

In 1998, Stephen Cecchetti, at the Federal Reserve Bank of New York, expressed confidence in monetary policy rules. He supports rules for central bank policy on the grounds that if they are not present, the "dynamic inconsistency problem leads to high steady inflation." An additional reason offered is "the importance of policy transparency" (Cecchetti 1998: 10). Interestingly, Cecchetti claims that an independent central bank is in a better position to make believable pledges to secure a low inflation policy. The difficulty is that independence and accountability appear to be incompatible. The solution, and he cites Blinder (1997) and Bernanke and Mishkin (1997) as the proponents, is policy transparency. There is accountability if the policy makers are forced to announce their goals and explain their actions to achieve them.

Explicit goals or targets for inflation have been announced in several countries including Australia, Canada, Sweden, and the United Kingdom. The announcement is the transparency solution and it means that any later policy actions are better understood and, therefore, uncertainty and instability may be reduced. To formulate an operational rule for central bank policy, more information and general agreement on the impact of policy actions on prices and outputs is required. Further, the impact of shocks upon the chosen goals when the source of the shocks emanates from outside the system must be better understood (Cecchetti 1998: 1–14).

Almost 20 years ago, Karl Brunner anticipated the arguments concerning transparency and accountability. In a "Shadow Open Market Committee" position paper in March 1981, entitled "Policymaking, Accountability, and the Social Responsibility of the Fed," he suggested that the Fed set a benchmark level of desired money growth to match its desired rate of price change. Then, the Fed should set rules for money growth in the long run and announce them to the public. Finally, the actual growth of the money supply should be subject to a control procedure allowing for a small tolerance level. If the desired rate is not achieved in any year, members of the FOMC should submit their resignations to the president. The president may accept the resignations and choose a new team, or he may consider their explanations and refuse the resignations. As Brunner emphasizes, his proposal is meant to draw attention to the inadequate accountability of a very important agency which affects the welfare of the nation in many ways (Brunner 1997: 117–118).

In January 2000, the FOMC proceeded to make its decisions known to the public sooner, and with greater clarity. The FOMC announced its approval of modifications to the Committee's disclosure procedures at its 21 December meeting. At the FOMC meeting scheduled for February, the following procedures, aimed at improving communications with the public, will take effect: (1) immediately following every FOMC meeting, a statement will be issued to the public; (2) in the statement, a new language for assessing future developments will be used to described the FOMC's consensus concerning risks to attaining its long run goals of price stability and sustainable economic growth. Comments on risks of inflationary pressures or economic weakness will be included (*Federal Reserve Bulletin* 2000: 217). In fact, the FOMC has observed these new requirements at its meeting of 15 May 2001. It voted to release a statement to the press shortly after the meeting on its domestic policy directive aimed at reducing the federal funds rate, and to include the following sentence: "Against the background of its long-run goals of price stability and sustainable economic growth and of the information currently available, the Committee believes that the risks continue to be weighted mainly toward conditions that may generate economic weakness in the foreseeable future" (*Federal Reserve Bulletin* 2001: 544).

In May 2000, Daniel L. Thornton tested the hypothesis that if the Fed makes its intentions known, the market will respond more closely to the Fed's intentions. The study was reported in an article entitled "Lifting the Veil of Money from Monetary Policy: Evidence from the Fed's Early Discount Rate Policy," which appeared in the *Journal of Money, Credit and Banking* in May 2000. The obverse of the hypothesis is when the Fed does not make its intentions known, the market responds in a manner inconsistent with the Fed's intentions. Thornton's findings support the hypothesis but the empirical analysis is limited to the discount rate tool only. He indicates that the advantages of conducting monetary policy more openly appear to have been recognized in eight countries that have established explicit inflation targets, including Canada, Sweden, and the United Kingdom, and four countries that have medium-term inflation objectives: France, Germany, Italy, and Switzerland (Thornton 2000a: 155–167).

INFLATION

Inflation targeting became continuously more popular with central banks during the 1990s. It entails a numerical inflation target which is flexible in that it is set for the medium run with attention to stability conditions. The Maastricht Treaty states that the primary goal of the Eurosystem is price stability. The definition of price stability offered by the system in October 1998 was annual increase of less than 2 percent in the "Harmonized Index of Consumer Prices." There has been frequent mention that emphasis should remain on the medium term and on gradualism and stability. However, two problems have not been addressed: the lower bound for inflation has not been decided, and the Eurosystem has not been as transparent as it could be with its unwillingness to publish internal forecasts and minutes of the European Central Bank (ECB) and the meetings of the General Council of the Eurosystem. Since its creation in 1998, the ECB has attempted to maintain communication with external researchers and academicians. Lars Svensson, author of the article in which these comments appeared, is optimistic about the future monetary policy of the Eurosystem (Svensson 2000: 95–98).

From the contrasting point of view, Benjamin Friedman, in the *American Economic Association Papers and Proceedings* (1992), stressed that unemployment should be the top priority for the FRS. According to Friedman, anticipated inflation has a mild effect on the value of money. Unanticipated inflation causes an inequitable distribution of income, but unemployment reduces national product and has substantial social effects related to crime, drug addiction, and homelessness. Friedman suggests that the FRB needs to be urged to reorder its priorities (Friedman 1992: 310).

Daniel L. Thornton is not as certain about the mildness of the effect on money. He writes that money facilitates exchange because it reduces the cost of exchange. It has such a large cost advantage over barter and credit that anticipated inflation is unlikely to cut down on its use. Although it continues to serve as a medium of exchange, money's role as a standard of value diminishes. The welfare costs of inflation are probably significant because of this occurrence as the efficiency of credit markets deteriorates along with the uncertainty of inflation and its effects on goods, labor, and financial markets, and the increased costs of using money (Thornton 2000b: 35–62).

Monetary and financial stability conditions were the subject of the study called "Price Stability and Financial Stability: The Historical Record," which was published in the Federal Reserve Bank of St. Louis *Review* in 1998. Michael D. Bordo and David C. Wheelock, authors, remark that in many countries, the primary objective of monetary policy since 1988 has been controlling fluctuations in the price level. Not all economists agree with the viewpoint, but Anna Schwartz (1988) has claimed that a central bank which maintained price stability would not only promote financial stability but would reduce the need for lender-of-last-resort intervention. Furthermore, in a later work, "Comment on 'Debt-Deflation and Financial Instability: Two Historical Explorations' by Barry Eichengreen and Richard L. Grossman" (1997), she claims that unexpected disinflation raises the real burden of nominal debt above expectations concerning it while lowering the nominal return to investment below anticipations of that return. Bordo and Wheelock conclude from their study of periods of financial instability in Canada, the United Kingdom, and the United States, that the Schwartz hypothesis seems to be correct. Disinflationary environments have been the typical setting for periods of severe financial instability since Civil War times, although with some exceptions (Bordo and Wheelock 1998: 41–62).

In the United States, the 1990s have been a decade of low inflation, and many observers consider it a reflection of the changed relationship between economic growth and inflation. Robert W. Rich and Donald Rissmiller find that other than the standard reasons for explaining inflation behavior in the past, the largest influence, currently, has been the continuing deep decline in relative import prices (Rich and Rissmiller 2000: 1–5).

Although there are economists who claim that some ongoing inflation stabilizes economic performance, James M. Bullard and Alvin L. Marty find the arguments faulty or questionable. They have studied the stability-through-inflation argument in a 1998 issue of the Federal Reserve Bank of St. Louis *Review*. Bullard and Marty find, after examining models since 1954 proposed by Arifovic Cagan, Marimon and Sunder, Phelps, and Vickrey, that not much remains of the argument under either adaptive expectations or under rational expectations. In addition, in the case of rational expectations, the argument is reversed and stability achieved only on the high inflation segment of the Laffer curve. According to the *Routledge Dictionary of Economics* (Rutherford 1992), adaptive expectations is defined as "The expected value of an economic variable at a future date measured by the weighted average of all previous values of the variable" and, rational expectations is defined as "Individuals, when making decisions, it is assumed, have all relevant information, including knowledge of the structure of the economic system, and that any errors in the analysis of that information are attributable to random forces" (pp. 5, 383).

Other objections to the theory of rational expectations have been raised by Herbert Geyer in "Changes in Budget Policy Goals and Instruments: Five Decades of Development in the United States of America." Geyer comments on the topic of rational expectations concerning its arguments that lead to a "policy ineffectiveness theorem." He claims that in the world where uncertainty is present, it is difficult to argue that expectations can be formed when, according to those who follow the rational expectations concept, the only policies that are effective are those not expected and not anticipated in economic behavior (Geyer 1985: 51).

With respect to the alleged association of unemployment and inflation, it has tended to fluctuate over the years, which is particularly evident in reports concerning the "misery index." On page 30 of the *Budget FY 2001*, reference is made to the fact that, after the years of expansion, the misery index is at its lowest ebb in 30 years. The combination of an employment rate that fell to 4.2 percent last year, the lowest since 1969, and an inflation rate based on the core consumer price index (CPI) of 1.9 percent, the lowest since 1965, results in the lowest misery index rate since the 1960s.

In the 1960s, the full employment rate was set at a 4 percent rate of unemployment. Economists believed that any lower unemployment rate would generate an accelerating inflation. Therefore, the full employment/unemployment rate was named NAIRU, or the "nonaccelerating-inflation rate of unemployment" (Council of Economic Advisers 1999: 24). NAIRU was thought to be higher from 1975 into the 1980s than it had been in the 1960s. In the 1990s, it was thought to have dropped again. In the February 1999 *Economic Report of the President*, it was estimated to be approximately 5.3 percent, and the figure was the rate implicit in the administration's 1999 forecasts. The 2000 budget assumptions revised the NAIRU downwards to 4.8 percent, and the 2001 budget assumptions lowered it further to 4.2 percent for calendar year 1999 (*Analytical Perspectives* 2000: 11; 2001: 12).

The *Economic Report of the President 2000* announced that the unified deficit had steadily diminished between 1993 and 1997. In 1998, the budget was in surplus for the first time since 1969, and then again in 1999.

The surplus in 1998 resulted in an almost $51 billion reduction in debt held by the public. At the end of July 1999, the debt held by the public was $3.65 trillion (*Analytical Perspectives* 2000: 21–32; CEA 2000: 21–34).

DEBT AND DEBT MANAGEMENT

When the budget is in deficit, the Treasury issues more securities than are maturing and can select the issues so as to affect the maturity profile of the debt. When the budget is in surplus, the Treasury is retiring more debt than it is issuing. The maturity profile of the debt is determined by the outstanding debt which remains. When and how the Treasury reduces debt is determined by the type of security and maturity dates of the outstanding marketable debt. As of July 1999, outstanding marketable debt consisted of 57 percent in notes with a maturity of two to 10 years, 20 percent in bills with a maturity of one year or less, 20 percent in bonds with a maturity of 10 or more years, and 3 percent in notes and bonds that are inflation indexed (see Chapter 7, Table 14, note 2).

The stated profile of securities affects interest payments and liquidity, how often the Treasury must go to market, how it can reduce debt held by the public, and its ability to respond to market changes. The Treasury chose to reduce notes volume and issued more bills in 1999. Average maturity of the debt was thereby shortened. In FY 1997 and FY 1998, OMB and CBO underestimated revenues. The 1998 debt reduction concentrated on reducing bills. Average maturity of the debt lengthened from 5 years, 3 months at the beginning of 1997 to 5 years, 8 months in May 1998. Cash management bills are the Treasury's most flexible debt management instrument with maturities ranging from a few days to about 6 months and, besides, they mean lower interest payments. The average maturity of the outstanding debt had lengthened to 5 years, 9 months in February 1999 but returned to 5 years, 6 months by March 1999 as the Treasury attempted to curb the trend.

In addition to modifying the type of Treasury security sold, more flexibility in debt management is achieved through reopening an existing issue rather than opening a new issue, repurchasing outstanding Treasury securities before maturity dates, and redeeming callable securities before their maturity dates (GAO 1999c: 1–18).

Rudi Dornbusch explained several connections between "Debt and Monetary Policy: The Policy Issues" at a conference held by the International Economic Association at the Deutsche Bundesbank in Frankfurt, Germany in the late 1990s. His statement refers to four different ways in which to look at issues involved in the relationship between monetary policy and debt:

1. Large debts invite inflation which reduces the debt burden.
2. Large debts interfere with sound monetary policy as higher interest rates encourage more debt in a continuous cycle.
3. Private sector balance sheets may become more fragile and monetary policy may be used for other purposes than the price stability objective.
4. An open question is the relationship between the transmission effects of monetary policy and the existing stock of debt (Dornbusch 1998: 3–4).

PRIVATE DEBT AND PUBLIC DEBT

James L. Clayton, an economic historian at the University of Utah, is concerned with the immense size of both public and private debt internationally in his book *The Global Debt Bomb* (2000). Clayton admits the public debt is huge but so is the private debt. In 1999, private sector debt was almost 130 percent of GDP in the United States. Even in the spendthrift times of 1928, the private sector debt attained the same level of GDP, but no more. The problem of private debt has spread internationally and, in both Germany and Japan, private sector debt exceeds GDP. Clayton's book is dedicated to persuading the public and the policy makers that there is a global debt bomb crisis, and he makes some suggestions concerning how to diffuse the bomb before it explodes (Clayton 2000: ix–x).

Clayton informs the reader that it is only recently that the term "debt" became known as "credit." The concept of debt evolved into credit during the early twentieth century when the installment plan was introduced. Before that, debt was considered dangerous and morally wrong. Benjamin Franklin and Andrew Carnegie were two well-known individuals who spoke out against living beyond one's means. By the late 1920s, U.S. citizens accepted spending as the norm and turned away from the old Victorian values of saving and paying cash for all purchases. Private debt went from 119 percent of GDP in 1920 to 219 percent in 1933.

Up until the 1930s, continues Clayton, the budgets of governments were expected to be balanced just as they were for families. Governments should not live beyond their means either. John Maynard Keynes changed the outlook with his fiscal remedy for the depression and unemployment, compensatory government spending. Beginning in the 1970s, the public debt as a percentage of GDP, began to rise, while private debt increased even more rapidly. By the late 1980s, U.S. household debt was over 100 percent of after-tax income annually. Federal participation in U.S. credit markets after 1990 was at least 45 percent of the funds available, according to Clayton. Public debt in industrial countries has been rising rapidly for the past 20 years. The OECD has reported an average gross public debt of 41 percent of GDP in 1970 and, by 1997, the figure was practically twice as high. The main reason for higher public debt ratios in industrialized nations from the

1970s to the 1980s was the rapid rise in public entitlement programs—public pensions, medical care, and income transfer programs. In all these countries, government spending was greater than tax revenues and large deficits had to be financed.

From 1980 to 1995, the gross public debt of the industrialized countries grew from approximately 40 percent to 70 percent of GDP. Public entitlement programs were also increasing. Clayton offers seven reasons why nations found their capacity to fund the new commitments reduced: (1) productivity slowdown, (2) the ratio of inexperienced young workers and fewer older experienced ones increased, (3) the ratio of manufacturing employment to total employment declined, (4) economic growth went down and income disparities rose, (5) costly government regulations, (6) increased public spending, and (7) reduced personal saving rates (Clayton 2000: 45–103).

Growing deficits can be attributed in part to rising real interest rates. As the demand for funds rises, it costs more to finance debt. Nations began to borrow in foreign markets. By the end of 1997, 32.3 percent of the U.S. public debt was owned by foreigners; by 1998, 32.7 percent was owned by foreigners, and by 1999, 35.3 percent. Interest on the debt paid to foreigners rose from 33.6 percent of total interest on debt held by the public to 36.5 percent in 1998, and to 39.5 percent in 1999 (*Analytical Perspectives* 2000: 280).

Clayton writes that discussions of the alleged impacts of deficits and the public debt have consisted of the following issues:

1. It does not matter whether the government raises taxes or borrows now to pay for increased spending, the Ricardian equivalence theorem.
2. The association of rising public deficits with rising real interest rates.
3. The tendency of large and continuing public deficits to successfully compete against private needs for credit and investment.
4. Large deficits now mean future generations have to pay higher taxes.
5. Large public deficits result in large balance of payments deficits.
6. Increasing public debt tends to lead to increasing public debt.

The Ricardian equivalence theorem was developed by R. Barro and published in the *Journal of Political Economy* in his article "Are Government Bonds Net Wealth?" (1974). Essentially, the theorem says current taxation or borrowing have the same effect because individuals realize that taxes must rise in the future if debt finance is chosen. Because of their awareness of this relationship, individuals increase their saving to match the increased government spending so that the economy is not stimulated by the deficit finance (Rutherford 1992: 397–398).

The other issues mentioned by Clayton are part of the classical doctrine that has been described by Jesse Burkhead in his pioneering work *Government Budgeting* (1956) (Meyer 1989a: 23–24). Recently, the answer to the question of whether the growing proportion of public debt held by foreigners is a burden to the United States has been said to depend, according to Alan S. Blinder, on what is done with the borrowed funds, how soon the lenders want their money back, and whether the new status as the world's largest debtor mars the reputation of the United States as a sovereign nation (Blinder 1991: 209–226).

MONETARY POLICY AND INTEREST RATES

No discussion of monetary policy and debt policy can be complete in the present era of global capital mobility without mention of interest rates and the issues they raise. *Interest Rate Volatility* (1996) is the title of a penetrating work by Gerald A. Hanweck and Bernard Shull. Interest rate changes, according to Hanweck and Shull, are hazardous to banking health and practices. Variations in interest rates affect everyone so that there are large responses when it happens. If the interest rate drops sharply, depositors may wish to withdraw their funds, bank liquidity may lessen, income will probably drop. In the case of a rise in interest rates, the value of fixed assets drops and causes net worth of banks to decrease as well. The possibilities of these events have contributed to provisions and regulations in the law, which are continuously updated, to meet the problems created by interest rate changes and their impact on debt instruments. Such considerations were found to be necessary in the 1920s when the Federal Reserve used open market operations to curb borrowing and restricted access to the discount window. In the 1950s, the FRS recommended that banks hold short-term Treasury securities to be sold, if necessary, when deposit withdrawals or higher interest rates made funds scarce.

More recently, the problems have been met by establishing risk-based capital requirements such as those included in the Financial Institution Reform, Recovery, and Enforcement Act of 1989 (FIRREA) and further expanded by FDICIA in 1991. Hanweck and Shull comment that interest rate risk is not entirely eliminated by the use of capital requirements even if the correct measure for calculating it is found. Banks have been using different means to lower interest rate risk such as shortening their asset maturities in some cases and lengthening them in others. At the present time, there is no single, clear-cut solution and each bank needs "to manage their interest rate risk independently of regulating requirements" (Hanweck and Shull 1996: 1–2, 32, 167).

The impact of changes in interest rates on government programs had been recognized by Leon H. Keyserling, former chairman of the CEA, more than 20 years ago. Keyserling has said that an oversight on the part of the Federal Reserve policies has been their neglect of impacts on income flows.

In particular, policies with respect to interest rates have increased the cost of housing loans while those with respect to private debts have caused income transfers from borrowers to lenders such that they account for a great deal of the regressivity in income distribution. Increases in interest rates on total public and private debt from 1952 to 1978 were up 160 percent for a total of $1.54 trillion. The interest costs have imposed a huge burden on the federal budget. During the period from 1965 to 1979, it is estimated by Keyserling that the average annual costs in current dollars of "excess interest costs," the increased costs arising from increased interest rates from the base year of 1952, were $10.8 billion (Keyserling 1979a: 133–134).

A more recent budget issue has been the Treasury's interest rate changes for the trust funds which were examined by the GAO. A statutory formula is used by the Treasury to set the interest rate earned on trust fund balances for Social Security and Medicare. The calculation of interest rates in the case of the government trust funds was changed in 1980 and 1998. Inquiries were made in January 1999 of the Treasury Assistant General Counsel for Banking and Finance as to whether the Secretary of the Treasury had the right to change the method of computing the interest rates. The response was affirmative and, furthermore, the Treasury has no obligation to apply the new policy retroactively. The Associate Director, Budget Issues, at the GAO, Susan J. Irving, agreed with the finding.

The effects of the 1980s changes increased the rates for the Social Security and Medicare Trust funds by one-eighth of a point over what it would have been in certain years. The Treasury estimated the increased revenue difference was $1.4 billion for Social Security and $0.4 billion for Medicare combining the years 1988, 1992, 1997, and 1998. In December 1998, the 1980 change means higher future revenue from 1999 to 2013. The estimated increase on existing investments is $4.3 billion for Social Security and $0.5 billion for Medicare, according to the Treasury (GAO 2000a: 1–5).

CREDIT: ON AND OFF BUDGET

The significant issue in trying to cope with the various forms of credit extended to the private sector is evaluating whether the federal government has succeeded in capturing a net benefit for society by its actions. One of the purposes of the Government Performance and Results Act (GPRA) was to help measure the government's efforts in the area. Long-range strategic plans and annual performance plans gauge agency progress in credit and insurance. In particular, the four kinds of measures employed are: inputs or resources used, outputs or goods and services produced, outcomes or gross effects achieved by the programs, and net impacts or effects net of those that would have happened without the program. They are studied for their contributions to program success. The goal of net impacts for federal credit programs is to exclude anything that might have been attained with private credit only. The programs are concerned with a net increase in home ownership, a net increase in graduates of higher education, a net increase in small businesses, a net increase in exports, and a net increase in jobs. The goals imply reaching individuals who would not be able to obtain private credit. Often, it indicates lending to more risky borrowers for more risky purposes. When it does, it means finding ways to help the borrowers repay their loans. There is a social goal as well as a financial one.

The OMB developed a tentative set of principles for restructuring credit programs to improve performance in FY 2001:

1. To justify a program, it must be demonstrated that private credit markets cannot reach the federal goal.
2. To undertake a program, it must be shown that it is the best way to achieve the federal goal in comparison to other approaches.
3. To provide a program, it must be established that its benefits exceed its costs.

Other features of the restructuring program concerned program design, operations, and monitoring. All the information contained is based on OMB Circular A-129. A revised version of Circular A-129, issued in 2000, prescribes policy and procedures for justifying, designing, and managing federal credit programs and for collecting non-tax receivables. It sets principles for designing, preparing, budgeting, and improving the efficiency of federal credit programs. In addition to other purposes, it sets standards with respect to credit card and guaranteed loan programs and the collection of delinquent debt (OMB 2000: 2). In *Analytical Perspectives* (2000), federal credit is viewed in terms of four sectors: Housing Credit Programs and Government Sponsored Enterprises (GSEs), Education Credit Programs and GSEs, Business and Rural Development Credit Programs and GSEs, and International Credit Programs. In the first group, Departments of Housing and Urban Development (HUD), Veterans Affairs (VA), and Agriculture (USDA) furnished $177 billion of loans and loan guarantee commitments in 1999. About 1 of 6 single-family mortgages originating in the United States obtained aid from one of the following programs: HUD's Federal Housing Administration (FHA) operates the Mutual Insurance Fund, VA Program, or USDA's Rural Housing Service Program.

In the second sector, the Department of Education aids in financing student loans through the Federal Family Education Loan Program and the William D. Ford Federal Direct Student Loan Program. It is expected that loans totaling nearly $42 billion will be made in 2001.

With respect to small businesses in the third sector, the Small Business

Administration increased its annual loan volume by 62 percent from 1993 to 1999, or from $7.4 billion to $12.1 billion. The Farm Credit System (FCS), also part of the third sector, has been improving its financial condition and performance. Loan volume amounted to $69.7 billion in September 1999, up from 1992 but below the $80 billion level recorded in the early 1980s. In the last sector of federal credit, the international credit programs are described. They are offered by seven federal agencies including the Departments of State, Defense, and the Treasury. Loans, loan guarantees, and insurance are available for foreign private and foreign government borrowers. In 1998, official direct and guaranteed credit flows were $24 billion; in 1992, they were $25 billion. The credit assistance is for U.S. exporters, for developing nations, and to help stabilize international financial markets. Insurance programs in the federal credit section consist of deposit insurance, pension guarantees, disaster insurance, and crop insurance (*Analytical Perspectives* 2000: 187–207). At the close of 1999, federal direct loans outstanding were $234 billion and guaranteed loans were $976 billion. These loans and loan guarantees were mostly for business, education, exports, and housing.

The GSEs net loans outstanding were $2.4 trillion including asset-backed securities guaranteed by the GSEs. GSEs are not part of the federal government and their securities carry no federal guarantee. However, Congress has granted the Secretary of the Treasury the right to purchase, if he so chooses, up to $2.25 billion of obligations of Freddie Mac and Fannie Mae, up to $1 billion of Sallie Mae, up to $4 billion of the Federal Home Loan Bank system, and $1.5 billion of Farmer Mac under certain conditions.

The reasons for federal intervention for credit and insurance all rest on the understanding that government can improve on the market outcome. *Analytical Perspectives* (2000) lists six situations where the government might accomplish the objective:

1. Information failures, when financial institutions are better informed and have been required to provide information to borrowers;
2. Externalities, when students require credit assistance for their college education;
3. Economic disequilibrium, when financial hard times occur and the existence of deposit insurance can prevent panic;
4. Failure of competition, when foreign governments intervene in the conduct of free trade;
5. Incomplete markets, when insurance is not provided, as in the case of catastrophic events; and
6. For redistributive purposes, when subsidies to disadvantaged areas need to be provided.

The Appendix (2000) to the federal budget contains additional statistics and information on the GSEs, which are not a part of the unified budget totals. In the Appendix there are five separate institutions or groups of institutions called GSEs that are examined. They include the Student Loan Marketing Association (SLMA or Sallie Mae), the Federal National Mortgage Association (FNMA or Fannie Mae), and the Federal Home Loan Mortgage Corporation (FHLMC or Freddie Mac); the Farm Credit System (FCS), composed of the Agricultural Credit Bank and Farm Credit Banks; the Federal Agricultural Mortgage Corporation (FAMC or Farmer Mac); and the Federal Home Loan Banks (FHLB).

Sallie Mae, as all the rest of the GSEs, is a private company sponsored by the federal government. It was created in 1972 and must be liquidated by 30 September 2008 as required by recent legislation. It purchases insured student loans from eligible lenders and loans to lenders secured by insured student loans, government or agency securities, or other acceptable collateral known as warehousing advances. In addition, it advances funds to state agencies for student loan purposes, it provides a secondary market for non-insured loans, and it may purchase and underwrite student loan revenue bonds, among other authorized activities.

At the end of 1999, the SLMA had more than $37.8 billion direct loans outstanding and guaranteed student loans of $13.5 billion, according to the statement submitted by the GSE but not reviewed by the president. The FNMA is a federally chartered, privately owned company established in 1938. As of 30 September 1999, the FNMA held a net mortgage portfolio of $50 billion and had net outstanding guaranteed mortgage-backed securities of over $670 billion. The FHLMC is federally chartered and privately owned also. As of 30 September 1999, the FHLMC had $315 billion in its mortgage portfolio and $739 billion in outstanding guaranteed mortgage backed securities.

The FCS's major entities are the Agricultural Credit Bank (ACB), the Farm Credit Banks (FCB), and direct lender associations. Their establishment goes back to the 1920s and 1930s. Direct loans at the end of 1999 included $18.1 billion by the ACB and $45.8 billion by the FCB. The FHLB system was chartered in 1932 and its influence in the residential housing finance market is substantial. Direct loans outstanding at the end of 1999 were $306.8 billion (*Appendix* 2000: 1251–1258).

FEDERAL FINANCING BANK

In 1974, the Federal Financing Bank (FFB) began operations as an entity in the Treasury Department. It is a government financial intermediary originally intended to purchase debt from federal agencies that are authorized to borrow from the public, to purchase guaranteed loan assets from federal agencies or to make loan asset sales, and to make direct loans to borrowers when the loans are guaranteed by a federal agency. Currently, the first purpose is in frequent use. The FFB's purchase of debt from a federal agency enables the substitution of Treasury borrowing for agency from the public, because the FFB borrows from the Treasury to finance the purchase. The transactions are intragovernmental and are excluded from the gross federal debt, as it would be double counting to add Treasury borrowing from the public—to provide the FFB with the funds to purchase the agency securities—to the agency borrowing from the FFB. However, amounts the agencies borrow from other funds, for example, agency debt held by the government accounts, are included in the federal debt. The difference is that the Treasury did not borrow from the public to enable these accounts to purchase the securities (*Analytical Perspectives* 1999: 264; *Analytical Perspectives* 2000: 275; Meyer 1989a: 39).

An example of the intragovernment transaction may be observed in a situation that occurred in 1996 in which Congress was involved. Agencies that borrow from the FFB are not subject to the statutory debt limitation and the Treasury used this advantage to raise cash when the debt limit was reached at that time. The transactions began with a swap by the FFB of a great deal of its holdings of the Tennessee Valley Authority (TVA) and U.S. Postal Service debt with the Civil Service Retirement and Disability Fund (CSRDF). It ended with the TVA prepaying all of its $3.2 billion of debt securities held by CSRDF in 1998. Congress provided for this possibility together with an appropriation to FFB to cover the prepayment charges in the Omnibus Consolidated and Emergency Appropriations Act of 1999. Concurrently, it prohibited the TVA from borrowing at the FFB in the future. The TVA borrowed from the public to finance the prepayment (*Analytical Perspectives* 2000: 275).

CONTINGENT LIABILITIES

In 1997, the federal government acknowledged in a Department of Treasury statement that total contingencies were almost $5,500 billion, or $5.5 trillion, according to Marvin Phaup and David F. Torregrosa. These contingencies consist mainly of federal deposit insurance commitments of $3.5 trillion and federal guarantees of loans to students, home buyers, and farmers and others of $650 billion. Phaup and Torregrosa report an additional $3.4 trillion which were not included in the Treasury statement, of which about $2.0 trillion securities were issued by the GSEs including Freddie Mac and Fannie Mae; $1.1 trillion is federal pension insurance guarantees of private firms' pension plans; and $400 billion is crop and flood insurance programs. The figures represent total risk exposure and not the expected payout under any of the programs. The federal government does not budget for contingencies except in the case of expected losses on federal direct loans and guarantees. The budget includes the discounted present value of net expected losses on direct and guaranteed loans at the time the loans are made, as directed by the Credit Reform Act of 1990.

Another instance of contingent liabilities is that of the on-budget revolving or trust fund. Cash collections in excess of present period insurance payments are credited to these fund accounts as they are earmarked for the purpose. By law they must be invested in government securities and, therefore, the trust fund assets, the securities, become a liability of the Treasury Department. As the transactions are intragovernmental, they cancel each other, and the net result is zero (Phaup and Torregrosa 1999: 700–702).

In the *Consolidated Financial Statements of the United States Government of Fiscal 1997* (U.S. Treasury 1997), the federal government reports commitments with federal insurance and loan programs of $2.97 trillion. The amounts are for flood insurance, crop insurance, bank deposit insurance, and other commitments. Guarantees of housing, agriculture, and education loans were listed at a face value of more than $712 billion on 30 September 1997. The figures represent the maximum theoretical risk exposure. Notes to the financial statements refer to other contingencies, in particular, litigation. The U.S. Court of Federal Claims has 125 supervisory goodwill cases that are likely to result in government payments for damages, but the amount cannot be estimated at this time. The GSEs were specifically excluded from the statements along with the Board of Governors of the FRS (U.S. Treasury 1997: 9–10, 55, 66).

At the beginning of the report, Secretary of the Treasury Robert E. Rubin states, "Never before has the United States Government attempted to assemble comprehensive financial statements covering all of its myriad activities and to subject those financial statements to an audit" (U.S. Treasury 1997: 1). He continues that the statements must be improved with respect to their reliability as the GAO could not render an opinion about them.

In the *1999 Financial Report of the United States Government* (GAO 2000d), the second of these reports under the new title, there are separate listings of "Commitments," Contingencies," and "Loan and Loan Guarantee Programs," all as of 30 September 1999. Commitments refer to contractual commitments in three separate categories that will require future payments. They include Long-Term Capital Losses of $1.8 billion, Undelivered Orders of $405.0 billion, and Other Commitments, such as for National Oceanic and Atmospheric Administration satellites and weather systems, of $5.6 billion, the largest in the total categories of $10.8 billion for Commitments.

Contingencies contains three categories. Insurance programs amount to $60.5 billion with the two largest of the programs consisting of the Export-Import Bank of $40.9 billion and the Pension Benefit Guarantee Corporation of $19.0 billion. Contingencies includes Unadjucated Claims of $2.3 billion and Other Contingencies of $77.7 billion, the largest of which is the Multi-lateral Development Banks of $67.4 billion.

In the Loan and Loan Guarantee Programs, Direct Loans sum to $236.1

billion with Rural Development of $68.9 billion, the largest of these. Guaranteed loans amount to $1.05 trillion with the FHA obtaining the largest share of $551.4 billion. The GSEs are specifically excluded from the statements along with the Board of Governors of the FRS (GAO 2000d: 74–75, 88–90, 109).

In the notes accompanying Commitments and Contingencies, contingencies are explained and the financial treatment of loss contingencies is illustrated. A contingency is an existing situation or condition where a possible loss may or may not occur. If the loss is probable, the financial treatment requires it to appear on the balance sheet. If the loss is less than probable but more than remote, it is considered reasonably possible and calls for a footnote disclosure. If the loss is remote and the chance of it occurring is slight, financial treatment calls for no disclosure, which is the case, also, if the contingencies would result in a gain.

Litigation is mentioned with respect to pending cases concerning supervisory goodwill at savings and loan institutions, harbor maintenance fees, Medicare cost report settlements, and other matters. Ultimate costs cannot be estimated at the time of the report. There is mention in the 1999 report that the government has unused statutory lines of credit to the GSEs amounting to $10 billion (GAO 2000d: 88).

FEDERAL PARTICIPATION IN CREDIT MARKETS

The financing of deficits by the federal government together with the Loan and Loan Assistance Programs mean substantial participation in the credit markets in some years. Total net borrowing, or its counterpart, total net lending, in the credit markets was $1.1 trillion dollars in 1999. Of the total, federal and federally guaranteed borrowing was just under −$28 billion or −2.6 percent of total borrowing, representing the government's participation rate. In contrast, the GSEs borrowing amounted to almost $346.8 billion, or a participation rate of 31.8 percent. On the lending side, federal and federally guaranteed lending in 1999 amounted to slightly more than $74 billion, or a participation rate of 6.8 percent. Lending represents a greater participation rate for the federal government than borrowing in 1999.

The GSEs lending in 1999 is listed as $284 billion, or a participation rate of 26 percent. In their case, the GSEs seem to borrow more heavily than they lend. They did more borrowing than lending in 1996, 1998, and 1999. In 1995 and 1997, the reverse was true but participation rates for borrowing and lending were approximately half as much.

In the past two decades, federal and federally guaranteed *lending* participation rates were highest in 1980 at 16.6 percent, while federal and federally guaranteed *borrowing* participation rates were highest in 1990 at 37.2 percent of total net lending and borrowing by domestic nonfinancial sectors in the credit market. Financial sectors are excluded to eliminate double counting. For the GSEs, both borrowing and lending participation rates have increased since the 1970s by 5 to 6 times their initial position in 1970 of 5.6 percent for GSE lending and 5.9 percent for GSE borrowing. Participation rates for borrowing by GSEs have exceeded those for federal and federally guaranteed borrowing since 1996, while GSEs lending participation rates have exceeded those for federal and federally guaranteed lending since 1990 (*Analytical Perspectives* 2000: 239, 279, 282; *Budget of the United States Government FY 2001* (2000): 420).

FEDERAL BUDGET DOCUMENTS

Analytical Perspectives, Budget of the United States Government (various fiscal years)

Appendix, Budget of the United States Government (various fiscal years)

Budget Information for States (various fiscal years)

Budget of the United States Government (various fiscal years)

Budget System and Concepts (various fiscal years)

A Citizen's Guide to the Federal Budget (various fiscal years)

Historical Tables, Budget of the United States Government (various fiscal years)

For monetary and financial information and statistical tables concerning the Budget of the United States Government for any fiscal year, consult:

Federal Reserve Bulletin
Treasury Bulletin

All of the above documents are available in electronic format. Consult the following web sites, for example:

http://www.federalreserve.gov/
http://www.ustreas.gov/
http://www.whitehouse.gov/OMB/budget

The budget on CD-ROM for FY 2001 may be purchased from Superintendent of Documents, U.S. Government Printing Office, Washington, DC 20402. Official federal government information may be obtained from the U.S. Government Printing Office online at http://www.gpo.gov/usbudget.

CONCLUDING COMMENTS

Because the federal budget has served as a fiscal document since 1921, it has not furnished information on the vital role of money in accomplishing budget objectives, nor has it explained the many financial activities of the Federal Reserve System in that respect. The manner in which fiscal measures are implemented through the use of money and financial operations might be outlined in the budget while continuing to maintain the integrity of the Fed's independence. Perhaps one or two available options and their possible contributions could be offered. Monetary and fiscal policy are related although there is disagreement over the analytical connections between them. There has been much debate concerning the importance of monetary policy as opposed to fiscal policy but, in practice, fiscal policy cannot accomplish the desired goal(s) without the eventual assistance of monetary policy.

In past years, the attention to the rising public debt as a result of rising public deficits led to congressional actions to attempt to curb the trend. It is not clear whether the legislative limits to spending or the growing economy with sharply rising tax revenues is responsible for the recent reversal to surpluses. Another related issue that needs further study is the reason for the more rapid and continuing increase in private sector debt. However, though deficits vanished in 1998 and 1999, the growing debt has not. Debt management policies deserve additional development in the budget, particularly those involving the government accounts, the trust funds. The topic of interest rates and debt management, as well as the use of interest rates as a tool of monetary policy, as an incentive for productive and financial investment, and the ways in which these events affect income distribution requires thorough examination.

In general, improved financial reporting for credit programs remains one of the most important objectives to be achieved. All costs incurred in extending credit to anyone, or any institution, should be reflected in budget totals. The off-budget agencies, the GSEs, have enormous impacts on the economy through their participation in credit markets for agriculture, education, and housing. They enjoy many special privileges as federally chartered institutions with implicit federal approval of their operations. If, however, their functions, in whole or in part, can be performed efficiently and effectively by the private sector, then a readjustment of their status may be in order.

The number and size of the federal budget documents is overpowering. If the major budget document could be modified to more closely resemble *A Citizen's Guide to the Federal Budget* (2000), it would draw a larger audience. The guide is written clearly and concisely. It describes federal spending within the framework of total spending together with relating that spending to the budgets of seven other nations. The same treatment for revenues might be valuable to aid understanding of the variations in tax bases among countries. The tables included in the 40-page guide, as compared to the 433 pages of the *Budget FY 2001*, are easy to read and well presented. They might be of greater usefulness if the tables furnished data on several past fiscal years rather than presenting predictions for future years. As the on- and off-budget sections are so controversial, the section could be expanded to explain the mechanisms of the trust funds in more detail. The same suggestion might apply to the financing and debt sections. Especially members of Congress, as elected delegates of citizens of the United States, would appreciate the attention to clarity, directness, and relevance of the message in a worldly context.

Part II

An Overview of the Budget Process

Chapter 3

Executive Formulation

The President of the United States has many duties to perform, but there are none so important on the domestic scene as those he must perform as chief provider and manager of the federal budget. In this chapter, the president's duties and the duties of his main helpers, the OMB in the Executive Office of the President (EOP) and the Treasury Department, are outlined. Information concerning the budget cycle and several reforms in the executive branch relating to the National Performance Review, downsizing, cost-benefit analysis, federalism, and the Internal Revenue Service (IRS) is furnished. The connection between the National Income and Product Accounts (NIPA) and the federal budget is discussed.

THE PRESIDENT AND THE BUDGET

There was no comprehensive executive budget process before the Budget and Accounting Act of 1921. Before that time, the Secretary of the Treasury received estimates of planned spending directly from the agencies. With the introduction of the 1921 Act, presidents were required to prepare and transmit expenditures and revenue estimates to the Congress annually. The Bureau of the Budget (later the OMB) was established to help the president in formulating and executing the budget. It remains the principal source of the executive's budget power (Schick 1994a: 49).

According to Louis Fisher (1997), a single executive was chosen by the authors of the Constitution because it was a way of achieving unity, responsibility, and a national perspective. Many of the defects and problems suffered by the Continental Congress were eliminated by introducing an executive office. Nevertheless, there have been changes in the manner in which the EOP operates. There is a great deal more delegation of power than formerly, through the use of staff assistants, advisors, agency and commission heads, and the Cabinet, which includes the secretaries of 14 executive departments.

The duties of the President of the United States are described in Article II, sections 2 and 3 of the Constitution. His powers consist of those associated with his position as Commander in Chief of the Armed Forces and, also, of filling vacancies in the Senate if they occur during a recess of that body. However, section 3 specifies his fundamental peacetime purposes:

He shall from time to time give to the Congress information of the state of the Union, and recommend to their Consideration such measures as he shall judge necessary and expedient; he may, on extraordinary Occasions, convene both Houses, or either of them, and in Case of Disagreement between them with Respect to the Time of Adjournment, he may adjourn them to such Time as he shall think proper; he shall receive Ambassadors and other public Ministers; he shall take Care that the Laws be faithfully executed; and shall Commission all the Officers of the United States. (*Constitution of the United States of America* 1974: 7)

After the passage of the Budget and Accounting Act of 1921, the president acquired the additional duties of providing for a comprehensive executive budget and overseeing the Budget Bureau created to aid him in formulating the budget (Meyer 1989a: 47).

According to the *Analytical Perspectives* volume of the *Budget of the United States Government FY 2001*, resource allocation in the public interest is the primary purpose of federal budgeting. For example, resources should be moved into programs that help provide national defense and health care. In order to do so, the budget must stipulate the money to be spent on each program and the amount of revenues to be collected. It is the president and the Congress who make these decisions and they are written and explained by the OMB and the CBO with the aid of the congressional committees (*Analytical Perspectives* 2000: 445–446).

THE BUDGET CYCLE

There are currently three main phases of the budget cycle: (1) executive formulation of the budget, (2) congressional formulation and action on the budget, and (3) budget execution. Formerly, there was a fourth phase, audit and review of the budget (Meyer 1989a: 75–90). Initially, it is the president who provides the general budget and fiscal policy guidelines for the coming year. There may be changes proposed for the current year; if so, they are included along with the data on the most recently completed fiscal year for comparative purposes. Funding levels for at least four years beyond the coming year are provided.

The budget calendar is as follows:

Between the first Monday in January and the first Monday in February:	Budget transmitted by the president with a sequestration preview report.
Six weeks later:	Budget committees receive reports of budget estimates from congressional committees.
April 15:	Action to be completed on congressional budget resolution.
May 15:	Annual appropriations bills may begin to be considered by the House.
June 15:	Reconciliation action to be completed.
July 15:	Mid-session review of the budget transmitted by the president.
August 20:	Sequestration preview updated by OMB.
October 1:	Fiscal year begins.
15 days after the end of a session of Congress:	Final sequestration order issued by OMB. Sequestration order issued by the president, if needed. (*Analytical Perspectives* 2000: 449)

In spite of the timetable specified in the law and described above, there have been times when the budget documents were not transmitted according to these dates. Sometimes, it has been because an outgoing president is not required to transmit a budget, and other times it has been because of lateness with appropriations acts and tax laws considered in the previous budget cycle. Presidents have dealt with these problems by transmitting abbreviated budgets stating "with more information to follow later," and sometimes presidents have submitted a budget supplement (*Analytical Perspectives* 2000: 446).

During the formulation phase which begins in the spring or at least nine months before the January or February transmission of the budget to Congress, the president, the OMB director, and other individuals in the EOP are continually in communication with other heads of departments and agencies to settle matters of budget policy and evaluation. All of these discussions are reliant upon projections of the economic outlook which are developed jointly by the CEA, OMB, and the Treasury Department.

The decision-making process begins in the autumn when agencies forward their budget requests to OMB for review. The OMB and the agencies resolve any issues that arise among themselves or involve officials of the White House, as needed. By late December, these matters are completed and formal preparation of the budget and its accompanying documents begins.

It is at this point that the vital basis of the budget estimates is considered. The economic and technical assumptions with respect to the nation's growth rate, interest rates, the unemployment rate, and so forth, are studied (*Analytical Perspectives* 2000: 445). The single most important basis for determining the growth of the economy is that developed by the Bureau of Economic Analysis for the NIPA, although it is continuously subject to revision.

NATIONAL INCOME AND PRODUCT ACCOUNTS

The National Bureau of Economic Research (NBER) developed the first set of national income accounts in the 1930s as an extension of its studies on factor incomes. Simon Kuznets, who directed the work received the 1971 Nobel Prize for his role in the project.

In 1993, the United States formally adopted the newly revised System of National Accounts (SNA) which had been developed by Sir Richard Stone, the 1984 Nobel laureate. The United Nations had been the first to publish it in 1953. Internationally, the adoption of SNA means a more consistent basis for comparing economic activity across countries (Popkin 2000: 215–224). The NIPA are used to measure economic progress. They need to be improved and supplemented. For example, nonmarket worktime, natural resources, and the environment should be presented as supplemental information. Research and development, physical, human and environmental capital should appear in separate but related accounting forms, according to Michael J. Boskin. Adding these items to the NIPA is not appropriate at present because of continued difficulties in their interpretation and measurement. The Bureau of Economic Analysis has continued to make improvements in the accounts including the move from GNP to GDP, chain weighting, better price and output indexes (Fisher ideal), using the SNA system, and others. Major revisions of the 1999 accounts were the inclusion of software under the investment heading and "the backcasting to 1978 of the geometric mean aggregates of price quotes to reduce lower-level substitution bias." The adjustment raised real GDP growth for the entire 1990s decade (Boskin 2000: 248).

Definitions of GNP and GDP are given in *A Glossary of Terms Used in the Federal Budget Process* (GAO 1993a) as follows:

GNP: The value of all final goods and services produced by labor and capital supplied by residents of the United States in a given period of time, whether or not the residents are located within the United States. (p. 50)

GDP: The value of all final goods and services produced within the borders of the United States in a given period of time, whether produced by residents or nonresidents. (p. 50)

GNP was formerly used in the budget documents as the basis for many tables reflecting budget sums, such as receipts or outlays, as a percentage of GNP. Currently, the new basis used is GDP.

Many significant problems remain in forecasting statistics that reflect an ever-changing economy. Some of those mentioned by Boskin are: the continuous launching of new products, the changes in the quality of products, introduction of new technology and innovation; the changing uses of time for the household member and the worker; and other demographic, capital, structural, and international trade arrangements. Previous improvements to measured GDP have led to its increase. The outcome of the above changes are uncertain (Boskin 2000: 249–252).

Furthermore, the frequent and important revisions of NIPA definitions and statistical procedures have led to considerable difficulties in interpreting budgetary numbers over time. There is no doubt that the assumptions concerning the various components of the national income accounts and the economic projections which are based upon this information can affect budget estimates significantly. The *Budget FY 2000* reports on page 9 of *Analytical Perspectives* (1999) that it is prudent to base budget estimates on a conservative set of economic assumptions, close to the consensus of private sector forecasts.

THE TREASURY

The Treasury Department and the FRS are the hub of all financial operations for the federal government. Their importance cannot be overstated when it comes to the efficient and effective performance of government's financial activities. However, the FRS is an independent entity with no formal role in federal budget making, which is considered a fiscal proposition. The FRS undertakes duties on behalf of the Treasury Department in the execution phase of the budget process. The following information from the *United States Government Manual 1999/2000* (Office of the Federal Register 1999) offers an overview of the broad array of functions that the Treasury Department performed, with the aid of 143,000 civilian employees, at the end of September 1999, or 7.8 percent of total executive branch employees of 1,280,000 at that time. The Treasury Department is the third largest executive branch employer after the Defense Department, 666,000 or 36.5 percent, and the Veterans Department, 219,000 or 12.9 percent. Total federal personnel, excluding uniformed military personnel, was 2,749,000 at the end of September 1999 (*Historical Tables* 2000: 280–281). According to *Analytical Perspectives* (2001), federal employment in the executive branch (measured by full-time equivalents) in 2001 totaled 1,814,300. The Defense Department remains the largest employer. Total federal personnel (measured by total positions filled) as of September 2000 was 4,128,596, of which 1,420,495 represented military personnel on active duty (*Analytical Perspectives* 2001: 214–215).

The Department of the Treasury formulates and recommends economic, financial, tax, and fiscal policies, in addition to acting as financial agent for the U.S. government. Also, it enforces the law, and manufactures coins and currency. Among the bureaus of the department that are involved in budget and related matters are the Financial Management Service, the IRS, and the Public Debt. Also, there are assistant secretaries for economic policy, financial institutions, fiscal affairs, legislative affairs, tax policy, and an inspector general for tax administration (Office of the Federal Register 1999: 446–447).

According to Barry H. Potter and Jack Diamond (in an article which appeared in *Finance and Development* in September 2000), Treasury systems rely on four basic elements: (1) a treasury department within the finance ministry that forwards government payments and collects receipts through its field offices; (2) a treasury account in the central bank to contain the government's financial resources; (3) a general ledger for the treasury to account for government operations; and (4) a financial plan and accompanying financial management for the public sector.

In the year 2000, Treasury payment systems and ledgers were introduced in every country but Treasury ledgers and financial management were taking longer than anticipated to develop. Part of the problem was due to budget formulation issues with respect to such items as: lack of information on spending patterns, inadequate classification systems, or lack of cooperation between Treasury and Budget departments. The other part of the problem relates to poor governance in the manner of use of off-budget accounts, in-kind transactions, and netting practices.

The International Monetary Fund (IMF) is drawing up a guide for budget preparation based on its *Code of Good Practices on Fiscal Transparency* to help further the course of improved overall budget management (Potter and Diamond 2000: 36–39).

OFFICE OF MANAGEMENT AND BUDGET

The primary budgetary functions of the OMB, according to the *United States Government Manual 1999/2000*, are:

1. To aid the President in promoting effective government by overseeing the organizational structure and managerial methods of the executive branch to assure the establishment of intended results.
2. To aid in cultivating efficient systems for implementing government activities and interagency collaboration.
3. To aid in formulating and preparing the government's fiscal program and the budget.
4. To plan and develop information systems to provide the executive with program performance data.
5. To plan and implement evaluation efforts to aid the executive in assuring program efficiency, performance and objectives (Office of the Federal Register 1999: 100).

The OMB is the single largest unit in the EOP. The office was created by Franklin D. Roosevelt in 1939 and the then Bureau of the Budget moved from the Treasury Department to its new presidential home. Physically, OMB is located across the street from the White House and operates with little public visibility, but with a great deal of informational sources, analytical expertise, and presidential clout. Shelly Lynne Tomkin, author of *Inside OMB Politics and Process in the President's Budget Office* (1998), suggests that OMB is situated at the nerve center of the federal government and exerts a strong impact on public policy outcomes.

The OMB, or the Bureau of the Budget, was established in 1921 by the passage of the Budget and Accounting Act of 1921 that provided for the first federal budget in the United States. The Bureau's major purpose is to assist and advise the president by providing information on issues and making recommendations concerning resource allocation. The president also uses OMB as a go-between for interagency disputes. OMB had a $50 million budget, or almost one-fourth of the total budget of $212 million allocated to the EOP in 1998. OMB had a staff of 518 in that year, which is more than one-fourth of the EOP staff of 1,600 individuals. EOP consists of the White House staff, the Office of the Vice President, the National Security Council, and the CEA, among other entities.

The largest OMB unit is the Budget Review Division (BRD), and within it are the Budget Analysis and Systems Division and the Budget Review and Concepts Division. These groups are the ones that prepare and coordinate the president's budget proposals. For example, the Budget Concepts branch of the Budget Review and Concepts Division prepares and presents the "Balances of Budget Authority," a separate compilation included with the annual budget documents. The Budget Review branch coordinates and prepares the final form of the budget for its transmission to Congress. It monitors each stage of the congressional appropriations process.

The BRD prepares overall economic projections and serves as a connecting link between the executive and the legislature. Furthermore, with the passage of deficit limiting legislation in the 1980s, the BRD has acted as interpreter for those points in the law that were not clearly specified by Congress. There are three other branches of the OMB that are considerably smaller than BRD with its approximately 75-person unit. They are the Resource Management Office, which acts as a storehouse for agency programmatic information, the Budget Analysis, or Fiscal Analysis Division prior to the early 1990s, and the Office of Economic Policy, which serves as part of the economic policy making quartet for the president. The other members of the group of four are the Treasury Department, the CEA, and the most recent member, the National Economic Council. However, when economic estimates and forecasting differences arise between the executive and the legislature, the Budget Analysis branch is a participant as well. The unit will act, then, as a representative of OMB in consultation with the CBO and the Senate and House Budget committees (Tomkin 1998: 17).

The OMB has a central computer system housed in the Budget Systems branch, the MAX system. It was introduced in 1994 when two previous systems were integrated into one. OMB has some legislative duties along with its budget-making role. These duties are assumed by the Legislative Reference Division (LRD), created in 1945, and they include clearance for agency-proposed legislation, advice to the president concerning his action on enacted bills, and formulation of presidential legislative initiatives.

There are offices in OMB devoted to government-wide management concerns: the Office of Federal Financial Management (OFFM), the Office of Federal Procurement Policy (OFPP), and the Office of Information and Regulatory Affairs (OIRA). In addition, there is a Legislative Affairs Office (LA) which acts as a go-between for OMB, the House and Senate Appropriations Committees, and the OMB's Office of Administration, Communications Office, and Office of the General Counsel.

In 1997, there were over 500 persons working at OMB and that number has remained fairly constant in the past several years. They are headed by the director of the OMB who has a difficult and responsible job of major importance to the president and the nation. Under the guidance of the president, the OMB director prepares the president's budget and formulates his policies into budget numbers. OMB's director must maintain communications not only with the White House, but with other members of the Cabinet agencies as well. In common with the FRS, the OMB operated for years in relative obscurity. Then gradually, the directors of the OMB became more visible as the media called upon them to express administration policies. Since the 1970s, they began to testify before Congress concerning the budget transmitted to Congress. This has encouraged the growth of a more significant and prominent role for the director, particularly in the area of domestic policy (Tomkin 1998: 25–28).

Another explanation for the decline in the relative standing of the OMB as an institution, even while the director became more prominent in the news, is that of Lance T. LeLoup. He sees the development of presidential budgeting as having led to more congressional input in budgeting and spending, including entitlements over recent years as a sort of backlash. Also, there has been a transition from the more detailed and specialized agency goals of budgeting, or microbudgeting, to the larger approach of looking at taxing and spending policies altogether, or macrobudgeting.

In the early years of federal budgeting, the executive budget was accepted in the form in which it was offered by the president, although the Congress would argue over priorities and dollar figures. Any budget reforms were made to clarify objectives and to improve budget analysis. Reforms involved Planning Programming Budgeting Systems (PPBS) in the 1960s, Management by Objective (MBO), and Zero-Based Budgeting (ZBB) in the

1970s. These programs addressed efficiency considerations and were directed at small organizational units and programs.

In 1974, Congress passed the Congressional Budget and Impoundment Control Act. It made changes in both the executive and congressional process and structure of budgeting. However, the major impact of the Act was to give Congress the upper hand in budgeting by limiting the presidential powers of impoundment and by permitting Congress to revise and restructure the priorities expressed in the executive budget.

The 1970s were eventful for another reason. Entitlement programs increased from 33 percent to 47 percent of the budget during the period. Programs were enlarged, benefits were increased, and inflation made costs rise. The programs that were substantially larger included Food Stamps, Social Security, Supplemental Security Income (SSI) and, in addition, Social Security became inflation indexed.

Congress and the OMB were continually involved in disputes over budget information, the reliability of budget and deficit projections, and political concerns. Discretionary fiscal policy was on the decline by the end of the decade and monetary policy came to the forefront. The 1980s saw the emergence of OMB as an external arm to Congress. The Central Budget Management System (CBMS) tracked the president's requests through the various stages of the congressional budget process. OMB introduced discussion of aggregates and multiyear trends in budget presentation to Congress instead of programs and line items. However, with the defense buildup and a large tax cut during these years, deficits were mounting up and reached more than $200 billion in each of the years 1983, 1985, and 1986 (LeLoup 1998: 210–221).

Probably the single most important factor in the declining importance of OMB in the budget process was the congressional attempt to reduce deficits and override executive budget power through several procedural changes and the adoption of the Balanced Budget and Emergency Deficit Control Act of 1985 (Gramm-Rudman-Hollings). The Act was not successful but it emphasized the general concern over budgetary politics so that presidential budgeting became more prominent as a public issue. OMB concentrated, at this point, on top-down budgeting while Congress continued working toward better ways of intruding its own priorities into the budget process. In 1990, the Omnibus Budget Reconciliation Act (OBRA), which included the BEA, succeeded in making a contribution toward deficit reduction. The mandatory deficit reduction method of G-R-H was dropped, and spending caps and a PAYGO system introduced. Congress and the president were under constraints that limited any particular increases in spending or reductions in taxing to be offset elsewhere in the budget (LeLoup 1998: 215).

Of all the changes in the institutional arrangements of federal budgeting, which continued into the 1990s and, in 1997, included the Balanced Budget

Act and the Taxpayer Relief Act, the largest change has been the growth of congressional budget making relative to that of the executive.

REFORM IN THE EXECUTIVE BRANCH: NATIONAL PERFORMANCE REVIEW

In 1993, the administration released a management reform report called National Performance Review (NPR) which started a lively debate about the federal bureaucracy. Although, in the first year, it simplified rules and procedures, reformed the procurement process, coordinated management activities, and encouraged innovations by federal managers, it did not lay the foundation for sustained success, according to Donald F. Kettl. At the end of 1993, the GAO analyzed the 384 major recommendations of the NPR report; it rejected only one of them, made no comment on 121, and formally accepted 262. The one rejection had to do with forming a coordinating council inside the Department of Labor (DiIulio 1995: 3). Kettl's comments were that working better and costing less were basically conflicting objectives in the NPR plan. In the end, the NPR did demonstrate that management in government, as in private business, does matter (Kettl 1995: 9–11, 81).

Donald Kettl, in "The Three Faces of Reinvention" in the Brookings Institution serial volume *Setting National Priorities* (1999), makes an even more definitive statement about the successes and failures of the NPR. He remarks that the federal government is not organized well enough to manage the government effectively. Now that the deficit in the unified budget has evaporated, there are two "quieter" deficits to challenge government: the gap between the nation's economic goals and their achievement, and the gap between the public's confidence in government and government's ability to satisfy that trust. Management reform is the cure for the first gap and success for this one can help to close the second gap (Kettl 1999: 445).

REFORM IN THE EXECUTIVE BRANCH: DOWNSIZING

According to Paul C. Light, author of *The True Size of Government* (1999b), President Bill Clinton declared in 1996 that the era of big government was over. At that time, there were approximately 1.9 million federal employees or almost 400,000 less than in 1968. If all the individuals who produce goods and services for the federal government were counted, the number is closer to 14.6 million individuals including those employed under federal grants, contracts, and under mandate to state and local government. The larger number still leaves out the uniformed military and postal service workers, which bring the final total to 17 million persons.

Light calls the additional workforce, those who are not receiving paychecks directly from the U.S. Treasury, the "shadow of government." He concludes that the shadow is designed to give the illusion of a smaller government. Actually, it makes government more complex and less accountable. Light recommends leaving aside the concept of head count constraints and letting departments and agencies use their alloted budget dollars to employ whatever workforce they find suitable and efficient (Light 1999b).

In Light's chapter, "Changing the Shape of Government" in *Setting National Priorities: The 2000 Election and Beyond* (Light 1999a) he emphasizes that "The days of a fully self-contained work force are long gone, never to return." Persons with almost every political preference are pleased to keep government looking small. Future cutbacks are certain, writes Light, but they should be planned and government should be carefully reshaped.

REFORM IN THE EXECUTIVE BRANCH: COST-BENEFIT ANALYSIS

A third reform is not fully underway but the need for it has arisen with the several proposals for reforming Social Security. It concerns the governmental use of cost-benefit analysis to determine whether a given long-term investment project is worthwhile undertaking from the viewpoint of the economy as a whole. Cost-benefit analysis was used, initially, as a technique for assessing the effects of the Flood Control Act of 1936. The theoretical justification for it was established by Sir John Hicks in his 1943 article on consumers' surplus (Rutherford 1992: 97).

The three most commonly used decision rules in cost-benefit analysis are: net present value (NPV), benefit/cost (B/C), and internal rate of return (IRR).

NPV = net present value is the discount rate of future expected returns from an investment project less the discounted value of expected costs.

B/C = benefit–cost ratio is the process of evaluating benefits and costs of a program to learn if benefits outweigh the costs.

IRR = internal rate of return is the discount rate which makes net present value of an investment project equal to zero.

Of the three rules, NPV is preferred because, ordinarily, it provides reliable ranking. The other two are less reliable, particularly with respect to differences in size of initial capital outlay, in the case of B/C, or size of project, in the case of IRR. Essentially, it is the calculations of costs and benefits in themselves that can lead to their over- or understatement. Tevfik F. Nas (1996) has stressed that identifying and accounting for consumer surplus, compensating and equivalent variation measures of a welfare change, real output effects, and the external effects of a project must be distinguished from redistribution outcomes in evaluating a project or program (Nas 1996: 67–171).

One of the most difficult assumptions to be made in the use of any of these decision rules relates to the choice of discount rate. Coleman Bazelon and Kent Smetters (1999) suggest that when a larger discount rate is used, cost and benefit in the future are given less weight than those in the near term. Therefore, choice of the discount rate can be a predetermining factor in evaluating government programs. The programs selected in this way cover a broad range of policy choices from whether to build an electricity generating dam to how to choose among reform plans for Social Security.

Bazelon and Smetters' article in the 1999 issue of the *Journal of Economic Perspectives* begins with the argument that the discounting of future benefits and costs should somehow be similar to the program's level of riskiness. If there is no uncertainty involved, say the authors, then economic theory would select a risk-free discount rate usually associated with a U.S. Treasury bill.

When it comes to private markets, there is risk involved and investors seek an additional premium called the "equity premium." It is quite large and has ranged from an average of 6 percent above the U.S. Treasury bill rate annually over the past century. Economists have not been able to explain the reason for the height of the risk premium within the standard neoclassical model.

However, Bazelon and Smetters argue that the government's programs are not risk-free and, in some cases, benefit-cost analysis should use a higher discount rate than the private market. One outcome of this decision is that more than one discount rate may be appropriate, depending on the government program being evaluated. For example, the very long-term, large project to which one applies a 6 or 7 percent discount rate may very likely see future benefits and costs shrink to nothing in the present. Therefore, it is common practice to use a lower discount rate in these cases. There are occasions when no discounting at all is used by government. Agencies do not ordinarily discount dollars spent within a single year, nor does congressional cash-based budget planning. The latter includes the mandatory spending in the congressional budget resolution, which covers a five-year period. Entitlements, most taxes, and debt interest are part of mandatory spending. Much of the mandatory spending is subject to PAYGO rules, which require that a proposed increase in spending in one section of the budget be offset by decreases elsewhere or increases in taxes. The absence of discounting leads to a trade-off between the past and the future. In other words, increase spending now, and pay for it later by cutting a future program.

In fact, even the use of risk-free discount rates typically favors current government spending because risky future benefits appear greater when discounted at a low rate. Another bias of the low discount rate is toward the purchase of assets rather than their lease. At the direction of the OMB, agencies are to choose the cheaper of two possibilities: leasing or buying. For leasing, the agency is to use a discount rate for costs of a U.S. Treasury Bond of equal maturity to the costs over the full life of the lease. But the same rate may be applied to buying the asset rather than the applicable commercial market rate. Thus, the bias turns toward purchasing the asset.

Bazelon and Smetters argue that similar biases arise in the analysis of the sale of government assets. The numerous proposals for reforming Social Security are faced with more difficult problems. The fundamental discounting issue relates to prefunding and equity investment and how to account for the riskiness of investment. Bazelon and Smetters conclude their study by claiming that government should not be discounting future costs and benefits of any of its programs any differently than the private market does. The present system tends to encourage more provision of goods and services by government along with an occasional greater redistribution between generations favoring the current one. These and related issues will have significant bearing on the resolution of Social Security reform (Bazelon and Smetters 1999: 213–228). Additional comments concerning improvements in the technique of evaluating long-run government projects include those of John K. Horowitz (2000) and others. A consensus has apparently developed during the past 15 years that medium-length projects should be evaluated using a market discount rate, one that reflects the opportunity cost of capital, in cost-benefit analysis. Medium-length projects are those with time frames of 40 years or less. For any longer period, decision makers do not agree.

Some economists believe that uncertainty should enter the calculations by using a lower discount rate for long-run projects. Others argue the same result—the lower discount rate—but because a social rate of return on investment is needed rather than the private one. Other contributions comprise one that questions the idea of being that concerned about future generations. Another uses the present value of consumption as a base rather than capital investment. There are suggestions, also, that present value point estimates should not be used alone but that different control strategies should be applied (Horowitz 2000: 424–425).

REFORM IN THE EXECUTIVE BRANCH: FEDERALISM

Executive Order 12612, originally issued in 1987, established basic principles and criteria for formulating and implementing policies that have implications for federalism. For example, executive agencies are directed to refrain as much as possible from initiating unvaried national standards for programs with implications of federalism. If it is necessary to develop such standards, it should be done in consultation with representatives of the states. In 1998, there was an executive order on federalism issued, but it was suspended and never went into effect. The National Governors' Association and others expressed concern that the order might give the federal government too much authority in making national policies, and besides, affected state and local governments had not been consulted about the order. Therefore, Executive Order 12612 remains in effect and the testimony offered here is concerning its specific requirements for agency implementation and government review. The statement was made by L. Nye Stevens, Director, Federal Management and Workforce Issues, General Government Division of GAO, before the Committee on Governmental Affairs of the United States Senate, in May 1999. An official of each executive department or agency is responsible for following up on the accomplishment of the directives and for deciding which policies should be assessed for federalism content. When an assessment is to be made and there is a "significant rule" involved, it must be submitted to OMB for review under another Executive Order, 12866 issued in 1993.

In the concluding section of the statement, Stevens notes that agencies have not prepared many federalism assessments. Of the three agencies visited, Environmental Protection Agency (EPA), Health and Human Services (HHS), and USDA, all had written guidelines prepared for implementation, but one had no written criteria for determination of when federal assessment would be necessary. The other two agencies between them had only one federalism assessment in which they cited the executive order in only 10 cases of almost 3,000 rules. In fact, only five federalism assessments had been prepared by agencies for more than 11,000 final rules issued in recent years. Even OMB, who includes federalism in its regulatory reviews, has no other specific agenda for ensuring that agencies observe the executive orders on federalism.

REFORM IN THE EXECUTIVE BRANCH: INTERNAL REVENUE SERVICE

This reform has been expected by persons both inside and outside government for some time. It is likely that there will be further developments. Initially, the movement began with an effort to establish the citizen's rights as a taxpayer. Under the Taxpayer Bill of Rights 1, the IRS had to explain clearly any actions it proposed to take against the taxpayer. Then, in Taxpayer Bill of Rights 2, section 101, the establishment of Taxpayer Advocate within the IRS was provided. The advocate serves as the Director of the Office of the Taxpayer Advocate, which is responsible to the Commissioner of Internal Revenue. The functions of the Taxpayer Advocate include assisting taxpayers and identifying problems associated with their dealings with the IRS. The advocate has the additional duties of preparing changes in administrative practices and suggesting legislative actions on behalf of the IRS that might aid in overcoming taxpayer problems. The Taxpayer

Advocate reports to the Committee on Ways and Means in the House of Representatives and the Committee of Finance in the Senate, on objectives for the coming fiscal year, by 30 June each year after 1995. The Advocate reports, also, to the committees on activities during the past fiscal year before 31 December. The later report is to include at least 20 of the most serious problems encountered by taxpayers and recommendations for improving taxpayer services. The Taxpayer Advocate replaced, according to the Act, the former position of Ombudsman and Office of Ombudsman established under the provisions of the Internal Revenue Code of 1986 (P.L. 104–68 [1996]: 1452–1455).

Two years later, the Internal Revenue Service Restructuring and Reform Act of 1998, or Restructuring Act, was passed. In the statement of James R. White, Director of Tax Policy and Administrative Issues of the General Government Division of the GAO on the first anniversary of the act, he explained the purposes and the general plan of the reform. Some of the major purposes of the act were to (1) emphasize serving the public and meeting the needs of taxpayers, (2) form new operating units to serve taxpayers with similar needs, (3) introduce training programs for employees to assure good customer service, and (4) take action to affirm taxpayers' rights.

In order to fulfill this agenda, Commissioner Rossotti has introduced a new mission statement and outlined a modernization strategy. In the mission statement, he promises the best quality service to taxpayers, application of the law with integrity and fairness, and increased productivity of employees by improvements in work environment. With respect to fulfilling this mission, the IRS "five levers of change" are (1)revamped business practices, (2) organizational restructuring, (3) management rules with clear responsibility, (4) balanced measures of performance, and (5) new technology (James White 1999: 1).

Even Director James R. White, while making these statements, recognizes the difficulty in achieving the goals. He comments that the IRS has been subject to "stovepipe management and a culture driven by enforcement statistics." In sum, White finds the agenda ambitious and notes the IRS has a poor track record for implementation. Nevertheless, he reports that the first steps have been taken in the initial modernization plan, which was blueprinted in May 1977 and has been updated in light of the new legislative recommendations. In the opinion of Director White, a central part of achieving cost-effective systems is the use of an incremental investment management strategy. The strategy requires breaking up larger system projects into a sequence of incremental steps. Each increment is tracked and monitored for its performance in meeting benefit and cost schedules on time and its reporting of the information to appropriate executive decision makers. The Commissioner's leadership and IRS efforts to meet the foregoing agenda are applauded by White, but the final success of serving taxpayers will rest with IRS managers and their efficient use of agency resources (James White 1999: 2–15).

BUDGETARY MANAGEMENT IN OTHER NATIONS

In spite of problems with budgetary management in the United States, it is uplifting to learn that budgetary management as practiced by the federal government has been a model for many other nations of the world. A. Premchand, who is associated with the IMF, ascribes the pervasive influence of U.S. budgeting to five factors: (1) countries who have been under U.S. administrative management; (2) countries who have received U.S. technical assistance; (3) countries who adopt budgetary innovations of the United States, such as performance budgeting; (4) transition economies who choose the United States as a representative democracy; and (5) countries who follow academic theories developed in the United States who have made similar innovations even though the U.S. methods were not adopted.

In common with other nations since the 1970s, innovations in budgetary management have followed similar paths. There has been a trend at reorganizing government in three main ways: downsizing, greater decentralization, and greater use of information technology. In addition, more managerial flexibility has developed with accountability emphasized and backed up by a reward or incentive structure. A significant innovation has been the development of internal competitive markets within government and more contracting out of services to encourage economic efficiency in the provision and delivery of goods and services (Premchand 1999: 83–85, 88–89).

CONCLUDING COMMENTS

One of the more serious difficulties in formulating the federal budget is deciding upon its underlying assumptions concerning such factors as the expected growth rate of the economy or the possible rise in the price level. The NIPA figures have been of invaluable assistance. There are two aspects of their employment that might be studied to improve their quality over time. One is the weighing of the advantages and disadvantages of frequent revisions of definitions or inclusions at one moment of time, versus a consistent set of numbers over a period of time. A second is, given the weaker reliability of long-range projections, determining what would be a reasonable and meaningful cutoff period for budget forecasts.

Although the Treasury and the OMB have important roles to play in budget making, more communication between them on the subject of the financial aspects of budgeting might be rewarding. Indirectly, the improvements in federal management instituted by NPR may contribute to correcting the situation. The techniques of cost-benefit analysis, their application, the time period under study, the factors to be included, the appropriate discount rate, and the proper accounting for uncertainty appear not to be developed to their full potential. As any federal program involves time, the significance of cost-benefit analysis increases with the size of the program and the length of its time frame. Social Security programs are on the high side of both these considerations. As for reforms concerning federalism and the IRS, it is too early to comment on the directions they may take. But, in general, the arrival of information technology, the competitive environment of government agencies, and the greater accountability of federal managers promises a more efficient government organizational structure.

Chapter 4

Congressional Action

The role of Congress in the budget process was minor compared to that of the president up until the 1970s. With the passage of the Congressional Budget and Impoundment Control Act of 1974, Congress gained the power to prepare its own version of the federal budget with the aid of its new office, the CBO. The CBO became the chief source of data related to budgeting, taxing, and spending legislation and performed analyses and evaluations of various programs and policy options for the Congress. Several significant budget acts followed that extended the budget powers of Congress, but later attempted to curb them as deficits grew ever larger. Today, budget reformers are concerned with entitlement programs, executive management, and legislative committee structure. The final section of this chapter deals with the relationship between the Congress and the FRS. Financial matters are vital to budget implementation and have been understated in their contribution to successful budget operations and outcomes.

CONGRESS AND THE CONSTITUTION

Compared to the executive branch and its hierarchy of authority, Congress is distinguished by its more loosely organized participants and their variety of opinions and values. It does not move quickly by design because this is an important feature of democratic government. The job list of Congress is a large, long, and indispensable one described in Article I, section 8 of the Constitution, beginning with:

The Congress shall have the Power To lay and collect Taxes, Duties, Imposts and Excises, to pay the Debts and provide for the common Defence and general Welfare

of the United States; but all Duties, Imposts and Excises shall be uniform throughout the United States;

and ending with:

To make all Laws which shall be necessary and proper for carrying into Execution
the foregoing Powers, and all other Powers vested by the Constitution in the Government of the United States, or in any Department or Officer thereof. (*Constitution
of the United States of America* 1974: 3–4)

Unlike the executive branch, Congress has the authorization under the
Constitution to collect revenues, to spend them to provide and support an
army and a navy, and to coin money to do so. However, like the president,
the Congress did not have the authorization to formulate a comprehensive
federal budget.

CONGRESSIONAL BUDGET ACT OF 1974

Approximately 50 years after the creation of the executive budget, the
congressional budget and budget process was established with the passage
of the Congressional Budget Act of 1974. Since that time, the process has
gone through several formal and informal changes. One of the more important changes has been with respect to the budget resolution. Originally,
there were two, but in the early 1980s, only one was retained as a constraint on Congress rather than its prior use as a goal (Schick 1994a: 96).

After the president submits his proposals, usually by late January or early
February, it is up to the Congress to accept, reject, or to modify them. In
other words, Congress can include new programs, change funding levels,
eliminate programs or taxes, add other sources of receipts, or affect total
receipts collected.

At the outset, under the requirements of the Congressional Budget Act
of 1974, Congress must decide on a budget resolution that provides levels
for total spending and receipts, the amount of surplus or deficit, and the
debt limit. The recommended budget levels are prepared by each standing
committee of the House and the Senate. There were 19 standing committees
in the House and 16 in the Senate reported in the *United States Government Manual 1999/2000* (Office of the Federal Register 1999). The standing committees report their decisions to the Budget Committee within each
body together with legislative plans for matters within each committee's
specialization. The Budget Committees then proceed to formulate the concurrent resolution on the budget. In the resolution, levels are set for budget
authority and outlays by total and by functional category as well as for
total receipts. The budget surplus or deficit and the level of the debt are
specified, also. The statutory limits that apply to changes in outlays and

receipts through 2002 for the president's budget apply equally to the budget resolution.

CONGRESS AND THE BUDGET PROCESS

At this point, Congress has the blueprint within which the congressional committees must operate. The first step before making appropriations, is for Congress to pass authorizing legislation that enables an agency to carry out a program. Sometimes, the legislation limits the amounts that can be appropriated for the program. There are one-year, multiyear, and permanent appropriations. It is possible for Congress to decide on appropriations for a program without any specific authorization for it. Then, Congress proceeds to furnish spending authority for certain purposes, usually in 13 appropriations acts annually. Actually, Congress votes on budget authority rather than the level of outlays. Budget authority is the authority granted by statute to incur financial obligations that will result in outlays. The House and Senate Appropriations Committees are allocated the amounts of budget authority and outlays within the functional category totals, according to their jurisdictions, by the Budget Committees. Subcommittees receive their allocations from the Appropriations Committees. In drafting spending bills, the subcommittees must keep totals within their allocations. Budget resolutions often contain reconciliation directives which necessitate changes in permanent laws affecting outlays and receipts by the authorizing committees. Amendments to the laws are then proposed by each designated committee (*Analytical Perspectives* 2000: 446). The congressional timetable calls for Congress to adopt the budget resolution by the fifteenth of April each year. Congress continually fails to meet that date. Whenever the budget resolution is passed, any bill that would enable a committee to overstep its allocation may be blocked if a member of Congress raises a point of order.

Appropriations bills originate in the House by tradition, but bills raising revenue originate there as provided by Article I, section 7 of the Constitution. The Appropriations Committees are divided into subcommittees, which hold hearings and study budget justification reports prepared by the appropriate agencies. The subcommittee drafts a bill on the basis of its findings, which must be approved by the committee, and then the full House, usually with amendments. The bill is forwarded to the Senate for a similar procedure. Any difference between the House and the Senate about the bill is referred to a Conference Committee consisting of members of both bodies. When they agree to a revision of the bill, it must be referred back to the House and the Senate for their approval before it can be forwarded to the president. The president can approve or veto the entire bill, not parts of it. He was granted a limited line item veto by the Congress in 1996, but it was declared unconstitutional in 1998 by the Supreme Court.

At the beginning of the fiscal year, if Congress has not completed action on appropriations bills, it may enact a joint resolution. A joint resolution enables agencies to continue operating until their appropriations have been enacted. There have been agency shutdowns when the president did not approve all the provisions contained in the resolution, but not for more than a few weeks. In late 1998, there were two short government-wide shutdowns. The annual appropriations acts control one-third of total spending, although they identify the spending for the greater part of federal programs. Two-thirds of total spending is associated with authorizing legislation or permanent laws. These programs include Social Security and interest on the public debt. The permanent laws generate most taxes and other receipts, also. Tax bills originate in the House Ways and Means Committee, while the Senate Finance Committee reviews the proposed tax bills. There may be reconciliation directives in the budget resolution that require changing permanent laws. The designated committees study the matter and draft the necessary legislation. The legislation may indicate revision of eligibility requirements, benefit formulas, or other changes. Sometimes, Congress furnishes an omnibus reconciliation act combining all the amendments in a single act. In this case, they and the appropriations acts may include, also, methods of enforcing agreements reached between the president and the Congress (*Analytical Perspectives* 2000: 446–447). It is the OMB and CBO who propose the estimates and calculations that determine whether sequestration is necessary. Sequestration is of two types: for discretionary appropriations or for mandatory spending legislation. In both cases, it refers to the cancellation of budgetary resources, under the provisions of the Budget Enforcement Act (BEA), previously provided in one of the two areas. If sequestration is necessary, the director of OMB explains the differences between the two reports to the president and Congress. The president is required by the BEA to issue a "preview" report in August, and a "final" report at the end of a session of Congress. In the event that a sequestration is too close to the end of the fiscal year and may be too unsettling, the BEA permits the use of a reduced cap for the next fiscal year in its place (*Analytical Perspectives* 2000: 449).

BASIC BUDGET LEGISLATION

Since the 1970s, the budget and the budget process have been substantially affected by six budget laws:

- the Congressional Budget and Impoundment Control Act of 1974 and amendments, which sets out the congressional budget process and restricts certain procedures of budget execution.
- the Balanced Budget and Emergency Deficit Control Act of 1985, known as the Gramm-Rudman-Hollings (G-R-H) Act, and amendments, which includes methods to prevent excess spending.

- the Budget Enforcement Act (BEA) of 1990, which amended the Congressional Budget and Impoundment Control Act and the Balanced Budget and Emergency Deficit Control Act and other key laws pertaining to the budget process.
- the Budget Enforcement Act of 1997, which specified the contents of the report accompanying the concurrent resolution and included new definitions of terms, commonly referred to as BEA requirements, for discretionary spending limits, PAYGO, sequestration, and others (*Analytical Perspectives* 2000: 460–461).
- the Federal Credit Reform Act of 1990 as amended by the BEA of 1997, which provided for the treatment of federal credit programs in the budget.
- the Government Performance and Results Act of 1993, which required agencies to prepare annual performance plans and reports.

The Congressional Budget and Impoundment Control Act of 1974, P.L. 93–344, is actually two acts: Titles I to IX are known as the Congressional Budget Act of 1974 (CBA), and Title X is known as the Impoundment Control Act of 1974. The purposes of the Acts are stated at the beginning: "An Act to establish a new congressional process; to establish Committees on the Budget in each House; to establish a Congressional Budget Office; to establish a procedure providing congressional control over the impoundment of funds by the executive branch; and for other purposes" (P.L. 93–344, 5 August 1974: 1657).

Over the period since the 1974 Act, presidents have proposed 1,200 rescissions totaling almost $76 billion. Congress accepted less than half of them, or 33 percent totaling just under $25 billion. Congress, over the same period, has initiated approximately $105 billion in rescissions to revise expenditure decisions or budgetary authority.

In 1999, there were proposed rescissions amounting to $35 million, Congress rescinded $17 million (*Analytical Perspectives* 2000: 449–450; Kepplinger 1999: 1–9). The Balanced Budget and Emergency Deficit Control Act of 1985 or Gramm-Rudman-Hollings, P.L. 99–177, as amended in 1987, introduced a new budget process timetable; provided for assessing the deficit and methods of deficit reduction; explained the methods and reporting of sequestration; established credit authority for direct loan obligations and loan guarantee commitments along with other requirements within a single budget resolution; returned all off-budget entities to the budget but removed Old Age and Survivors Insurance (OASI) and Disability Insurance (DI) from the budget while it retained their receipts and disbursements for calculating deficit targets under G-R-H; and initiated budgetary procedures involving OMB, CBO, and the Comptroller General of the United States, among other matters (Meyer 1989a: 30–32, 65–72, 87–89, 140).

The Budget Enforcement Act of 1990, P.L. 101–58 and the Budget Enforcement Act of 1997, P.L. 105–33, amended almost all of the budget laws previously mentioned and affected legislation up until 2003. The budget documents devote a good deal of space to the provisions of these laws. There are two types of spending described in the BEA: discretionary spending and direct spending. Discretionary spending or appropriations refers to budgetary resources provided in annual appropriations acts such as salaries and operating expenses. Direct spending, the language of the BEA, is more generally known as mandatory spending and it arises from permanent laws that authorize payments for specific purposes. Other than the Food Stamp program, which is included here although it is funded by appropriations acts, there are Medicare and Medicaid programs, unemployment insurance benefits, and farm price supports, to name a few. Receipts are usually controlled by the same rules within the permanent legislation.

There are different constraints placed upon mandatory spending and receipts than on discretionary spending. Caps, or spending limits, are used in the case of discretionary expenditures, whether it be for defense or nondefense spending. If the spending limits are exceeded, either for budget authority or budget outlays for a given category, the BEA requires sequestration to reduce the spending in that category. Ordinarily, sequestration means that spending for most programs in the category will be reduced by an equal percentage.

New mandatory spending and receipts are not subject to caps but, rather, to a procedure known as PAYGO, which is applicable to all laws enacted through 2002. The procedure requires that if legislation increases the deficit or reduces the surplus in the current budget year or the four upcoming years, another law must be passed to offset the change completely for each year the budget balance is affected. Mandatory programs that are not subject to special rules or are not exempt require a uniform reduction in spending. Exempted programs are several, including Social Security, interest on the public debt, Medicaid, and most unemployment benefits.

Other mandatory spending programs limit the size of sequestration so that, in all, only about 3 percent of total mandatory spending is subject to sequestration (*Analytical Perspectives* 2000: 447–449). There were many more requirements imposed on the budget process by the BEA of 1997. Some of these are specifications as to the contents of the report accompanying the resolution:

- comparison of total new budget authority, total outlays, total revenues, and the surplus/deficit contained therein with those of the president's budget.
- each major functional category must have estimates of discretionary and mandatory amounts for total new budget authority and total outlays.
- economic assumptions for all matters listed and any other assumptions considered.
- estimated tax expenditures for the president's budget and the resolution.
- significant changes in proposed levels of federal assistance to state and local governments.

- allocation of revenues among the major federal sources.
- share of investment in total federal budget outlays and gross domestic product in the president's budget and resolution.
- assumed levels of budget authority and outlays for public buildings with respect to construction and repair, and rental.

Section 311 of the CBA of 1974 was amended in the BEA of 1997 by placing strong limitations on any attempt by either congressional body to raise the level of total new budget authority or total outlays, or lower the level of total revenues after the passage of the concurrent resolution for the coming fiscal year, and ensuing fiscal years for which allocations have been provided, except in the case of war (BEA 1997: 686–687).

Subtitle B of the BEA of 1997 included amendments to the G-R-H of 1985. There were new definitions of terms presented. For example, budgetary resources means new budget authority, unobligated balances, direct spending authority, and obligation limitations. The following section explains the enforcement of discretionary spending limits. Its purpose is to extend these limits through FY 2002. The adjustments concern annual limits for "continuing disability reviews," defined as redeterminations under section 201 of the Social Security Act and those authorized under section 211 of the Personal Responsibility and Work Opportunity Act of 1996. The limits stated apply to administrative expenses for the Social Security Administration. The sum almost doubles over the five-year period for additional new budget authority in FY 1998 of $290 million, to $520 million in FY 2002. Additional outlays have the limitation of $338 million in FY 1998, and $520 million in FY 2002.

In the amendments to the 1985 Act, a statement appears concerning the term "discretionary spending limit," which is followed by a list of budget authority and outlay limitations for five years separated into defense, nondefense, and violent crime reduction categories. This time, there is hardly any increase in new budget authority, which is scheduled at $527 billion for FY 1998, and rises to $551 billion in FY 2002. Outlays rise by less, from $553 billion in FY 1998, to $561 billion in FY 2002 (BEA of 1997: 667–702).

In sections 10205 to 10208 of the BEA of 1997, subjects covered comprise the enforcement of PAYGO provisions, exempt programs and activities, and sequestration rules. The last sections of the amendments to the 1985 Act include section 10209, which concerns the baseline budget and budgetary treatment of trust fund operations. It recognizes that OASI and DI are exempt from any general budget limitation on expenditures and net lending. It provides that no law after the 1985 Act, except if one is in force at the time, may permit payments from the General Fund of the Treasury to any trust fund or vice versa. Finally, sections 10210 to 10213 offer details about a technical correction, judicial review, effective date, and matters affecting the PAYGO scorecard. Scorecard refers to measurement of budget effects of legislation, usually with respect to budget authority, receipts, and outlays as required by BEA (P.L. 105–33 5 August 1997: 703–712; *Analytical Perspectives* 2000: 463).

The Federal Credit Reform Act of 1990 (P.L. 101–58 a part of the BEA of 1990, began its existence as part of the Omnibus Budget Reconciliation Act of 1990. In it, Title V of the CBA of 1974 was amended to be called "Credit Reform.") Section 500 stated that this title may be cited as the Federal Credit Reform Act of 1990. The title had four purposes:

1. To improve measurement of costs of federal credit programs.
2. To state these costs in budgetary terms equivalent to that for federal spending.
3. To enhance resource allocation among credit programs and between credit programs and other spending programs.
4. To promote the form of benefits most suitable to beneficiaries. Among the many definitions of terms, such as "direct loan" and "loan guarantee" in the next section, are definitions of how to calculate each of them. For example:

The cost of a direct loan shall be the net present value at the time when the direct loan is disbursed, of the following cash flows:
   (i) loan disbursements;
   (ii) repayments of principal; and
   (iii) payments of interest and other payments by or to the government over the life of the loan after adjusting for estimated defaults, prepayments, fees, penalties, and other recoveries. (P.L. 101–58: 1554)

In 1997, an additional phrase was added after the last word, "recoveries":

including the effects of changes in loan terms resulting from the exercise by the borrower of an option included in the loan contract. (P.L. 105–33: 693)

The Government Performance and Results Act of 1993, P.L. 103–62, records the findings of Congress which are stated in harsh terms:

(1) Waste and inefficiency in Federal programs undermine the confidence of the American people in the Government and reduces the Federal Government's ability to address adequately vital public needs;
   (2) Federal managers are seriously disadvantaged in their efforts to improve program efficiency and effectiveness, because of insufficient articulation of program goals and inadequate information on program performance; and
   (3) Congressional policymaking, spending decisions and program oversight are seriously handicapped by insufficient attention to program performance and results.

Then, the Act continues by stating the ways in which the findings are to be corrected. Among the six purposes of the Act are: holding federal agencies accountable for the success of their programs; establishing program goals and measuring performance in reaching the stated goals; and improving internal management of the federal government.

The Act, requires agencies to propose both strategic plans and performance plans to be submitted to the OMB director. The strategic plan is a long-range plan of at least five years, containing a mission statement and overall goals and objectives. The performance plan is an annual plan, ordinarily quantifiable and measureable, that forms the basis for comparing actual program results with the performance goals. OMB may exempt any agency from these requirements if its annual outlays are $20 million or less. There are some administrative procedural requirements and controls for waiver in the performance plans if the director of OMB chooses to approve such waivers. They may be for such items as personnel staffing levels or limitations on remuneration. The Act provides, also, for pilot projects for performance goals, managerial responsibility, and performance budgeting. The final portion of the Act is primarily concerned with strategic planning and performance management for the U.S. Postal Service (P.L. 103–62: 285–296).

BUDGET REFORM AND THE PRIVATE SECTOR

Both Allen Schick, who spent many years researching and writing about the federal budget process, and Roy Meyers, a former analyst with the CBO from 1981 to 1990, have offered suggestions for reform of the congressional budget process. In the conclusion to his book *The Federal Budget* (1994a), Schick discusses four reforms in the budget process that together would strengthen the president's budget powers relative to the Congress: the line item veto, enhanced rescission authority, biennial appropriations, and a legally binding budget resolution. Schick observes that none of these reforms will get the budget under control if the concentration is on discretionary spending only. The serious problem of budget control rests with existing entitlement programs (Schick 1994a: 203).

In another work, written together with John F. Cogan and Timothy J. Muris, both of whom served as policy officials at the OMB, Allen Schick is concerned with the institutions of budgeting. In particular, in his chapter on "The Study of Microbudgeting" in *The Budget Puzzle* (1994b), he focuses on the role of Congress as opposed to the president, the spending power of the various congressional committees, and the actions of the appropriations committees. Congress has the advantage when it comes to microbudgeting, while the executive is stronger in matters dealing with the broad aggregates of budgeting. The decentralized situation of congressional committees gives the Congress the opportunity to have each committee specialized in different features of the budget. The specialization most often will depend on the concerns of the constituencies of members of the relevant committee. The president is not likely to object to any of these micro-budgeting issues but will dispute any changes in his proposals that jeopardize the executive's overall control of the federal budget. The pity is that the dispersion of spending power among the congressional committees, together with each committee acting in its own behalf, raises total spending and deficits more than any one committee would choose. Cogan has raised this argument and confirmed the outcome with examples from the late twentieth century. Schick argues, nevertheless, that the rise in both mandatory outlays and trust receipts could explain the rise in federal spending without the presence of dispersion of spending power in the Congress (Schick 1994b: 105).

The matters that are harder to explain, says Schick, are on the executive side of budgetary operations. Less is known about what happens in federal agencies not only concerning how they construct their budgets, but how they put them into effect. More information is needed about what happens between the time of the agency's requested budget and the final pattern of spending. These affairs would include apportionment, allotment, internal budgets, reprogramming requests, revolving funds, and so forth. Micro-budgeting works with financial data from the ground up. It is the first step toward a better look at the aggregative level (Schick 1994b: 105–157).

Roy T. Meyers, in his chapter on "Legislatures and Budgeting" in the book he edited, *Handbook of Government Budgeting* (1999), suggests that there are certain flaws in the congressional budget process that can be overcome. One of these flaws is the extraordinary number of rules and procedures which need to be reduced if decisions are ever to be made as scheduled. The debt limit process appears unnecessary given the many other new rules that accomplish the same objective since the 1974 Act. Another flaw is that power has become too decentralized. There are too many committees performing similar functions and seniority rights help to perpetuate this arrangement (Meyers 1999: 498).

CONGRESS AND THE FEDERAL RESERVE SYSTEM

Congress passed the Federal Reserve Act of 1913 that created the Federal Reserve System, the central bank of the United States. Since that time, it has not ceased legislating, affecting the budget status and independence of the system. For example, in the Omnibus Reconciliation Act of 1993 (P.L. 103–66), the 103rd Congress placed information in "Banking and Housing Provisions," Title III, concerning "National Depositors Preference," section 3001, and "Transfer of Federal Reserve Surpluses," Section 3002. In National Depositors Preference, it is stated that the case of liquidation of any insured depository requires a priority order for beneficiaries. The top two mentioned are (1) the receiver for administrative expenses, and (2) the depositor or any deposit liability of the institution.

In section 3002, there is a provision for an annual dividend of 6 percent on paid-in capital stock to the stockholders of the Bank after all expenses of a Federal Reserve Bank have been provided for or paid. Each Federal Reserve Bank, which is a chartered federal corporation, was capitalized with subscriptions from private banks which then became members of the Federal Reserve Bank and eligible for their services. Therefore, the private banks are the stockholders of each Federal Reserve Bank. Any net earnings remaining after payment of the dividend claims are fully met become the surplus fund for the Federal Reserve Bank. For FY 1997 and 1998, any amount in the surplus fund over 3 percent of the paid-in capital and surplus of member banks to the Federal Reserve Bank must be transferred to the Board of Governors for transfer to the General Fund of the Treasury. In addition, the Federal Reserve Banks must transfer to the Board for the Treasury's General Fund, $106 million in FY 1997, and $107 million in 1998. It is the Board of Governors who determines the allocation of these amounts to be paid by the individual Federal Reserve Banks (P.L. 103–66 1993: 337).

These payments by the FRS have varied in amounts over the years as Congress continually reassesses the extent of independence to be granted to the system. The original Federal Reserve Act of 1913 (P.L. 63–43) had a mixed public/private ownership and regional structure reflecting the traditional dislike, in the United States, for the concept of a central bank. In addition, the Secretary of the Treasury and Comptroller of the Currency served on the Board in "ex officio" capacity in order to limit executive branch influence but still recognize that the Federal Reserve Banks had the responsibility of holding the Treasury accounts.

It was Congress, nonetheless, which set up the FRS, and they realized that the system would be profitable. So they established a "franchise tax" which required the transfer of 50 percent of the Federal Reserve Banks' net income to the Treasury. The other 50 percent could become part of the Federal Reserve Banks' surplus as long as that surplus did not exceed 40 percent of the paid-in capital of member banks. If it did, 90 percent of net income was then due the Treasury (CBO 1985: 7–8).

With the Banking Acts of 1933 and 1935, the franchise tax was repealed. The Acts established, also, the Federal Deposit Insurance Corporation (FDIC) and prohibited Federal Reserve Banks from engaging in the securities, real estate, and insurance industries. The budgetary independence of the Banks became more pronounced and the GAO no longer had the power of auditing the Board of Governors. The provision meant that assessments of Federal Reserve Banks by the FRB were not subject to government control. This independence was paid for by an amount of $139 million, half the surplus of the FRS at the time, which was used to partially capitalize the FDIC. During the depression era, the FRS consistently supported Treasury security offerings with "pegged" interest rates. By 1943, bond and Treasury securities were the main activity of 50 percent of employees in the system. Open market functions were considerable during this period. The FRS earned millions and turned over thousands to the Treasury (CBO 1985: 3–9).

Congress and the Treasury were troubled by the existing arrangement. However, before any legislation was introduced, the FRS decided to pay interest on Federal Reserve Notes in the amount of almost 90 percent of its earnings. From 1947 to 1970, the FRS reduced its support of Treasury financing. The conflict between the president, the Treasury on one side, the Congress, the FRS on the other, finally was resolved with the "accord." The agreement between the two conflicting groups recognized their common purpose with respect to debt management and monetary policies. Both would work toward assuring that the financing of government requirements would be successful and minimize the monetization of the public debt.

The period of 1951 to 1970 was one of continued discussion concerning the independent exercise of monetary and credit power desired by the FRS, and the Congress seeking direct congressional control. In 1967, the President's Commission on Budget Concepts upheld the budgetary independence of the FRS by indicating that just its profits transferred to the Treasury should be included in the new unified budget. The Commission claimed the operations and the economic significance of the FRS activities were basically different from other government programs and activities.

During the 1970s, the monetary policy reporting duties of the FRS increased, although it continued to retain its independent status for policy and budgeting affairs. The Federal Reserve Reform Act of 1977 (P.L. 95–188) required occasional testimony by the Board chairman before banking committees and required the FOMC, which controls the level of bank reserves through open market operations, to announce publicly its yearly targets for the growth of the money supply. The Full Employment and Balanced Growth Act of 1978 (P.L. 95–523), the Humphrey-Hawkins Act, directed the FOMC to ascertain whether its monetary targets were in harmony with the president's goals for employment, output, and prices.

In 1978, another important law made the FRS more responsible to government and the public: The Federal Banking Agency Audit Act of 1978 (P.L. 95–326). In it, the GAO was given authority to audit the FRS, and FDIC, the Comptroller of the Currency, and the Financial Institution Examination Council. There were several exemptions from the audit including most of the activities of the FOMC and transactions with or for a foreign central bank.

Two years later, a complex banking law, the Depository Institutions Deregulation and Monetary Control Act of 1980, was enacted. The Monetary Control Act portion introduced charges for FRS services that had formerly been free to depository institutions. Members of the system were now required to set aside part of their assets as reserves without earning interest on them. Nominal interest rates rose during the 1970s and this provision became an expensive proposition. A decline in bank assets resulted, as both national banks and state banks have the option to withdraw from the U.S. "dual banking system," although under different arrangements. At this point, the FRS lowered reserve requirements and directed all types of depository institutions to observe them. FRS services were extended to encompass nonmember depository institutions. Additional fees for services were introduced (CBO 1985: 10–14).

THE CONGRESS AND THE FRS INTO THE TWENTY-FIRST CENTURY

The 1996 GAO report to congressional requesters, entitled *Federal Reserve System: Current and Future Challenges Require Systemwide Attention*, outlined the basic mission of the FRS. It can be explained in terms of its major responsibilities. There are five functions which it performs: (1) conducting monetary policy, (2) maintaining stability of financial markets, (3) providing services to financial institutions, (4) providing services to the Treasury and other government agencies, and (5) supervising and regulating banks and bank holding companies (GAO 1996: 30–31). On 26 July 1996, Charles A. Bowsher, Comptroller General of the United States, appeared before the Senate Committee on Banking, Housing and Urban Affairs to offer testimony with respect to the GAO's recent report of 1996 on the FRS. In his comments, he remarked that the FRS is not like other federal agencies because it is self-financing. Expenses of the system are deducted from its revenues and the balance is transferred to the Treasury. From 1988 to 1994, average annual revenue for the system was $22 billion as compared to average annual expenses of $2.5 billion. The FRS has returned to the Treasury each year amounts ranging from $15 billion to $24 billion.

Interest income accounted for practically 90 percent of the system's revenues in 1994, and it is expected that approximately that proportion will continue. The interest income is earned on U.S. securities that the FRS holds as collateral for over $380 billion of Federal Reserve notes that circulate in the U.S. economy as paper currency. Other revenues derive mainly from fees charged financial institutions for providing services such as check clearing and electronic fund transfers.

The largest expenses of the FRS are the operating costs of the Board of Governors and the 12 regional Federal Reserve Banks. In 1994, these costs were $2 billion, a 48 percent increase since 1988. The operating costs are primarily for payment systems and other financial services to government agencies and to banks. Of a total staff of about 26,000 over 20,000 Federal Reserve employees (approximately 80 percent of the system's total staff) were involved in these activities in 1994. The balance of employees were performing either economic policy activities (2,300) or bank supervision and regulation (3,000). As of December 1999 there was a total of 23,288 officers and employees of the Federal Reserve Banks (12) and Federal Reserve Information and Technology, according to the *86th Annual Report 1999* of the Board of Governors of the Federal Reserve System. The total decreased to 23,056 as of 31 December 2000 (Board of Governors of the FRS 1999: 353; 2000: 341). The GAO report finds that the FRS is losing ground in its most important activity, furnishing financial services. Its costs are rising and its volume of business and market share is declining along with changing requirements for its supervisory activities. Increased cost consciousness is recommended, particularly as the limits on discretionary spending in the budget get tighter. However, the GAO recommends to the FRS and the Congress, which must approve any changes in both structure and operations of the FRS, that these would be desirable. The GAO emphasizes that it is important not to make any changes that might threaten the independence of the FRS in setting U.S. monetary policy (Bowsher 1996: 38–41).

The FRS has shown a marked improvement in terms of cost recovery since 1996, the year of the GAO report. The *Annual Report 1999* states that revenue for priced services (payment systems and financial services) was $835.9 million. Other income related to priced services was $31.7 million. Costs related to priced services amounted to $775.7 million (including imputed costs that would have been increased, such as income taxes, if the services had been provided by a private firm). A net income of $92 million resulted. These figures mean that priced services recovered 104.2 percent of total costs, which includes $57.2 million of imputed profit on pretax return on equity that would have been earned had the services been furnished by a private firm. The imputed costs and profits are part of the specifications of the Monetary Control Act of 1980. The Act requires the FRS to set fees for providing priced services, such as check collection, Fedwire funds transfer, and net settlement and automated clearing house (ACH) services to depository institutions that recover all direct and indirect costs over the long run. For the decade of the 1990s, the Reserve Banks have recovered 101.1 percent of their priced services costs (Board of Governors of the FRS 1999: 152–153). According to the *Annual Report 2000*, that number has been revised downward to a recovered amount of 100.8 percent of their priced services. The recovery rate for the year 2000 was listed as 101.1 percent of costs, including as before the imputed costs and imputed profit (Board of Governors of the FRS 2000: 145).

J. Kevin Corder, in *Central Bank Autonomy: The Federal Reserve System in American Politics* (1998), raises the issue of why Congress allows central bank autonomy to continue. It is not, he writes, because they are uninterested in monetary policy outcomes. In fact, special investigations of monetary policy and the FRS have been conducted by congressional committees in 1950, 1952, and 1966. Since the 1970s, there have been congressional advocates for including the FRS in the appropriations process and detailed government audits. In addition, there have been recommendations for changing the composition of the Board of Governors and the Humphrey-Hawkins Act that required its chairman to make frequent reports to Congress on the activities of the FRS (Corder 1998: 12–13).

Currently, the most important issue is not the extent of independence of the central bank but how quickly it can streamline its financial service operations. Jamie B. Stewart, Jr., First Vice President and Chief Operating Officer of the Federal Reserve Bank of New York, made the following comments about the extraordinary changes in telecommunications technology and computing at an international banking operations seminar. The seminar was sponsored by the payment network, Society for Worldwide Interbank Financial Telecommunications (SWIFT). He reported that the FRS is still defining strategies to improve its services in the face of pervasive changes occurring in the financial services industry. The FRS has updated Fedwire, the FRS electronic funds and and securities transfer system, in a number of ways. Fedwire is expected to attain greater integration with other nations' payment systems as it further develops and expands as a part of the global payment system (Stewart 2000: 1–5).

CONCLUDING COMMENTS

Two of the reasons the U.S. Constitution is the oldest written constitution in the world is because it is short and it leaves room for interpretation. The problems with the budget and the budget process are the over-abundance of rules, regulations, limitations, and legal procedures. The case of rescissions in terms of numbers and time spent is an excellent example. The Budget Enforcement Act of 1990 and the Budget Enforcement Act of 1997 have redefined previous acts, budget terms, and spending limitations. Together, they have led to an almost entirely revamped budget process. Until the executive and the legislative branches recognize their common purposes as they did at the time of the "accord," the citizens will not be well served. An offspring of the primary difficulty is that of entitlements, or mandatory spending; and ordinary, or discretionary spending. Increasing one without limit at the expense of the other does not make good budget sense. At one time, Congress had "sunset" laws in place which were meant to require review of programs on a staggered cycle basis to establish whether goals had been achieved or not and if the programs should be continued.

The independence of the FRS is a proposition defended by many economists, political scientists, government officials, and others. The matter that needs additional consideration is that which faced the 1967 President's Commission on Budget Concepts and should be reviewed: (1) to what extent FRS activities should be included in the budget, (2) to what extent audits and general accountability should apply, and (3) to what extent the FRS should participate more formally in the budget process and its aftermath reviews.

Chapter 5

Budget Execution

In this chapter, the emphasis is on the budget execution phase as the time and place of executive action. The OMB, acting as a manager and supervisor, must apportion funds according to congressional appropriations. More recently, OMB has acquired the formalized task of reviewing annual performance plans and strategic plans of the various executive agencies. The Treasury and the FRS play a vital part in the intragovernmental financial transactions required and provide the financial services necessary to finance the deficit or dispose of the surplus. Budget totals vary over the period from inception to actualization. These variations are discussed in this chapter along with information concerning transfer of funds within and between budget accounts. A fundamental aspect of this stage of the budget process is accountability and control of operations throughout the fiscal year. Although there is no official audit and review stage for the budget process, and for the overall success of the annual budget in reaching its planned goals, all the participants are at work to achieve that objective. The financial audits of the GAO for 1997, 1998, and 1999 are examined and an overview of a projected federal balance sheet is offered.

BASIC ELEMENTS

The budget execution phase is the same as the budget's fiscal year. For FY 2001, it began 1 October 2000 and ended 30 September 2001. Although it is listed in the budget documents as the final phase of the budget process, that statement does not recognize departments', agencies', and overall government review of performance and results of the budget act and the auditing procedures of the same group plus the GAO. Formerly, until 1984, there had been a fourth phase, called Audit and Review. As improvements to the techniques for these purposes continue to be made, undoubtedly the fourth phase will be reinstated.

In the 1970s, the approach to the executive phase of the budget process had changed from its previous outlook. Even though the execution of the budget remained an executive responsibility, as it is now, Congress had begun to intervene by changing its initial decisions and introducing independent checks on particular transactions. Originally, the concept of legislative authorization had been that the legislature authorizes expenditures as a ceiling on spending and, therefore, the executive has no obligation to reach that ceiling. The concept was rejected, formally, by the passage of the Congressional Budget and Impoundment Control Act of 1974 (Meyer 1989a: 280–281). Government agencies cannot spend or obligate the government to spend, before Congress has made an appropriation. Agencies are limited to the amount appropriated and for the purposes specified by law. The AntiDeficiency Act provides, also, that the president apportion the funds to most executive agencies. The apportionments are made by the OMB in four monthly installments but, in some cases, by activities. Agencies can request different time periods during the year as circumstances require. Supplemental appropriations are enacted by Congress if unanticipated events occur during the fiscal year. It is possible that appropriations granted are not needed, in which case the president may propose not to spend the funds as permitted by the Impoundment Control Act of 1974. However, his decision must meet with congressional approval or he is forced, by law, to spend the funds in question. The president has two choices in withholding funds: one is temporary but must be spent by the end of the fiscal year except in certain circumstances, called deferral; the other is a permanent cancellation of budget authority, called rescission. Deferrals take effect immediately and are used, for example, to provide for contingencies or to enable savings because of greater efficiency or changes in requirements. They may not be used for policy reasons. Rescissions may take effect only if Congress passes a law within 45 days approving them. Otherwise, the president must permit the funds to be spent immediately after the 45 days have passed. Rescissions can be for any reason. There is a provision that 20 percent of the members of either House can insist on a floor vote on a presidential rescission proposal (*Analytical Perspectives* 2000: 449–450).

REFORMS IN MANAGEMENT AND CONTROL

The essential features of the execution process are management and control of government operations. There have been many contributions to improving these features through legislation and executive order. The following are representative of major reforms.

The first financial management reform, after the passage of the Budget and Accounting Act of 1921, was an executive order issued under the authority provided in the Economy Act of 1932 to institute accounting forms, systems, and procedures. The Bank Act of 1933 improved management and financial control throughout the federal government and the banking system. The Reorganization Act of 1939 not only moved the Bureau of the Budget into the Executive Office of the President (EOP), but made it an agency concerned with program review.

The Budget and Accounting Procedures Act of 1950 stressed accounting and internal controls at each agency that integrated with those of the Treasury, and full information and control of funds as a basis for budget preparation and execution. The Comptroller General was made responsible for setting the accounting principles and standards that should be followed. He, together with the director of the OMB and the Secretary of the Treasury, were to continuously work at improving government financial and accounting systems. In 1956, the Budget and Accounting Procedures Act was amended to inject cost-based budgeting for the federal government to continue the development of agency accounting systems subject to the GAO review. However, agencies were not confined to any specific framework and the procedures and accounting systems developed, according to law, were different from one another. General revenue sharing in the 1960s and 1970s suffered, also, from accounting inconsistencies and, therefore, problems for auditors until OMB issued guidelines in 1971 as specified in its Circular A-102. Finally, the Uniform Single Audit Act of 1984 simplified audit requirements and made all state and local governments subject to audit.

Supplementing the six budget acts outlined in the chapter on congressional action, financial management in budgeting was facilitated by the Inspector General Act of 1978 and its amendment in 1988 that established offices of Inspectors General in federal agencies and departments. Through their diligent work in auditing and supervising, they saved the government billions of dollars over the first decade of their existence (Joyce 1999: 599–619). Significant legislation of the 1980s and 1990s which helped create an improved financial management structure and led to a better framework in which decisions about the allocation of government's financial resources could be made, included the following legislation: the Federal Managers' Financial Integrity Act (FMFIA) of 1982, in which faster flows of information to the president and improved methods of accountability were achieved. The Chief Financial Officers Act (CFO) of 1990, in which financial management reform was centralized and government-wide policies to attain them were established in the existing management and power center, the OMB; the Government Management Reform Act (GMRA) of 1994, in which federal management reform begun with the 1990 Act continued and quicker employment of the new reforms was provided; the Federal Financial Management Improvement Act (FFMIA) of 1996, in which the general ledger and accounting principles as they related to maintaining financial management systems was detailed; the Debt Collection Improvement Act of 1996, in which all payments by the federal government must be forwarded by electronic funds transfer by January 1999.

Agencies have found the tasks related to achieving the goals of the above Acts to be overwhelming given their resources. Jones and McCaffery conclude their assessment by observing that with the existing spending ceilings on discretionary expenditures, agencies and departments may have to make the choice between increasing or decreasing computers, software, training, and decreasing or increasing staff personnel (Jones and McCaffery 1999: 53–81).

PERFORMANCE BUDGETING

Perhaps the most promising and forward-looking budget innovation of recent years is the introduction of performance-based budgeting. Professor Philip G. Joyce explains, early in his chapter "Performance-Based Budgeting," in the *Handbook of Government Budgeting* (1999), that a major challenge of the study was terminology. Therefore, he begins by giving his definitions of four major performance measurement concepts: inputs, activities, outputs, and outcome.

Inputs are the resources used for a given program and, most of the time, are easily measured in dollars; for example, teacher salaries in education. However, indirect costs of programs can raise measurement problems. Activities are the operations performed by the agency. Again, in education, these can be represented by teacher hours of preparation. Outputs are the results of an agency's immediate operations. In the education category, an appropriate example might be the number of students who passed the course.

Outcomes are concerned with the results or success of the program overall. In education, the relevant figure might be the number of students who passed the course with a grade of C or better.

The performance measurement system, altogether, should combine these four measures in such a way as to reveal the cost of achieving a given outcome (Joyce 1999: 597–599). Of course, additional qualitative information would be necessary to establish the relationship between these measures and any social objectives sought.

During the 1990s, the Chief Financial Officers Act of 1990 and the Federal Accounting Standards Advisory Board (FASAB) employed performance measures in their federal financial reporting. The National Performance Review was the strongest effort before current attempts to use performance measures. Prior to the performance technique, the federal government used other management tools with the purpose of evaluating programs in terms of objectives. Joyce gives his own historical perspective on the development of management reforms. The focus shifts from management control to management objectives, unlike the development pictured by Jones and McCaffery.

At the time of the 1921 Act creating the federal budget system, central methods of administrative control were emphasized. From the 1930s through the 1950s, the Budget Bureau was evaluating many river and water projects with the method known as cost-benefit analysis, a more specific decentralized approach.

By the 1960s, Planning, Programming, Budgeting, Systems (PPBS) emerged, beginning with its introduction in the Department of Defense in 1965. By the 1970s, two new evaluation techniques replaced PPBS, Management by Objectives (MBO), and Zero-Based Budgeting (ZBB). All of the techniques were too ambitious in their goals, requiring extraordinary amounts of data and cooperation among many executive departments. Perhaps the most serious failing was their neglect of the outlook and objectives of the Congress in the budgeting process (Joyce 1999: 601–603; Meyer 1989a: 8–10).

Joyce points out some of the difficulties associated with the employment of performance budgeting. One of the primary problems is identifying objectives, particularly in cases where several departments or agencies are involved. Others include the need for full cost accounting of inputs including indirect costs, not only in terms of output but with respect to outcomes; the need for common denominators of performance across the various activities of government; the need for greater flexibility for agency managers to use resources to improve performance which would require, among other items, more authority and accountability for their actions. One very significant item that must be added to the list is the incentives offered to government officials to motivate them to recognize the benefits of adopting a performance orientation (Joyce 1999: 610–618).

In 1999, Congress decided to investigate initial agency experiences with the new management technique and began to hold hearings and receive testimony. Paul L. Posner and Christopher J. Mihm, directors in two different divisions of the GAO, offered statements before the Subcommittee on Government Management, Information and Technology, Committee on Government Reform of the House of Representatives on 1 July 1999. Mihm's statement began with a description of the two approaches to the use of performance budgeting indicated by the Results Act: (1) The preparation of an annual performance plan for each program activity budget by an agency; the purpose is to have the agency clearly demonstrate the funding level associated with each of its performance goals. (2) Five agencies are to be chosen by the director of OMB in FY 1998 and 1999, to propose budgets for some major operations of the agency that vary in levels of performance according to different appropriated fund amounts. These pilot performance budgets would act as an alternative form of the president's budget for FY 1999. However, these pilot programs were not under way at the time of the statements of Posner and Mihm.

Among the problems with performance budgeting is the fact that objectives or outcomes of the process are difficult to measure, say Posner and Mihm, because of the presence of nonfederal agents, such as state and local governments, contractors, and other third parties. Measurement is made difficult, also, by the lengthy performance horizons necessitated in such cases as health, safety, and research. Entitlement programs pose a particular challenge in that they predominate in federal spending, on the basis of eligibility requirements. Often these programs inspire more attention to outputs, such as prompt payments to individuals, rather than outcomes such as maintaining a standard of living (Posner 1999: 3–5).

In a report made in February 1999, three months earlier, the GAO comments on some agency initiatives in connecting inputs to outcomes or results. Performance plans in FY 1999 attempted to change budget structures to accommodate performance plans, integrated performance information with budget justifications, and devised crosswalking performance plans with budget structures. The Administration for Children and Families (AFC) consolidated over 60 program activities to show their contribution to 10 strategic objectives (GAO 1999d: 13, 28–29).

However, it has been eight years since the enactment of GPRA, and progress toward the use of performance information in managing programs has been disheartening, according to a statement in *The President's Management Agenda FY 2002* (OMB n.d.). At the beginning of the report, a message from President George W. Bush states, "I am pleased to send to the Congress a bold strategy for improving the management and performance of the federal government."

One of the major areas examined in the agenda is that of budget and performance integration. Among the issues to be resolved are:

1. Appropriate definitions of agency performance measures and their integration into budget submissions;

2. Greater control over resources by program managers;

3. Availability of timely and complete information;

4. Failure of the current budget to reflect the full cost associated with each program; and

5. A U.S. citizen should be able to view and compare the performance and cost of the various government programs. (OMB n.d.: 1, 27–28)

THE ROLE OF THE TREASURY AND THE FEDERAL RESERVE SYSTEM

The Treasury is constantly active in the financial markets as typified by the next report by Hillery and Thompson from the Federal Reserve *Bulletin* of April 2000. There are relatively few persons, however, who realize that the actual operations and the records of market transactions are performed by the Federal Reserve Banks.

Federal Reserve Banks are required to act as fiscal agents and depositories of the United States when directed by the Secretary of the Treasury, consistent with the provisions of the Federal Reserve Act of 1913. Hillery and Thompson (2000) furnish the following data and information on activities of the Federal Reserve Banks.

In performing services for the Treasury in 1999, the Federal Reserve Banks processed 288 million government checks and $823 million in government payments by direct deposit, collected $2.1 trillion in business taxes, and originated approximately 13 million book entry transfers totaling $179 trillion. These activities were related to their services in receiving bids for auctions of Treasury securities to finance the public debt and issue securities in book entry form. The Federal Reserve Banks maintain the Treasury's deposit accounts, receiving federal taxes and receipts and processing checks. The GAO conducts an annual audit of the Treasury's essential financial reporting and accounting systems so that it can certify the *United States Consolidated Financial Statements* as required by statute. Because the Federal Reserve is so intimately associated with the Treasury operations including furnishing the data, the GAO also reviews the Federal Reserve networks and systems that involve Treasury transactions. It was in 1915 that the Reserve Banks were established as the Treasury's depositories. From that time, U.S. government funds were transferred from national banks to the Treasury accounts at each of the Federal Reserve Banks. The accounts continue to be maintained and, at the end of each day, they are combined at the Federal Reserve Bank of New York. An end-of-day balance of $5 billion is the current Treasury cash goal. The amount has been as high as $52.2 billion on 30 April 1997 because of high tax receipts.

The single largest collection undertaking within the federal government is that of business taxes. Initially, it was a paper-based tax collection system as businesses made tax payments according to a predetermined schedule. In 1986, the Treasury and the Federal Reserve introduced two pilot electronic systems for tax collections. Then, the Congress passed the North American Free Trade Agreement Implementation Act (NAFTA) in 1993, which permitted the Secretary of the Treasury to mandate the employment of electronic methods for business taxes. The act specified financial goals for speeding up federal tax collections for 1994 and beyond.

Two depository institutions were selected by the Treasury in 1994 to be financial agents for electronic collections. Tax payments of $1.7 trillion passed through electronically via the Automated Clearing House System (ACH) in 1999. Only taxpayers with annual tax liabilities of $200,000 or more are required to submit electronic payments. With the electronic payment method, the Treasury may access the collected funds on the due date.

At the end of 2000, it is planned that the Reserve Banks will move to a centralized tax collection system. Actually, it was not until 6 September 2001 that the Treasury announced that businesses and individuals can pay all their federal taxes using the Internet. The federal government's newest option is a further development of the Electronic Federal Tax Payment System, EFTPS-Online, which was started in 1996 (U.S. Treasury 2001: 1).

Other duties of the Reserve Banks include forecasting government cash requirements, reporting on government-wide collections, and collection of delinquent debt. The Federal Reserve not only collects for the Treasury but, in addition, it disburses. Paper and electronic payments for the government consist of federal salaries and benefits, interest, vendor payments, and other government agency obligations such as those of the Federal Home Loan Mortgage Corporation or the Social Security Administration.

Most of the government's payments are disbursed electronically from funds on deposit with the Federal Reserve Banks. For recurring payments, the government uses the ACH system; and this is the system used for the payment of Social Security benefits. A basic advantage of the ACH system is the reduction of lost, stolen, or forged Treasury checks. Approximately three-fourths of all government payments made by ACH by the end of 1999 were forwarded in this way. The Federal Reserve Banks participate, also, in intragovernmental financial management, permitting federal agencies to transfer balances to one another among other services. Reserve Banks are most important in carrying out the Treasury's financing operations to cover the federal deficit and to refinance maturing debt. Treasury auctions are conducted by the Federal Reserve. Treasury auctions have become more streamlined and work time in their preparation and completion has significantly shortened. The recent decrease in the need for the government to borrow has meant a reduction in the number of auctions and the amounts sold, and the introduction of Treasury buyback operations. The first redemptions occurred in March 2000. The Federal Reserve Bank of New York is in charge of buyback operations for the Treasury (Hillery and Thompson 2000: 251–255).

THE TREASURY, THE FEDERAL RESERVE BANKS, AND THE PUBLIC DEBT

The Treasury has financed the public debt by issuing printed or engraved securities on paper since 1782. It was not until 1968 that investors were offered the option of having their securities entered into accounts on the books of the Reserve Banks instead. The book entry system continues to expand its availability to various types of investors. All new Treasury securities were issued in book entry form as of August 1986. At present, there are two book entry systems for marketable Treasury securities: Treasury Direct and the National Book-Entry System (NBES).

The NBES became a single system rather than the 12 commercial book entry systems of 1998. It expedites the safekeeping and transfer of U.S. bills, notes, and bonds, U.S. agency securities, mortgage-backed securities issued by the FNMA, and by the FHLMC, and securities of some international organizations, such as the World Bank. By January 2000, the safekeeping part of the NBES had about $42 trillion in securities at par value. During 1999, the Fedwire securities transfer system had processed over 13 million book entry transfers. The average daily volume of securities transfers in the same year totaled $13.4 million.

The Treasury Direct system has been a convenient system for smaller investors since 1986, since it makes book entry securities available. The system records interest due and redemption proceeds with the aid of ACH transfers to the investor's depository institution account. There were 700,000 of these active accounts by the beginning of 2000; and, they held approximately $85 billion of Treasury securities.

U.S. Savings bonds are another tool of the Treasury for financing expenditures and, at the same time, promoting saving. There are numerous series of savings bonds and several, such as First Liberty Loan Funds and the Series E Savings bonds have been used to finance the world wars. Current offerings of savings bonds include Series EE, Series HH, and Series I. The last series has its rate of return inflation indexed. For savings bonds, too, the Federal Reserve Banks act as fiscal agent for the Treasury. During 1999, they issued 49 million savings bonds valued at $4.6 billion. Savings bonds are almost exclusively issued on paper.

Since 1917, Federal Reserve Banks have been reimbursed for their services on the government's behalf. However, the banks were not fully reimbursed until 1992 when Congress enacted permanent, indefinite appropriations legislation to provide monies for public debt–related operating expenses of Reserve Banks. These payments were for services performed for the Bureau of the Public Debt. In 1998, another appropriations bill was passed to permit other federal agencies to reimburse the Reserve Banks for expenses incurred in providing services for them. As the authors explain, reimbursement to the Federal Reserve Banks for their work as fiscal agents and depositories is important for two reasons: (1) costs of these services should be included in appropriations reports or congressional management of agency programs will be faulty; and (2) services provided at no or less than true cost tend to be overused and inefficient. Reimbursement to the FRS in 1998 amounted to $290 million (Hillery and Thompson 2000: 255–259).

VARIATIONS IN BUDGET TOTALS

In *Analytical Perspectives* (2000), intrayear variations in estimated to actual totals for receipts, outlays, and surplus for 1999 are compared with current service estimates for FY 1999 as transmitted to Congress in February 1998. Current services estimates, or baseline estimates, give outlays, receipts, deficits, or surpluses, and budget authority, as they would be if existing laws remain unchanged. The purpose of this section is to separate the reasons for the intrayear variations into three categories: policy differences, economic differences, and technical reestimates.

For FY 1999, current services receipts were approximately $1,729.8 billion, current services outlays were $1,732.4 billion, and the current services deficit was $2.6 billion. For the same year, actual receipts were $1, 827.5 billion, actual outlays were $1,703.0 billion, and the actual surplus was $124.4 billion. Accordingly, there are differences between the two sets of figures as reported in the budget documents of: receipts—$97.6 (actually, $97.7) billion; outlays—$29.4 billion; and deficit/surplus—$127.0 billion. *Analytical Perspectives* proceeds to identify the causes of the total change in the three categories as they relate to policy, economic differences, or technical reestimates. The largest explanatory factor for the increase in actual receipts above the current services estimate, amounting to $60.9 billion of the total difference of $97.6 billion, is for technical reestimates. The reestimates were largely due to greater-than-expected collections of individual income taxes and estate and gift taxes.

There are two big explanatory factors for the decrease in actual outlays below the current services estimate, amounting to $20.3 billion and $19.1 billion of the total difference of $29.4 billion: technical estimating differences and economic conditions, respectively. These figures together total more than the original difference of $29.4 billion because policy changes moved in the opposite direction, increasing outlays by $10.0 billion at the same time. The combined effects of the differences in receipts and outlays are necessarily responsible for the $127 billion difference between the actual surplus achieved and the initial current services deficit. The largest net impact appears to be from changes in technical reestimates, which decreased the deficit by an estimated $81.2 billion of the total difference of $127 billion. Economic conditions decreased the deficit, also, by $55.9 billion, but policy changes moved to increase the deficit by $10.0 billion.

Actual and estimated outlays for mandatory and related programs for FY 1999 are considered in *Analytical Perspectives* (2000) in an accompanying table. In the table, outlays dropped by $35.0 billion due, primarily, to less-than-expected spending in the human resource programs, such as Social Security and Medicare. Finally, there is a table called "Reconciliation of Fiscal Amounts for 1999" that brings together Treasury totals for receipts, outlays, and surplus of 30 September 1999, and totals as published in the budget. Federal family education loans and transactions of the United Mine Workers of America benefit funds were the sources of major adjustments needed to bring the two records into agreement *Analytical Perspectives* 2000: 367–371).

Another way to view intrayear variations in budget totals is to look at comparative data on initial, supplementary, and actual federal budget totals. In a previous work on U.S. budgeting, the comparisons were drawn among the initial estimate for a given fiscal year, say 2001, listed in the president's budget released February 2000; the supplementary estimate that appears in the next year's budget, FY 2002, released February 2001; and the actual figures that appear in the budget of FY 2003 that is expected to be transmitted to Congress in February 2002. In that scheme, the differences between initial and supplementary estimates signified, mainly, policy changes, as congressional formulation and action was meant to have been completed before the issuance of the president's next fiscal year budget. The differences between supplementary and actual figures would represent, mainly, changes in economic conditions over the year of budget execution. Technical and forecasting errors might occur in either phase.

The original idea for the analysis described was inspired by work conducted at the French Bureau of the Budget in the Ministry of Finance in Paris, France. Computer printouts on the French budget contained comparisons of intrayear changes in technical and forecasting categories of French finance law. These figures and comparable ones for the United States appeared on pages 292 to 305 of the author's doctoral dissertation, which was read, and accepted for the Graduate Faculty in Economics of the City University of New York by Herbert Geyer, Chairman of Examining Committee and Executive Officer on 15 April 1978. The U.S. budget documents, in comparison, by bringing in the current services estimates, is using a baseline that assumes no policy changes initially, and then compares the actual figures to outlays, receipts, surplus, or deficit to that baseline. There is no distinction made in this framework between policy changes originating with the president or the Congress, and no detailed explanation of how the separation of technical reestimates and economic conditions was achieved.

BUDGET TRANSFERS

Budget transfers may be appropriated funds shifted from one account to another or shifted within one account for a new purpose, reprogramming; or they can be funds accelerated or decelerated in the spending, including impoundment; or funds that serve as reserves for contingencies and lump sum appropriations; or funds used for unforeseen purposes, such as covert financing (Meyer 1989a: 83). Any of these changes must be within the limitations of the budget law. In some cases, Congress grants general transfer authority entailing permission to move up a certain sum of a certain percentage of the agency appropriation. Reprogramming is more difficult to track, although Congress has established thresholds, in a few cases, whereby it must be notified of the reprogramming action. In the Department of Defense, for example, the threshold has been set at $10 million for certain reprogramming. The department, itself, has complex rules and forms for reprogramming actions that are filed with the Congress (Schick 1994a: 168–175).

In the *United States Government Annual Report Fiscal Year 1999* (U.S. Treasury), in the table entitled "Appropriations, Outlays and Balances by Department," there is a column headed: "Transfers, Borrowings, and Investments" and its total is given as almost −$18.4 billion, while outlays are reported as almost $1.9 trillion for the FY 1999 budget. In the 642 page Appendix to this document, the column heading reads "Transfers, Borrowings, and Investments (net)," and each term is defined. Transfers are, in most cases, "for the benefit of advancing appropriation accounts." The amounts listed in the column are made with reference to the account in which the funds were initially placed. Therefore, the negative sign reflects the transfer of funds from the original account. In addition, the column includes the net amount of actual borrowings made during the fiscal year, the net par value of sale and purchases of government agency securities, and public debt, and net cash advances to government cashiers. The appendix table is given in more detail than in the annual report by separation into departments, and then reduced in the footnotes into appropriations and appropriations transfers. For example, the Department of the Treasury covers pages 414 to 439 in the Appendix with totals given by bureaus and other entities within the Treasury accounts. Most of the accounts are numbered "20." Contained in the system, the FFB is assigned the number 20, and its "Outlays (net)" were $1.1 billion and its "Transfers, Borrowings and Investments (net)" were −$3.1 billion. "Total, Interest on the Public Debt" is assigned number 20, also, and "Outlays (net)" were $353.1 billion and nothing in the transfer column. "Total, Public Debt Retirement, 20, has no "Outlays (net)," but "Transfers, etc.," were almost −$17.0 billion.

In the condensed table following the detailed accounts, totals are furnished for "Net Appropriations and Appropriations Transfers" of almost $10.5 billion. "Appropriations Amount" of almost $9.7 billion, and "Net Appropriations Transfers" of approximately $0.8 billion (*Appendix* n.d.: 414–439).

THE ROLE OF THE GENERAL ACCOUNTING OFFICE

In the *United States Government Manual 2001/2002* (Office of the Federal Register 2001), the description of the activities of the GAO has been revised from earlier versions. In this edition, the GAO is called "the investigative arm of the Congress," whose duties include the examination of matters pertaining to the receipt and disbursement of the public funds. In addition to the functions that had been assigned to the GAO by the Budget and Accounting Act of 1921, which established the agency, a new one appeared in the 1974/1975 edition that directed the GAO to suggest improvements in government operations such that greater efficiency and effectiveness might be achieved. In the 2001/2002 edition a broader description is offered: "Over the years, the Congress has expanded GAO's audit authority, added new responsibilities and duties, and strengthened GAO's ability to perform independently" (Office of the Federal Register 2001: 48).

Under activities in the 1999/2000 edition of the *Manual*, the GAO's basic responsibility is explained as one of supporting Congress. To accomplish the goal, the GAO audits, evaluates, and reviews government activities and programs either at congressional request or according to existing laws. Also, the GAO offers legal services, such as aid in drafting legislation or interpreting existing legislation; it conducts investigations of civil or possible criminal misconduct; it issues the *Government Auditing Standards* for audits of the various aspects of government activities; and it submits reports on the results of GAO projects, on request, to various levels of government as well as foreign governments and to the public, in print and by electronic access.

With respect to auditing and accounting policy, the Comptroller General, who is the director of the GAO, joins with the Secretary of the Treasury, and the director of the OMB as one of the principal members on the Federal Accounting Standards Advisory Board (FASAB) (Office of the Federal Register 1999: 47–50; Meyer 1978: 330; Meyer 1989a: 85).

The 1994 revision of *Government Auditing Standards* superceded the 1988 revision and was scheduled to be effective for financial and performance audits after 1 January 1995. In the chapter "Reporting Standards for Financial Audits," it is stated that generally accepted government auditing standards (GAGAS) have incorporated the American Institute of Certified Public Accountants (AICPA) four generally accepted standards. The report must state whether (a) the financial statements presented are in accordance with generally accepted accounting principles; (b) if they are not, the cases must be identified and the current period compared to the previous period; (c) information enclosed in the financial statements is assumed adequate if not otherwise mentioned in the report; (d) an expression of opinion, or if no opinion is given concerning the financial statements, the reason needs to be explained by the auditor with reference to the detail of his investigation.

Statements on Auditing Standards (SAS) have been issued by AICPA, and then are contained in the chapter together with additional standards concerning: communications with audit committees and others recording compliance with GAGAS, reporting on observance of laws and regulations and on internal controls, treatment of privileged and sensitive information, and distribution of reports (GAO 1994: 47–61).

It is not only the GAO that exercises control through audit over the nation's finances; there is self-review by the executive branch performed by the hub of budget formulation and execution matters, the OMB. For example, the *Federal Financial Management Status Report and Five Year Plan* of June 1999 (Office of Management and Budget 1999) was the eighth annual report submitted to fulfill the requirements of the Chief Financial Officers Act (CFO) of 1990. It was prepared by the OMB and the CFO Council. The plan accompanying the report includes information required by the CFO Act, the Debt Collection Act of 1982, as amended, and the Federal Financial Management Improvement Act of 1996 (FFMIA).

The CFO Council was authorized by the CFO Act to investigate essential federal financial issues. Members of the Council consist of the CFOs and Deputy CFOs of the 24 largest federal agencies, senior officials of OMB and the Treasury Department. During the year ending June 1999, OMB and the CFO Council worked together and the report describes their accomplishments and future goals in six key areas: improving financial management systems, increasing financial management accountability, developing human resources, employing new debt collection tools and better management of receivables, introducing electronic commerce for better financial management, and improving supervision of federal grant programs.

The improvement of financial management systems is necessary for one last objective: to achieve an unqualified opinion on the 1999 *Consolidated Financial Statements of the United States Government* (Meyer 1989a: 89; U.S. Treasury 1997: 1). In fiscal year 1997, after annual publication of unofficial consolidated financial statements in the *Treasury Bulletin* since FY 1985, the Treasury issued an auditable public document as part of its efforts to improve efficiency and management of the federal government. However, as Secretary of the Treasury Robert E. Rubin stated in his accompanying message, the GAO was unable to render an opinion because many areas of the statements needed substantial improvements. The commitment according to the secretary, is to achieve an unqualified opinion from the GAO on the consolidated financial statements for FY 1999 (Meyer 1989a: 89; U.S. Treasury 1997: 1).

The GAO was unable to furnish an unqualified opinion for the 1998 *Financial Report of the United States Government*, the successor to the 1997 consolidated financial statements, either, because of several obstacles. One of the most important of the functional issues is that most agencies had difficulties in identifying and eliminating transactions between federal government entities. In particular, the Department of Defense and the Department of Transportation do not have auditable information concerning the dollar value of property, plant, and equipment and inventory held for their domestic and international operations. Other obstacles related to inadequate reporting of costs of loans and loan guarantee programs in the USDA, DOE, HHS, HUD, and VA. The balance of the list of obstacles to an unqualified opinion consists of environmental and disposal liabilities, health benefits and other liabilities, improper payments, and unreconciled disbursements; and the reported change in net position of the government-wide financial statements needs to be more effectively reconciled with the budget surplus or deficit.

The Joint Financial Management Improvement Program (JFMIP), established in 1998 and funded by the 24 agencies, selected by Congress in 1996, is working with OMB to develop systems requirements, solve the necessary integration issues, develop testing apparatus, serve as federal financial information clearing house, and to enable communication with the private sector to further the several goals.

All of the efforts on behalf of improved federal financial management have the federal government's program performance goals as part of the framework. The CFO Council is working jointly with OMB, the General Services Administration (GSA), the Office of Personnel Management (OPM), and the Treasury to establish standards, to develop policies, and to remove any problems that may intrude on agency work reforms (Office of Management and Budget 1999: 5–15).

FEDERAL FINANCIAL AUDIT FOR FISCAL YEAR 1999

Testimony was offered by David M. Walker, Comptroller General of the United States, in March 2000 concerning the government's financial statements for FY 1999. The statement also contains information about the progress of individual agencies in achieving financial accountability under the provisions of the Chief Financial Officers Act of 1990, the Government Management Reform Act of 1994, and the Federal Financial Management Improvement Act of 1996. Congress had established the requirement for annual audited financial statements for 24 major federal departments and agencies starting with FY 1996. In that year, only six agencies fulfilled the goal of unqualified opinions of their financial statements. At the time of this testimony, 13 of the 24 major agencies had received unqualified opinions on their FY 1999 financial statements. One of these was the Social Security Administration (SSA), which completed and filed the statement six weeks after the close of the fiscal year and more than three months before the statutory deadline of 1 March.

Another major hurdle was overcome in October 1999 when the AICPA accepted federal accounting standards as a satisfactory method of accounting. The acceptance occurred even though a large percentage of the federal government's assets, liabilities, and net costs are found in the Department of Defense and the department, as a whole, had not been able to file auditable financial statements.

The GAO concludes that there are serious deficiencies in the financial statements of the U.S. government for FY 1997, 1998, and 1999. Reliability of information in any of the government's financial reports or any other financial management information is, therefore, questionable. The testimony continues that the financial systems of agencies are in poor condition and financial information is not reliable for managing daily government operations. Financial auditors reported that 19 of 22 major agencies in FY 1999 had financial management systems that did not fully comply with federal accounting standards and financial systems as required under the Federal Financial Management Improvement Act (Walker 2000: 1–5).

In another report to the president and the leaders of the two houses of Congress by the Comptroller General, dated 20 March 2000, he offers the information that the OMB, the Treasury, and the GAO are at work with other government agencies to furnish suggestions for solving the problems mentioned in the audit. Some agencies have made progress toward achieving the financial management goals, among them the SSA. The GAO has indicated the most grave cases as high risk and these comprise, in part, financial management at DOD, IRS, the Federal Aviation Administration, the Forest Service, along with information security. However, the problems of identifying and eliminating intragovernmental transactions and systematizing of financial statements need the continued coordinated support of the Treasury and the OMB (GAO 2000c: 37–38).

According to the letter addressed to the president of the Senate and the Speaker of the House on 31 March 2000, accompanying the *Financial Audit: 1999 Financial Report of the United States Government* (GAO 2000d) and signed by David M. Walker, Comptroller General, there are "certain significant financial systems weaknesses" which affect the reliability of the financial statements and information contained in the financial report. Some major problems concern (1) accounting and reporting of assets located principally at the Department of Defense; (2) estimating costs of major federal credit programs and loan guarantee liabilities, principally at the Department of Agriculture; (3) estimating costs and reporting on amounts of disposal and environmental liabilities, principally at the Department of Defense; (4) preparing the federal government's financial statements, accounting for intragovernmental transactions, and consistently recording information and reconciling the results of government operations with budget outcomes. Other deficiencies include mistaken payments amounting to billions of dollars annually that the government cannot attempt to reduce because their extent is unknown, computer security leaks that leave financial and other sensitive information open to loss or fraud, and material control shortcomings that harm tax collection estimates.

The Comptroller General draws attention, also, to release of updated information, as of 1 January 2000, on 30 March 2000, about Social Security and Medicare (Part A) which contains the trustees' new projections on contributions and expenditures that are substantially different from the government's 1999 financial report, which was issued the following day,

31 March 2000. GAO comments that Congress and the public may be puzzled and lose confidence in government financial reporting. Moreover, as the facts and the assumptions about the programs are so critical to assessing the solvency of the two programs, the Comptroller General, in the appendix to the letter, compares the two reports on Social Security and Medicare. The GAO comparison is included as Table 1. The document, known as the *Financial Report of the United States Government Fiscal Year 1999* (GAO 2000d), covers the entire executive branch but only parts of the legislative and judicial branches. These two branches are not required by law to submit complete financial statements to the Treasury. The FRS is not included either, as it is recognized as an independent entity. As is the custom, the privately owned but Government Sponsored Enterprises (GSEs), such as Fannie Mae, Freddie Mac, Sally Mae, and the FHLB, are also excluded. The basis of accounting for the financial statements is the accrual method. In contrast, cash-based accounting reports transactions when cash is paid or received; and, it is the method generally used in budget reporting. Accrual-based accounting reports transactions when the events causing the transactions occur (GAO 2000d: 108–109).

THE FEDERAL BALANCE SHEET

There is a chapter in the *Analytical Perspectives* (2000) entitled "Stewardship: Toward a Federal Balance Sheet." In it, there is an attempt to provide an overview of the government's financial resources, present and future claims on them, and the taxpayers' position as a result of government's acquisition of resources. As the text states, there are serious limitations to available data, and therefore the chapter's determinations "should be interpreted with caution." There are three parts to the discussion: (1) the assets and liabilities of the federal government; (2) the net position of the government beginning with an estimate of net federal liabilities as a result of the budget FY 2001 as a proportion of GDP and then projected up to 2070; and (3) information on national wealth and government's contribution to that wealth. In Table 2–4 of *Analytical Perspectives* (2000), national wealth consists of federal investments in physical assets, education capital, and research and development capital. The government's contribution represents $4.8 trillion, or 7 percent of total national wealth. This is lower than the 9 percent figure computed for the mid-1980s. However, the numbers are uncertain, to a great extent because of stong assumptions made in the preparation of the estimates (*Analytical Perspectives* 2000: 17–44).

CONCLUDING COMMENTS

The stress and strain placed on government agencies by the several new financial management acts and procedures, including performance bud-

Table 1

Comparison of Selected Information on the Social Security and Medicare (Part A) Trust Funds Included in the Boards of Trustees' Annual Reports, Dated 30 March 2000, and the *Fiscal Year 1999 Financial Report of the United States Government*

	Trust Fund	Trustees' Report	Financial Report
First Year Outgo Exceeds Tax Income Excluding Interest	Social Security	2015	2014
	--OASI	2016	Not Reported
	--DI	2007	Not Reported
	Medicare – Part A	2010	Not Reported
Year Trust Fund Is Exhausted	Social Security	2037	2034
	--OASI	2039	2036
	--DI	2023	2020
	Medicare – Part A	2023	2015
Present Value of Additional Resources Needed	Social Security	Not Reported	$2,935 billion
	--OASI	Not Reported	2,413 billion
	--DI	Not Reported	522 billion
	Medicare – Part A	Not Reported	$2,935 billion
Actuarial Deficit as a Percentage of Taxable Payroll Over the 75 Year Projection Period	Social Security	1.89%	Not Reported
	--OASI	1.53%	Not Reported
	--DI	0.37%	Not Reported
	Medicare – Part A	1.21 %	Not Reported
Actuarial Deficit as a Percentage of Taxable Payroll in Year 75	Social Security	6.18 %	Not Reported
	--OASI	5.40 %	Not Reported
	--DI	0.78 %	Not Reported
	Medicare – Part A	3.28%	Not Reported

Key: OASI = Federal Old-Age Survivors Trust Fund; DI = Federal Disability Insurance Trust Fund.

Note: Trustees' information is as of 1 January 2000. *Financial Report* information is as of 1 January 1999 for Social Security, and as of 30 September 1999 for Medicare (Part A).

Sources: GAO (2000c, 2000d: 4).

geting, outweighs the gain of having the Treasury, the OMB, and the GAO working together. More leeway for agency-initiated actions might achieve better results and more quickly. The relationship between the Treasury and the FRS is a more intimate affair. Literally, the two control a goodly portion of the money wealth of the nation. Accountability, transparency, and the very best record keeping possible should be the ultimate, if not the immediate, goal for the continued health of the finances of the United States. Extensive studies and investigations by the General Accounting Office have made considerable progress in this direction.

Part III

Budget Content and Presentation

Chapter 6

Trends in Budget Totals

Over time, budget totals in all the major categories have increased except for one, deficits. The government budget figures, as prepared by OMB, report that for fiscal years 1998 and 1999, the unified budget was in surplus; and it is expected that the trend will continue for future years. The major categories that are examined in this chapter include: outlays and receipts, their composition and their shares as a fraction of GDP; total government expenditures and receipts as percentages of GDP; direct loans and loan guarantees; on-budget and off-budget totals; federal funds and trust funds outlays; receipts and deficits or surpluses; percentage distribution of budget authority by agency; and the growth of the gross federal debt, consisting of that held by the public and the government accounts since 1940.

FEDERAL FINANCES AND GROSS DOMESTIC PRODUCT

It was not until World War II that the federal budget began to rapidly increase in size. Receipts and outlays for FY 1941 were $8.7 billion and $13.7 billion, respectively. A decade later, in FY 1951, receipts were $51.6 billion, and outlays were $45.5 billion. By 1981, receipts were more than 11 times the 1951 figure, at $599.3 billion, and outlays leaped by 15 times their 1951 level to $678.2 billion. The estimate for FY 2001, two decades later, shows an escalation in receipts over the period since 1981 of approximately 3.4 times the 1981 level to $2.02 trillion, and for outlays, to 2.7 times the 1981 level to $1.83 trillion.

These changes are more easily understood, and perhaps more informative, when viewed in the context of their relationship to GDP. GDP is the value of all final goods and services produced within the United States in a specific period of time by either residents or nonresidents. It differs from GNP, which is defined as the value of all final goods and services produced by residents of the United States who furnish their labor and capital in a specific time period, even if the residents are not located in the United States. Alternatively, GNP is the sum of purchases of final goods and services by individuals and governments, gross private domestic investment including changes in business inventories, and net exports or exports less imports (GAO 1993a: 50).

GNP was formerly used for comparisons within the budget documents; and it appeared in tables prepared by the author in the first edition of *Evolution of United States Budgeting* (1989). Figures offered in the chapter tables are not comparable for this reason and because of other revisions performed by the Bureau of Economic Analysis of the Department of Commerce. As percentages of GDP presented in Table 2, receipts had been growing relatively slowly, remaining in the single-digit numbers until 1942, when they suddenly skipped from 7.6 percent to 10.1 percent of GDP. By the end of World War II, in 1945, they had more than doubled to 20.4 percent. The following year, they dropped back to 17.6 percent and 14.4 percent in 1950, but they hovered around 17 or 18 percent of GDP for most of the 1950s and for most of the next four decades until 1997, when receipts equaled 19.3 percent. By 1999, they were 20.0 percent; and they are estimated to reach 20.1 percent in FY 2001. Outlays were highly volatile during the period from 1930 to 1941. They began at 3.4 percent of GDP and ended at 12.0 percent, but they did not follow a smooth path in between. Outlays doubled in 1942 to 24.4 percent of GDP and doubled again by 1943 to 43.6 percent. After 1944, they gyrated, once more, between a low of 11.6 percent in 1948 and a high of 20.5 percent of GDP in 1968, for the period through FY 1974. The most frequently repeated percentages for the period were 17 and 18 percent of GDP. In FY 1975, outlays were 21.3 percent of GDP and attained a height of 23.5 percent in 1983. Outlays remained over 21.0 percent of GDP until 1995, when they began to decline to 18.7 percent of GDP in FY 1999. In FY 2001, outlays are estimated to drop to 18.3 percent of GDP.

COMPOSITION OF OUTLAYS

One of the most noticeable aspects of the period from 1988 to 1999, as shown in Table 3, is that outlays for national defense began to decline from almost $304 billion in 1989 to nearly $275 billion in 1999, while nondefense items rose. As a percentage of total outlays, national defense began the period at 27.3 percent and ended, in FY 1999, at 16.1 percent. Corresponding figures for nondefense outlays were 72.7 percent in 1988, and 83.8 percent in 1999. Payments for individuals in the nondefense category appear to be largely responsible for the gain.

TOTAL GOVERNMENT EXPENDITURES: FEDERAL, STATE, AND LOCAL

During the 1990s, a private sector study investigated federal expenditures within the setting of total government spending for all levels of government. The summary of the report, entitled *Public Expenditures in the United States 1952–1993* by John E. Dawson and Peter J. E. Stan (1995), published by RAND, a nonprofit institution, expresses the report's objectives and findings. Among the study's goals are: to present federal, state, and local government expenditures in a different perspective; to identify the next century's policy agenda with respect to public expenditures; and to introduce methods of illustrating public expenditures that clarify their purpose for government policy makers and the average citizen.

Four classification schemes of expenditures are chosen to achieve these purposes: functional, level of government, economic type, and on- or off-budget. Within the four groups, trends in public expenditures are compared to the economic growth of the United States from 1952 to 1993, stressing those components of expenditures with the greatest impact. During the 41-year period, total government expenditures, including federal, state, and local, rose to 33.1 percent of GDP from the starting point of 26.3 percent. The increase is due to a large increase in nondefense expenditures combined with a smaller drop in defense spending and veterans' compensation.

In terms of the functional category, the largest increase in spending occurred for Social Security, Medicare, education, welfare, and police/corrections. With respect to the level of government, state and local expenditures have risen more sharply than the federal. In 1993, they were 13.0 percent of GDP and had been 6.9 percent in 1952, while federal expenditures rose by less than one percent of GDP over the same period.

In the economic types of expenditure category, all of the growth in public expenditures resulted from an increase in transfer and interest payments, which accrue primarily to the poor, the elderly, and creditors. For most of the period, purchases of goods and services maintained their status of 18 to 20 percent of GDP.

In the last classification, on- and off-budget expenditures, Social Security and Medicare compose most of the rise in the off-budget section of the budget. In 1993, they amounted to 6.7 percent of GDP and they represented 1.5 percent in 1951. On-budget expenditures increased by only 2.4 percentage points to 27.7 percent of GDP in 1993, from a level of 25.3 percent in 1952. Net interest payments were the largest explanation for this growth, although interfund transactions, which rose by 0.9 percentage points of GDP for the period, were deducted from the final sums (Dawson and Stan 1995: xi–xiii).

Expenditures since 1993, the last year of the RAND study, have shown a drop in all the categories functionally and by level of government. Total

Table 2
Summary of Receipts, Outlays, and Surpluses or Deficits (–) as Percentages of GDP, 1930–2005

Year	GDP (in billions of dollars)	Total			On-Budget			Off-Budget			Medicare Solvency
		Receipts	Outlays	Surplus or Deficit (–)	Receipts	Outlays	Surplus or Deficit (–)	Receipts	Outlays	Surplus or Deficit (–)	
1930	97.4	4.2	3.4	0.8	4.2	3.4	0.8	—	—	—	—
1931	83.7	3.7	4.3	-0.6	3.7	4.3	-0.6	—	—	—	—
1932	67.5	2.9	6.9	-4.1	2.9	6.9	-4.1	—	—	—	—
1933	57.4	3.5	8.0	-4.5	3.5	8.0	-4.5	—	—	—	—
1934	61.1	4.8	10.7	-5.9	4.8	10.7	-5.9	—	—	—	—
1935	69.5	5.2	9.2	-4.0	5.2	9.2	-4.0	—	—	—	—
1936	78.4	5.0	10.5	-5.5	5.0	10.5	-5.5	—	—	—	—
1937	87.7	6.1	8.6	-2.5	5.8	8.6	-2.8	0.3	'	0.3	—
1938	88.8	7.6	7.7	-0.1	7.2	7.7	-0.5	0.4	'	0.4	—
1939	88.9	7.1	10.3	-3.2	6.5	10.3	-3.8	0.6	'	0.6	—
1940	96.5	6.8	9.8	-3.0	6.2	9.8	-3.6	0.6	'	0.6	—
1941	113.9	7.6	12.0	-4.3	7.0	12.0	-4.9	0.6	'	0.6	—
1942	144.2	10.1	24.4	-14.2	9.5	24.3	-14.8	0.6	'	0.6	—
1943	180.0	13.3	43.6	-30.3	12.7	43.6	-30.9	0.6	'	0.6	—
1944	209.0	20.9	43.7	-22.8	20.3	43.6	-23.3	0.6	0.1	0.6	—
1945	221.4	20.4	41.9	-21.5	19.8	41.8	-22.0	0.6	0.1	0.5	—
1946	222.9	17.6	24.8	-7.1	17.1	24.7	-7.6	0.6	0.1	0.5	—
1947	234.9	16.4	14.7	1.7	15.8	14.6	1.2	0.6	0.1	0.5	—
1948	256.6	16.2	11.6	4.6	15.6	11.5	4.1	0.6	0.1	0.5	—
1949	271.7	14.5	14.3	0.2	13.9	14.1	-0.3	0.6	0.2	0.5	—
1950	273.6	14.4	15.6	-1.1	13.6	15.4	-1.7	0.8	0.2	0.6	—
1951	321.3	16.1	14.2	1.9	15.1	13.8	1.3	1.0	0.4	0.6	—
1952	348.9	19.0	19.4	-0.4	17.9	18.9	-1.0	1.0	0.5	0.5	—
1953	373.1	18.7	20.4	-1.7	17.6	19.8	-2.2	1.1	0.6	0.5	—
1954	378.0	18.4	18.7	-0.3	17.2	18.0	-0.7	1.2	0.8	0.4	—

114

Year										
1955	0.3	1.0	1.3	-1.0	16.3	15.3	-0.8	17.3	16.6	395.3
1956	0.3	1.2	1.5	0.6	15.4	15.9	0.9	16.5	17.4	427.6
1957	0.2	1.3	1.5	0.6	15.7	16.2	0.8	17.0	17.8	450.5
1958	0.1	1.8	1.7	-0.7	16.3	15.5	-0.6	17.9	17.3	460.6
1959	-0.1	1.8	1.7	-2.5	16.9	14.4	-2.6	18.7	16.1	491.8
1960	·	2.1	2.0	0.1	15.6	15.7	0.1	17.7	17.8	519.8
1961	0.1	2.2	2.3	-0.7	16.2	15.5	-0.6	18.4	17.8	530.9
1962	-0.2	2.4	2.2	-1.0	16.4	15.4	-1.3	18.8	17.5	568.6
1963	-0.1	2.5	2.4	-0.7	16.1	15.4	-0.8	18.5	17.8	600.2
1964	·	2.4	2.5	-1.0	16.0	15.0	-0.9	18.5	17.5	642.3
1965	-0.1	2.4	2.4	-0.2	14.8	14.5	-0.2	17.2	17.0	688.2
1966	0.5	2.8	2.5	-0.4	15.2	14.8	-0.5	17.8	17.3	757.2
1967	0.3	2.5	3.0	-1.6	16.9	15.3	-1.1	19.4	18.3	811.7
1968	0.4	2.6	2.9	-3.2	17.9	14.7	-2.9	20.5	17.6	870.0
1969	0.6	2.7	3.0	-0.1	16.7	16.6	0.3	19.3	19.7	949.4
1970	0.3	2.7	3.3	-0.9	16.6	15.7	-0.3	19.3	19.0	1,013.7
1971	0.3	3.0	3.3	-2.4	16.4	14.0	-2.1	19.4	17.3	1,081.7
1972	·	3.1	3.4	-2.2	16.4	14.2	-2.0	19.6	17.6	1,178.5
1973	0.1	3.5	3.5	-1.2	15.2	14.1	-1.1	18.7	17.6	1,313.6
1974	0.1	3.8	3.7	-0.6	15.1	14.5	-0.4	18.7	18.3	1,441.7
1975	-0.2	3.9	4.0	-3.5	17.4	13.9	-3.4	21.3	17.9	1,559.2
1976	-0.3	4.0	3.8	-4.1	17.4	13.3	-4.2	21.4	17.2	1,735.9
TO	-0.2	4.2	3.9	-2.9	16.7	13.8	-3.2	20.9	17.7	459.2
1977	-0.1	4.1	3.9	-2.5	16.6	14.1	-2.7	20.7	18.0	1,974.6
1978	·	4.0	3.8	-2.5	16.6	14.2	-2.7	20.7	18.0	2,219.5
1979	-0.2	4.0	3.9	-1.5	16.1	14.6	-1.6	20.1	18.5	2,504.9
1980	-0.2	4.2	4.1	-2.7	17.4	14.8	-2.7	21.6	18.9	2,731.8
1981	·	4.4	4.3	-2.4	17.7	15.3	-2.6	22.2	19.6	3,060.3
1982	·	4.7	4.4	-3.7	18.4	14.7	-4.0	23.1	19.1	3,231.1
1983	·	4.3	4.3	-6.0	19.2	13.2	-6.0	23.5	17.4	3,441.7
1984	·	4.3	4.3	-4.8	17.8	13.0	-4.8	22.1	17.3	3,846.5

Table 2 (continued)

Year	GDP (in billions of dollars)	Total			On-Budget			Off-Budget			Medicare Solvency
		Receipts	Outlays	Surplus or Deficit (-)	Receipts	Outlays	Surplus or Deficit (-)	Receipts	Outlays	Surplus or Deficit (-)	
1985	4,141.6	17.7	22.9	-5.1	13.2	18.6	-5.4	4.5	4.3	0.2	....
1986	4,398.3	17.5	22.5	-5.0	12.9	18.3	-5.4	4.6	4.2	0.4	....
1987	4,653.9	18.4	21.6	-3.2	13.8	17.4	-3.6	4.6	4.2	0.4	....
1988	5,016.6	18.1	21.2	-3.1	13.3	17.2	-3.9	4.8	4.0	0.8	....
1989	5,406.6	18.3	21.2	-2.8	13.5	17.3	-3.8	4.9	3.9	1.0	....
1990	5,738.4	18.0	21.8	-3.9	13.1	17.9	-4.8	4.9	3.9	1.0	....
1991	5,927.9	17.8	22.3	-4.5	12.8	18.3	-5.4	5.0	4.1	0.9	....
1992	6,221.7	17.5	22.2	-4.7	12.7	18.2	-5.5	4.9	4.1	0.8	....
1993	6,560.9	17.6	21.5	-3.9	12.8	17.4	-4.6	4.8	4.1	0.7	....
1994	6,948.8	18.1	21.0	-2.9	13.3	17.0	-3.7	4.8	4.0	0.8	....
1995	7,322.6	18.5	20.7	-2.2	13.7	16.8	-3.1	4.8	3.9	0.9	....
1996	7,700.1	18.9	20.3	-1.4	14.1	16.4	-2.3	4.8	3.9	0.9	....
1997	8,182.8	19.3	19.6	-0.3	14.5	15.8	-1.3	4.8	3.8	1.0	....
1998	8,636.3	19.9	19.1	0.8	15.1	15.5	-0.3	4.8	3.7	1.1	....
1999	9,115.4	20.0	18.7	1.4	15.2	15.2	*	4.9	3.5	1.4	....
2000 estimate	9,571.9	20.4	18.7	1.7	15.5	15.3	0.2	5.0	3.4	1.5	....
2001 estimate	10,041.3	20.1	18.3	1.8	15.1	14.9	0.1	5.0	3.4	1.6	0.2
2002 estimate	10,502.4	19.8	18.0	1.8	14.8	14.7	*	5.0	3.3	1.6	0.1
2003 estimate	10,982.8	19.6	17.9	1.7	14.6	14.6	*	5.0	3.3	1.7	....
2004 estimate	11,502.0	19.4	17.7	1.7	14.5	14.5	*	4.9	3.2	1.7	....
2005 estimate	12,084.5	19.4	17.6	1.8	14.4	14.4	*	5.0	3.2	1.8	....

Notes:

* 0.05 percent or less.

Budget figures prior to 1933 are based on the "Administrative Budget" concepts rather than the "Unified Budget" concepts. GDP, percentages of GDP, deflators, and constant dollar amounts for years prior to 1960 are OMB estimates based on detailed historical GDP series for which revised data are not yet available from the Bureau of Economic Analysis. For additional details, see the Special note on GDP and Constant Dollar Amounts in the Introduction to the Historical Tables (2000).

Source: Historical Tables (2000), Table 1.2.

government expenditures for 1993, in Table 4, appear to have been rees-timated downward to 31.4 percent of GDP, and then to 28.0 percent in 1999. In the economic type of expenditure category, all the major groups declined from 1993 to 1999: defense and international from 4.7 to 3.2 percent, net interest from 3.1 to 2.5 percent, and Social Security and Med-icare from 6.8 to 6.5 percent of GDP. Table 4, entitled "Total Government Expenditures: 1960–1999," views the progression of total government ex-penditures in current dollars as a percent of GDP in a similar manner to the Dawson and Stan report. In the table, total government expenditures rose by 2.3 times during the period from 1960 to 1970, and by almost 3 times during the period from 1970 to 1980; or, total expenditures were $124.8 billion in 1960 and increased by 1980 to $820.5 billion. In 1990, total government expenditures amounted to $1.79 trillion, and by 1999, they had reached $2.6 trillion, so that spending in current dollar terms had risen by less over the two decades than previously, or by a little more than 3 times their size in 1980 as a percentage of GDP.

TOTAL GOVERNMENT RECEIPTS

From 1960 to 1970, and again from 1970 to 1980, total government receipts more than doubled in size. Alternatively, receipts in 1960 of $129.3 billion rose by slightly more than 5.8 times to total government receipts in current dollars of $755.6 billion in FY 1980 as reported in Table 5. How-ever, as a percentage of GDP, the rise over the 20-year period appears much smaller, 24.9 percent in 1960 to 27.7 percent in 1980. Checking the GDP column, the difference is explained by the rise in GDP by 5 times its initial size of $519.8 billion in 1960, to $2.73 trillion in 1980. The last two decades have seen a slowdown in the growth of total government receipts in current dollars. In 1980, receipts were $755.6 billion, in 1990, receipts were $1.58 trillion; and in 1999, receipts were $2.73 trillion. For the same years, total government receipts as a proportion of GDP began in 1980 at 27.7 percent, actually dropped in 1990 to 27.4 percent; then rose again by 1999 to 29.9 percent. Checking the GDP column, once more, the reason is the slowdown in GDP increase from an initial size in 1980 of $2.73 trillion to approximately two times that size in 1990 at $5.74 trillion. By 1999, GDP in current dollars less than doubled to finish the last decade of the twentieth century at $9.12 trillion.

Another significant outlook on federal receipts is gained by seeing them according to source. In FY 1960, when revisions were completed by the Bureau of Economic Analysis, Table 6 shows that individual income taxes were the largest component, representing 7.8 percent of a total of 17.8 percent in government receipts as a percentage of GDP, both on- and off-budget. By 1980, individual income taxes represented 8.9 percent of total tax receipts and 18.9 percent of GDP. This increase was smaller propor-

Table 3
Composition of Outlays

Category	1988	1989	1990	1991	1992	1993	1994	1995	1996
In millions of current dollars									
Total outlays	1,064,489	1,143,671	1,253,198	1,324,403	1,381,684	1,409,512	1,461,902	1,515,837	1,560,572
National defense [1]	290,361	303,559	299,331	273,292	298,350	291,086	281,642	272,066	265,753
Nondefense:									
Payments for individuals	500,656	536,030	584,090	650,263	727,646	782,678	822,098	874,558	909,393
Direct payments [2]	(438,222)	(468,677)	(506,958)	(557,766)	(615,461)	(658,389)	(686,866)	(728,765)	(761,795)
Grants to State and local governments	(62,434)	(67,353)	(77,132)	(92,497)	(112,185)	(124,289)	(135,232)	(145,793)	(147,598)
All other grants	52,720	54,322	57,952	61,837	65,562	69,171	75,195	79,130	80,175
Net interest [2]	151,838	169,018	184,380	194,482	199,373	198,736	202,957	232,169	241,090
All other [2]	105,881	117,953	164,060	183,885	130,033	105,226	117,781	102,369	101,781
Undistributed offsetting receipts [2]	-36,967	-37,212	-36,615	-39,356	-39,280	-37,386	-37,772	-44,455	-37,620
Total nondefense	774,129	840,112	953,867	1,051,111	1,083,334	1,118,426	1,180,260	1,243,771	1,294,819
In billions of constant (FY 1996) dollars									
Total outlays	1,348.1	1,394.9	1,478.0	1,498.9	1,517.2	1,507.7	1,530.3	1,550.6	1,560.6
National defense [1]	364.0	369.0	354.3	309.3	327.0	314.1	297.9	281.8	265.8
Nondefense:									
Payments for individuals	638.6	654.9	683.8	730.9	796.9	834.0	857.3	892.0	909.4
Direct payments [2]	(559.0)	(572.6)	(593.5)	(626.9)	(674.0)	(701.5)	(716.2)	(743.3)	(761.8)
Grants to State and local governments	(79.6)	(82.3)	(90.2)	(103.9)	(122.9)	(132.5)	(141.1)	(148.7)	(147.6)
All other grants	65.4	65.3	67.1	69.4	72.6	74.7	79.2	80.9	80.2
Net interest [2]	189.6	203.2	213.6	217.2	217.7	211.6	211.2	236.6	241.1
All other [2]	142.9	153.0	207.2	220.6	150.1	115.8	125.6	106.0	101.8
Undistributed offsetting receipts [2]	-52.4	-50.4	-47.8	-48.5	-47.1	-42.5	-41.0	-46.8	-37.6
Total nondefense	984.1	1,026.0	1,123.8	1,189.6	1,190.1	1,193.6	1,232.4	1,268.6	1,294.8

As percentages of GDP

Total outlays	21.2	21.2	21.8	22.3	22.2	21.5	21.0	20.7	20.3
National defense [1]	5.8	5.6	5.2	4.6	4.8	4.4	4.1	3.7	3.5
Nondefense:									
Payments for individuals [2]	10.0	9.9	10.2	11.0	11.7	11.9	11.8	11.9	11.8
Direct payments [2]	(8.7)	(8.7)	(8.8)	(9.4)	(9.9)	(10.0)	(9.9)	(10.0)	(9.9)
Grants to State and local governments	(1.2)	(1.2)	(1.3)	(1.6)	(1.8)	(1.9)	(1.9)	(2.0)	(1.9)
All other grants	1.1	1.0	1.0	1.0	1.1	1.1	1.1	1.1	1.0
Net Interest [2]	3.0	3.1	3.2	3.3	3.2	3.0	2.9	3.2	3.1
All other [2]	2.1	2.2	2.9	3.1	2.1	1.6	1.7	1.4	1.3
Undistributed offsetting receipts [2]	-0.7	-0.7	-0.6	-0.7	-0.6	-0.6	-0.5	-0.6	-0.5
Total nondefense	15.4	15.5	16.6	17.7	17.4	17.0	17.0	17.0	16.8
Addendum: GDP ($ billions)	5,016.6	5,406.6	5,738.4	5,927.9	6,221.7	6,560.9	6,948.8	7,322.6	7,700.1

As percentages of outlays

Total outlays	100.0	100.0	100.0	100.0	100.0	100.0	100.0	100.0	100.0
National defense [1]	27.3	26.5	23.9	20.6	21.6	20.7	19.3	17.9	17.0
Nondefense:									
Payments for individuals [2]	47.0	46.9	46.6	49.1	52.7	55.5	56.2	57.7	58.3
Direct payments [2]	(41.2)	(41.0)	(40.5)	(42.1)	(44.5)	(46.7)	(47.0)	(48.1)	(48.8)
Grants to State and local governments	(5.9)	(5.9)	(6.2)	(7.0)	(8.1)	(8.8)	(9.3)	(9.6)	(9.5)
All other grants	5.0	4.7	4.6	4.7	4.7	4.9	5.1	5.2	5.1
Net Interest [2]	14.3	14.8	14.7	14.7	14.4	14.1	13.9	15.3	15.4
All other [2]	9.9	10.3	13.1	13.9	9.4	7.5	8.1	6.8	6.5
Undistributed offsetting receipts [2]	-3.5	-3.3	-2.9	-3.0	-2.8	-2.7	-2.6	-2.9	-2.4
Total nondefense	72.7	73.5	76.1	79.4	78.4	79.3	80.7	82.1	83.0

Table 3 (continued)

Category	1997	1998	1999	2000 estimate	2001 estimate	2002 estimate	2003 estimate	2004 estimate	2005 estimate
In millions of current dollars									
Total outlays	1,601,282	1,652,611	1,703,040	1,789,562	1,835,033	1,895,317	1,962,853	2,041,131	2,125,451
National defense [1]	270,505	268,456	274,873	290,636	291,202	298,390	307,363	316,517	330,742
Nondefense:									
Payments for individuals [2]	950,051	976,588	998,245	1,055,670	1,110,180	1,174,953	1,249,384	1,330,993	1,416,563
Direct payments [2]	(801,204)	(817,097)	(827,109)	(876,285)	(917,163)	(967,697)	(1,025,185)	(1,089,978)	(1,158,925)
Grants to State and local governments	(148,847)	(159,491)	(171,136)	(179,385)	(193,017)	(207,256)	(224,199)	(241,015)	(257,638)
All other grants	85,313	86,625	95,944	104,687	112,628	114,496	116,248	118,081	119,573
Net Interest [2]	244,016	241,153	229,735	220,314	208,312	198,626	189,301	177,530	163,768
All other [2]	101,370	126,983	144,688	161,316	158,327	157,837	147,758	144,791	143,296
Undistributed offsetting receipts [2]	-49,973	-47,194	-40,445	-43,061	-45,616	-48,985	-47,201	-46,781	-48,491
Total nondefense	1,330,777	1,384,155	1,428,167	1,498,926	1,543,831	1,596,927	1,655,490	1,724,614	1,794,709
In billions of constant (FY 1996) dollars									
Total outlays	1,572.5	1,604.8	1,626.3	1,670.3	1,674.3	1,689.5	1,708.2	1,733.6	1,761.7
National defense [1]	265.3	260.4	263.1	273.8	269.2	270.5	273.4	276.0	282.8
Nondefense:									
Payments for individuals [2]	932.5	948.9	951.9	980.1	1,006.6	1,039.3	1,077.1	1,118.4	1,160.2
Direct payments [2]	(786.4)	(793.9)	(788.7)	(813.6)	(831.6)	(856.0)	(883.9)	(915.9)	(949.2)
Grants to State and local governments	(146.1)	(155.0)	(163.2)	(166.5)	(175.0)	(183.3)	(193.3)	(202.5)	(211.0)
All other grants	83.7	83.6	90.6	96.2	100.9	100.0	98.9	97.9	96.7
Net Interest [2]	239.9	234.1	220.2	208.0	192.8	180.3	168.4	154.9	140.1
All other [2]	100.3	123.1	138.7	152.3	146.6	143.4	131.8	126.7	123.0
Undistributed offsetting receipts [2]	-49.3	-45.3	-38.3	-40.2	-41.7	-43.9	-41.5	-40.3	-41.0
Total nondefense	1,307.2	1,344.4	1,363.0	1,396.4	1,405.1	1,419.0	1,434.8	1,457.6	1,479.0

	19.6	19.1	18.7	18.7	18.3	18.0	17.9	17.7	17.6
Total outlays	19.6	19.1	18.7	18.7	18.3	18.0	17.9	17.7	17.6
National defense[1]	3.3	3.1	3.0	3.0	2.9	2.8	2.8	2.8	2.7
Nondefense:									
Payments for individuals	11.6	11.3	11.0	11.0	11.1	11.2	11.4	11.6	11.7
Direct payments[2]	(9.8)	(9.5)	(9.1)	(9.2)	(9.1)	(9.2)	(9.3)	(9.5)	(9.6)
Grants to State and local governments	(1.8)	(1.8)	(1.9)	(1.9)	(1.9)	(2.0)	(2.0)	(2.1)	(2.1)
All other grants	1.0	1.0	1.1	1.1	1.1	1.1	1.1	1.0	1.0
Net Interest[2]	3.0	2.8	2.5	2.3	2.1	1.9	1.7	1.5	1.4
All other[2]	1.2	1.5	1.6	1.7	1.6	1.5	1.3	1.3	1.2
Undistributed offsetting receipts[2]	-0.6	-0.5	-0.4	-0.4	-0.5	-0.5	-0.4	-0.4	-0.4
Total nondefense	16.3	16.0	15.7	15.7	15.4	15.2	15.1	15.0	14.9
Addendum: GDP ($ billions)	8,182.8	8,636.3	9,115.4	9,571.9	10,041.3	10,502.4	10,982.8	11,502.0	12,084.5

As percentages of outlays

Total outlays	100.0	100.0	100.0	100.0	100.0	100.0	100.0	100.0	100.0
National defense[1]	16.9	16.2	16.1	16.2	15.9	15.7	15.7	15.5	15.6
Nondefense:									
Payments for individuals	59.3	59.1	58.6	59.0	60.5	62.0	63.7	65.2	66.6
Direct payments[2]	(50.0)	(49.4)	(48.6)	(49.0)	(50.0)	(51.1)	(52.2)	(53.4)	(54.5)
Grants to State and local governments	(9.3)	(9.7)	(10.0)	(10.0)	(10.5)	(10.9)	(11.4)	(11.8)	(12.1)
All other grants	5.3	5.2	5.6	5.8	6.1	6.0	5.9	5.8	5.6
Net Interest[2]	15.2	14.6	13.5	12.3	11.4	10.5	9.6	8.7	7.7
All other[2]	6.3	7.7	8.5	9.0	8.6	8.3	7.5	7.1	6.7
Undistributed offsetting receipts[2]	-3.1	-2.9	-2.4	-2.4	-2.5	-2.6	-2.4	-2.3	-2.3
Total nondefense	83.1	83.8	83.9	83.8	84.1	84.3	84.3	84.5	84.4

[1] Includes a small amount of grants to state and local governments and direct payments for individuals.
[2] Includes some off-budget amounts; most of the off-budget amounts are direct payments for individuals (Social Security benefits).

Source: Historical Tables (2000), Table 6.1.

121

Table 4
Total Government Expenditures by Major Category of Expenditure as Percentages of GDP, 1960–1999

Fiscal Year	Total Government	Defense and International	Net Interest	Federal Payments For Individuals		Other Federal	State and Local From Own Sources (Except Net Interest)
				Social Security and Medicare	Other		
1960	24.0	9.8	1.5	2.2	2.5	1.9	6.1
1961	25.1	9.9	1.4	2.3	2.9	2.0	6.5
1962	25.5	10.2	1.4	2.5	2.6	2.3	6.6
1963	25.3	9.8	1.5	2.6	2.8	2.3	6.6
1964	25.2	9.3	1.5	2.5	2.5	2.9	6.6
1965	24.1	8.1	1.4	2.5	2.3	3.0	6.8
1966	24.6	8.4	1.4	2.7	2.2	3.2	6.7
1967	26.4	9.5	1.4	3.0	2.3	3.3	6.9
1968	27.9	10.0	1.4	3.3	2.5	3.4	7.3
1969	27.1	9.2	1.4	3.5	2.6	2.8	7.7
1970	27.5	8.5	1.5	3.6	2.8	3.0	8.1
1971	28.1	7.7	1.5	3.9	3.5	2.9	8.6
1972	28.3	7.1	1.5	4.0	3.8	3.2	8.5
1973	27.0	6.2	1.5	4.4	3.6	3.3	8.2
1974	27.3	5.9	1.5	4.6	3.8	2.9	8.6
1975	30.5	6.0	1.5	5.0	4.9	4.0	9.2
1976	30.6	5.5	1.7	5.2	5.2	3.9	9.1
TQ	30.1	5.4	1.7	5.2	4.7	4.1	9.0
1977	29.6	5.2	1.7	5.3	4.7	4.0	8.7
1978	29.1	5.0	1.7	5.3	4.3	4.5	8.4
1979	28.3	4.9	1.8	5.2	4.1	4.1	8.3

1980	30.0	5.4	1.8	5.5	4.7	4.1	8.6
1981	30.5	5.6	2.0	5.9	4.8	3.7	8.6
1982	31.9	6.1	2.4	6.3	4.8	3.3	9.1
1983	32.5	6.4	2.5	6.5	5.0	2.9	9.2
1984	30.7	6.-	2.7	6.2	4.3	2.5	8.8
1985	31.5	6.5	2.9	6.2	4.1	2.9	8.8
1986	31.4	6.5	3.0	6.2	4.1	2.6	9.0
1987	30.9	6.3	2.9	6.1	4.0	2.2	9.3
1988	30.4	6.0	3.0	6.0	3.9	2.2	9.2
1989	30.2	5.8	3.0	6.0	3.9	2.3	9.2
1990	31.2	5.5	3.1	6.2	4.0	3.0	9.5
1991	32.2	4.9	3.2	6.4	4.5	3.2	9.9
1992	32.2	5.1	3.2	6.7	5.0	2.3	9.9
1993	31.4	4.7	3.1	6.8	5.2	1.8	9.9
1994	30.8	4.3	3.0	6.9	5.0	2.0	9.7
1995	30.4	3.9	3.2	7.0	5.0	1.6	9.7
1996	29.9	3.6	3.1	7.0	4.8	1.7	9.6
1997	29.1	3.5	3.0	7.0	4.7	1.5	9.5
1998	28.5	3.3	2.8	6.8	4.5	1.8	9.4
1999	28.0	3.2	2.5	6.5	4.4	2.0	9.4

Source: Historical Tables (2000), Table 15.4.

Table 5
Total Government Receipts in Absolute Amounts and as Percentages of GDP, 1960–1999 (dollar amounts in billions)

Fiscal Year	In Current Dollars						As Percentages of GDP		
	Total Government Receipts	Federal Government Receipts			State and Local Government Tax Receipts (NIPA Basis)	Addendum: Fiscal Year GDP	Total Government Receipts	Federal Government Receipts	State and Local Government Tax Receipts (NIPA Basis)
		Total	On-Budget	Off-Budget					
1960	129.3	92.5	81.9	10.6	36.8	519.8	24.9	17.8	7.1
1961	134.1	94.4	82.3	12.1	39.7	530.9	25.3	17.8	7.5
1962	142.8	99.7	87.4	12.3	43.1	568.6	25.1	17.5	7.6
1963	152.6	106.6	92.4	14.2	46.0	600.2	25.4	17.8	7.7
1964	162.4	112.6	96.2	16.4	49.8	642.3	25.3	17.5	7.8
1965	170.8	116.8	100.1	16.7	53.9	688.2	24.8	17.0	7.8
1966	189.5	130.8	111.7	19.1	58.7	757.2	25.0	17.3	7.8
1967	212.8	148.8	124.4	24.4	64.0	811.7	26.2	18.3	7.9
1968	224.9	153.0	128.1	24.9	71.9	870.0	25.8	17.6	8.3
1969	268.2	186.9	157.9	29.0	81.3	949.4	28.3	19.7	8.6
1970	283.8	192.8	159.3	33.5	91.0	1,013.7	28.0	19.0	9.0
1971	287.2	187.1	151.3	35.8	100.1	1,081.7	26.6	17.3	9.3
1972	320.8	207.3	167.4	39.9	113.5	1,178.5	27.2	17.6	9.6
1973	357.2	230.8	184.7	46.1	126.4	1,313.6	27.2	17.6	9.6
1974	399.7	263.2	209.3	53.9	136.5	1,441.7	27.7	18.3	9.5
1975	426.8	279.1	216.6	62.5	147.7	1,559.2	27.4	17.9	9.5
1976	462.6	298.1	231.7	66.4	164.5	1,735.9	26.6	17.2	9.5
TQ	125.1	81.2	63.2	18.0	43.9	459.2	27.2	17.7	9.6
1977	543.5	355.6	278.7	76.8	188.0	1,974.6	27.5	18.0	9.5
1978	604.8	399.6	314.2	85.4	205.3	2,219.5	27.3	18.0	9.2
1979	683.3	463.3	365.3	98.0	220.0	2,504.9	27.3	18.5	8.8

Year									
1980	755.6	517.1	403.9	113.2	238.5	2,731.8	27.7	18.9	8.7
1981	865.5	599.3	469.1	130.2	266.2	3,060.3	28.3	19.6	8.7
1982	903.5	617.8	474.3	143.5	285.8	3,231.1	28.0	19.1	8.8
1983	911.4	600.6	453.2	147.3	310.8	3,441.7	26.5	17.4	9.0
1984	1,018.2	666.5	500.4	166.1	351.8	3,846.5	26.5	17.3	9.1
1985	1,115.1	734.1	547.9	186.2	381.0	4,141.6	26.9	17.7	9.2
1986	1,181.0	769.2	569.0	200.2	411.8	4,398.3	26.9	17.5	9.4
1987	1,298.6	854.4	641.0	213.4	444.3	4,653.9	27.9	18.4	9.5
1988	1,383.3	909.3	667.8	241.5	474.0	5,016.6	27.6	18.1	9.4
1989	1,503.0	991.2	727.5	263.7	511.8	5,406.6	27.8	18.3	9.5
1990	1,575.2	1,032.0	750.3	281.7	543.2	5,738.4	27.4	18.0	9.5
1991	1,630.3	1,055.0	761.2	293.9	575.3	5,927.9	27.5	17.8	9.7
1992	1,704.6	1,091.3	788.9	302.4	613.3	6,221.7	27.4	17.5	9.9
1993	1,805.0	1,154.4	842.5	311.9	650.6	6,560.9	27.5	17.6	9.9
1994	1,949.5	1,258.6	923.6	335.0	690.8	6,948.8	28.1	18.1	9.9
1995	2,077.8	1,351.8	1,000.8	351.1	726.0	7,322.6	28.4	18.5	9.9
1996	2,213.6	1,453.1	1,085.6	367.5	760.5	7,700.1	28.7	18.9	9.9
1997	2,381.3	1,579.3	1,187.3	392.0	802.0	8,182.8	29.1	19.3	9.8
1998	2,568.5	1,721.8	1,306.0	415.8	846.7	8,636.3	29.7	19.9	9.8
1999	2,726.4	1,827.5	1,383.0	444.5	898.9	9,115.4	29.9	20.0	9.9

Source: Historical Tables (2000), Table 15.1.

Table 6
Receipts by Source as Percentages of GDP, 1934–2005

Fiscal Year	Individual Income Taxes	Corporation Income Taxes	Social Insurance and Retirement Receipts			Excise Taxes	Other	Total Receipts		
			Total	(On-Budget)	(Off-Budget)			Total	(On-Budget)	(Off-Budget)
1934	0.7	0.6	*	(*)	--------	2.2	1.3	4.8	(4.8)	--------
1935	0.8	0.8	*	(*)	--------	2.1	1.6	5.2	(5.2)	--------
1936	0.9	0.9	0.1	(0.1)	--------	2.1	1.1	5.0	(5.0)	--------
1937	1.2	1.2	0.7	(0.4)	(0.3)	2.1	0.9	6.1	(5.8)	(0.3)
1938	1.4	1.4	1.7	(1.3)	(0.4)	2.1	0.9	7.6	(7.2)	(0.4)
1939	1.2	1.3	1.8	(1.2)	(0.6)	2.1	0.8	7.1	(6.5)	(0.6)
1940	0.9	1.2	1.8	(1.3)	(0.6)	2.0	0.7	6.8	(6.2)	(0.6)
1941	1.2	1.9	1.7	(1.1)	(0.6)	2.2	0.7	7.6	(7.0)	(0.6)
1942	2.3	3.3	1.7	(1.1)	(0.6)	2.4	0.6	10.1	(9.5)	(0.6)
1943	3.6	5.3	1.7	(1.1)	(0.6)	2.3	0.4	13.3	(12.7)	(0.6)
1944	9.4	7.1	1.7	(1.0)	(0.6)	2.3	0.5	20.9	(20.3)	(0.6)
1945	8.3	7.2	1.6	(1.0)	(0.6)	2.8	0.5	20.4	(19.8)	(0.6)
1946	7.2	5.3	1.4	(0.8)	(0.6)	3.1	0.5	17.6	(17.1)	(0.6)
1947	7.6	3.7	1.5	(0.8)	(0.6)	3.1	0.6	16.4	(15.8)	(0.6)
1948	7.5	3.8	1.5	(0.8)	(0.6)	2.9	0.6	16.2	(15.6)	(0.6)
1949	5.7	4.1	1.4	(0.8)	(0.6)	2.8	0.5	14.5	(13.9)	(0.6)
1950	5.8	3.8	1.6	(0.8)	(0.8)	2.8	0.5	14.4	(13.6)	(0.8)
1951	6.7	4.4	1.8	(0.8)	(1.0)	2.7	0.5	16.1	(15.1)	(1.0)
1952	8.0	6.1	1.8	(0.8)	(1.0)	2.5	0.5	19.0	(17.9)	(1.0)
1953	8.0	5.7	1.8	(0.7)	(1.1)	2.6	0.5	18.7	(17.6)	(1.1)
1954	7.8	5.6	1.9	(0.7)	(1.2)	2.6	0.5	18.4	(17.2)	(1.2)
1955	7.3	4.5	2.0	(0.7)	(1.3)	2.3	0.5	16.6	(15.3)	(1.3)
1956	7.5	4.9	2.2	(0.7)	(1.5)	2.3	0.5	17.4	(15.9)	(1.5)
1957	7.9	4.7	2.2	(0.7)	(1.5)	2.3	0.6	17.8	(16.2)	(1.5)
1958	7.5	4.4	2.4	(0.7)	(1.7)	2.3	0.6	17.3	(15.5)	(1.7)
1959	7.5	3.5	2.4	(0.7)	(1.7)	2.2	0.6	16.1	(14.4)	(1.7)

Year										
1960	7.8	4.1	2.8	(0.8)	(2.0)	2.2	0.8	17.8	(15.7)	(2.0)
1961	7.8	3.9	3.1	(0.8)	(2.3)	2.2	0.7	17.8	(15.5)	(2.3)
1962	8.0	3.6	3.0	(0.8)	(2.2)	2.2	0.7	17.5	(15.4)	(2.2)
1963	7.9	3.6	3.3	(0.9)	(2.4)	2.2	0.7	17.8	(15.4)	(2.4)
1964	7.6	3.7	3.4	(0.9)	(2.5)	2.1	0.7	17.5	(15.0)	(2.5)
1965	7.1	3.7	3.2	(0.8)	(2.4)	2.1	0.8	17.0	(14.5)	(2.4)
1966	7.3	4.0	3.4	(0.9)	(2.5)	1.7	0.9	17.3	(14.8)	(2.5)
1967	7.6	4.2	4.0	(1.0)	(3.0)	1.7	0.9	18.3	(15.3)	(3.0)
1968	7.9	3.3	3.9	(1.0)	(2.9)	1.6	0.9	17.6	(14.7)	(2.9)
1969	9.2	3.9	4.1	(1.1)	(3.0)	1.6	0.9	19.7	(16.6)	(3.0)
1970	8.9	3.2	4.4	(1.1)	(3.3)	1.5	0.9	19.0	(15.7)	(3.3)
1971	8.0	2.5	4.4	(1.1)	(3.3)	1.5	0.9	17.3	(14.0)	(3.3)
1972	8.0	2.7	4.5	(1.1)	(3.4)	1.3	1.0	17.6	(14.2)	(3.4)
1973	7.9	2.8	4.8	(1.3)	(3.5)	1.2	0.9	17.6	(14.1)	(3.5)
1974	8.3	2.7	5.2	(1.5)	(3.7)	1.2	1.0	18.3	(14.5)	(3.7)
1975	7.8	2.6	5.4	(1.4)	(4.0)	1.1	1.0	17.9	(13.9)	(4.0)
1976	7.6	2.4	5.2	(1.4)	(3.8)	1.0	1.0	17.2	(13.3)	(3.8)
TQ	8.4	1.8	5.5	(1.6)	(3.9)	1.0	0.9	17.7	(13.8)	(3.9)
1977	8.0	2.8	5.4	(1.5)	(3.9)	0.9	1.0	18.0	(14.1)	(3.9)
1978	8.2	2.7	5.5	(1.6)	(3.8)	0.8	0.9	18.0	(14.2)	(3.8)
1979	8.7	2.6	5.5	(1.6)	(3.9)	0.7	0.9	18.5	(14.6)	(3.9)
1980	8.9	2.4	5.8	(1.6)	(4.1)	0.9	1.0	18.9	(14.8)	(4.1)
1981	9.3	2.0	6.0	(1.7)	(4.3)	1.3	0.9	19.6	(15.3)	(4.3)
1982	9.2	1.5	6.2	(1.8)	(4.4)	1.1	1.0	19.1	(14.7)	(4.4)
1983	8.4	1.1	6.1	(1.8)	(4.3)	1.0	0.9	17.4	(13.2)	(4.3)
1984	7.8	1.5	6.2	(1.9)	(4.3)	1.0	0.9	17.3	(13.0)	(4.3)
1985	8.1	1.5	6.4	(1.9)	(4.5)	0.9	0.9	17.7	(13.2)	(4.5)
1986	7.9	1.4	6.5	(1.9)	(4.6)	0.7	0.9	17.5	(12.9)	(4.6)
1987	8.4	1.8	6.5	(1.9)	(4.6)	0.7	0.9	18.4	(13.8)	(4.6)
1988	8.0	1.9	6.7	(1.9)	(4.8)	0.7	0.9	18.1	(13.3)	(4.8)
1989	8.2	1.9	6.6	(1.8)	(4.9)	0.6	0.9	18.3	(13.5)	(4.9)

Table 6 (continued)

Fiscal Year	Individual Income Taxes	Corporation Income Taxes	Social Insurance and Retirement Receipts			Excise Taxes	Other	Total Receipts		
			Total	(On-Budget)	(Off-Budget)			Total	(On-Budget)	(Off-Budget)
1990	8.1	1.6	6.6	(1.7)	(4.9)	0.6	1.0	18.0	(13.1)	(4.9)
1991	7.9	1.7	6.7	(1.7)	(5.0)	0.7	0.9	17.8	(12.8)	(5.0)
1992	7.7	1.6	6.6	(1.8)	(4.9)	0.7	0.9	17.5	(12.7)	(4.9)
1993	7.8	1.8	6.5	(1.8)	(4.8)	0.7	0.8	17.6	(12.8)	(4.8)
1994	7.8	2.0	6.6	(1.8)	(4.8)	0.8	0.8	18.1	(13.3)	(4.8)
1995	8.1	2.1	6.6	(1.8)	(4.8)	0.8	0.9	18.5	(13.7)	(4.8)
1996	8.5	2.2	6.6	(1.8)	(4.8)	0.7	0.8	18.9	(14.1)	(4.8)
1997	9.0	2.2	6.6	(1.8)	(4.8)	0.7	0.8	19.3	(14.5)	(4.8)
1998	9.6	2.2	6.6	(1.8)	(4.8)	0.7	0.9	19.9	(15.1)	(4.8)
1999	9.6	2.0	6.7	(1.8)	(4.9)	0.8	0.9	20.0	(15.2)	(4.9)
2000 estimate	9.9	2.0	6.8	(1.8)	(5.0)	0.7	1.0	20.4	(15.5)	(5.0)
2001 estimate	9.7	1.9	6.8	(1.8)	(5.0)	0.8	0.9	20.1	(15.1)	(5.0)
2002 estimate	9.5	1.9	6.8	(1.8)	(5.0)	0.8	0.9	19.8	(14.8)	(5.0)
2003 estimate	9.3	1.8	6.8	(1.8)	(5.0)	0.7	0.9	19.6	(14.6)	(5.0)
2004 estimate	9.3	1.7	6.7	(1.8)	(4.9)	0.7	1.0	19.4	(14.5)	(4.9)
2005 estimate	9.2	1.7	6.7	(1.8)	(5.0)	0.7	1.0	19.4	(14.4)	(5.0)

Notes:

* 0.05 percent or less.

GDP, percentages of GDP, deflators, and constant dollar amounts for years prior to 1960 are OMB estimates based on detailed historical GDP series for which revised data are not yet available from the Bureau of Economic Analysis. For additional details, see the Special note on GDP and Constant Dollar Amounts in the Introduction to the *Historical Tables* (2000).

Source: Historical Tables (2000), Table 2.3.

tionately than that for social insurance and retirement benefits, which more than doubled from 2.8 percent in 1960, to 5.8 percent in 1980 as a fraction of GDP. Corporate income taxes followed the opposite path and dropped as a fraction of GDP from 4.1 percent in 1960 to 2.4 percent in 1980. The last identified receipts source, excise taxes started the period at 2.2 percent and dropped, also, to 0.9 percent of GDP. By 1990, personal income and Social Security taxes had continued to increase to 9.6 percent and 6.7 percent, respectively, while corporate income taxes and excise taxes dropped even lower to 1.7 percent and 0.7 percent of GDP.

DIRECT LOANS AND LOAN GUARANTEES

The federal budget no longer includes a credit budget. However, *Analytical Perspectives* (2000) provides an overview of direct loans and loan guarantees from FY 1995 to 1999 that is illustrated in Table 7. The following definitions may be helpful in interpreting the terms listed. An *obligation* is a binding agreement that leads to an immediate or future outlay. A legal obligation requires that budgetary resources be available. A *direct loan* is a disbursement of funds by the federal government under contract. The contract is made with a nonfederal borrower and stipulates the repayment of the loan with or without interest. A *subsidy* is equivalent to cost when applied to federal credit programs. A *guaranteed loan* is a nonfederal loan that has a federal guarantee attached to it. A *guaranteed loan commitment* is a binding agreement by the government to make a loan guarantee when certain conditions are met by the lender, the borrower, or other party to the loan agreement (*Analytical Perspectives* 2000: 461–463; GAO 1993a: 51).

DEFICITS AND SURPLUSES

When GNP was the base for percentage calculations, surpluses did not appear at all except for FY 1969. Table 1, which uses GDP as the base, reports small surpluses in 1951, 1956, 1957, 1960, 1969, and the more recent ones, 1998 and 1999. In the other fiscal years since 1952, deficits have ranged from a low of 0.2 percent in 1965 to a high of 6.0 percent of GDP in 1983. A special note appears in the introduction to *Historical Tables* (2000) concerning the use of GDP figures. The figures have been only partially revised to reflect the changes made in NIPA data. Revisions have been published back to calendar year 1959 only. Therefore, numbers quoted here are comparable for fiscal years 1960 and later (*Historical Tables* 2000: 1).

Another reference to the revision is made in the *Economic Report of the President February 2000* (Council of Economic Advisers 2000). The report states that in October 1999, the Bureau of Economic Analysis released its

Table 7
Summary of Federal Direct Loans and Loan Guarantees (in billions of dollars)

| | Actual | | | | Estimate | |
	1995	1996	1997	1998	1999	2000	2001
Direct Loans:							
Obligations	30.9	23.4	33.6	28.8	38.4	38.5	44.2
Disbursements	22.0	23.6	32.2	28.7	37.7	37.3	35.8
Subsidy budget authority [1]	2.6	1.8	2.4	6.5	2.6	-4.3	1.7
Loan Guarantees: [2]							
Commitments	138.5	175.4	172.3	218.4	252.4	255.1	289.0
Lender Disbursements	117.9	143.9	144.7	199.5	224.7	234.0	257.9
Subsidy budget authority [1]	4.6	4.0	3.6	2.6	4.3	3.2	0.8

[1] Excludes subsidy reestimates made prior to 1998.
[2] GNMA secondary guarantees of loans that are guaranteed by FHA, VA, and RHs are excluded from the totals to avoid double-counting.

Source: *Analytical Perspectives* (2000), Table 8.6.

benchmark revision of the GDP statistics that contained the revised annual sources and accounted for new data from the last full economic census five years before, as well as the benchmark input-output accounts for 1992. The modification permitted a change in accounting definitions and a correction to pre-1995 accounts to bring them into line with present methods of treating deflation. The biggest surprise, with respect to growth in the various GDP accounts, came from the new source data that showed productivity had been rising more quickly than had been formerly assumed (Council of Economic Advisers 2000: 81–82).

ON-BUDGET AND OFF-BUDGET TOTALS

Similar patterns apply for revenues and expenditures since 1980 in both the on-budget and off-budget receipts as a percentage of GDP, as seen in Table 2. The on-budget receipts were 14.8 percent in 1980, and by 1999 they had a small rise to 15.2 percent of GDP. Outlays, in contrast, started at 17.4 percent in 1980, and dropped to the same number as for receipts in 1999, 15.2 percent of GDP. The foregoing numbers resulted in an on-budget deficit of 2.7 percent of GDP in 1980 that dropped to 0.05 percent or less by 1999. The off-budget figures for receipts and outlays remain at approximately 4.0 to 5.0 percent of GDP throughout the 1980 to 1999 period. However, receipts gently rose while outlays, particularly after 1993, declined. By 1999, the difference between receipts of 4.9 percent and outlays of 3.5 percent was a surplus of 1.4 percent of GDP; whereas, at the beginning of the 20-year period in 1980, there had been a small deficit of 0.05 percent or less of GDP. The surplus is estimated to continue for FY 2001, but only as 0.1 percent of GDP on-budget, and 1.6 percent off-budget.

SURPLUS OR DEFICIT BY FUND GROUP

The unitary budget surplus and deficits so far described as fractions of GDP do not reveal the intimate detail of their composition. Table 8 does so by separating the components of the total budget surplus or deficit into the federal funds group and the trust funds group. The trust fund surplus almost doubled over the period from 1990 at $120 billion to just under $213 billion in 1999. The federal funds group remained in deficit for the entire period, although its size dropped from $341 billion in 1990 to $88 billion in 1999.

BUDGET AUTHORITY

Budget authority gives government officials the right to enter into obligations that require payment of funds now or later. Budget Authority is

Table 8
Receipts, Outlays, and Surpluses or Deficits (–) by Fund Group (in millions of dollars)

Fiscal Year	Receipts				Outlays				Surplus or Deficit (–)		
	Total	Federal Funds	Trust Funds	Interfund Trans- actions	Total	Federal Funds	Trust Funds	Interfund Trans- actions	Total	Federal Funds	Trust Funds
1990	1,031,969	635,838	566,931	-170,799	1,253,198	977,212	446,785	-170,799	-221,229	-341,374	120,145
1991	1,055,041	641,572	603,912	-190,443	1,324,403	1,022,667	492,179	-190,443	-269,361	-381,095	111,733
1992	1,091,279	656,296	636,125	-201,141	1,381,684	1,042,718	540,107	-201,141	-290,404	-386,422	96,018
1993	1,154,401	705,457	671,516	-222,571	1,409,512	1,060,952	571,130	-222,571	-255,110	-355,496	100,385
1994	1,258,627	775,027	694,016	-210,416	1,461,902	1,073,623	598,694	-210,416	-203,275	-298,596	95,321
1995	1,351,830	838,831	729,028	-216,029	1,515,837	1,102,097	629,769	-216,029	-164,007	-263,266	99,259
1996	1,453,062	917,134	775,748	-239,820	1,560,572	1,139,262	661,130	-239,820	-107,510	-222,128	114,618
1997	1,579,292	1,010,315	818,347	-249,370	1,601,282	1,158,244	692,408	-249,370	-21,990	-147,929	125,939
1998	1,721,798	1,113,467	870,967	-262,636	1,652,611	1,205,474	709,773	-262,636	69,187	-92,007	161,194
1999	1,827,454	1,164,384	937,639	-274,569	1,703,040	1,252,697	724,912	-274,569	124,414	-88,313	212,727
2000 estimate	1,956,252	1,260,599	988,810	-293,157	1,789,562	1,318,199	764,520	-293,157	166,690	-57,600	224,290
2001 estimate	2,019,031	1,292,574	1,056,750	-330,293	1,835,033	1,349,878	815,448	-330,293	183,998	-57,304	241,302
2002 estimate	2,081,220	1,318,068	1,107,725	-344,573	1,895,317	1,389,862	850,028	-344,573	185,903	-71,794	257,697
2003 estimate	2,147,489	1,353,930	1,154,709	-361,150	1,962,853	1,431,570	892,433	-361,150	184,636	-77,640	262,276
2004 estimate	2,236,091	1,411,485	1,215,598	-390,992	2,041,131	1,485,823	946,300	-390,992	194,960	-74,338	269,298
2005 estimate	2,340,896	1,470,782	1,289,005	-418,891	2,125,451	1,543,281	1,001,061	-418,891	215,445	-72,499	287,944

Notes:

Receipts and outlays have been adjusted in this table by including interfund offsetting receipts of federal funds and trust funds in each fund's receipt totals and excluding them from the outlay totals.

The surplus allocation for debt reduction is part of the president's overall budgetary framework to extend the solvency of Social Security and Medicare, and is shown in Table S-1 in Part 6 of the 2001 *Budget.*

Source: Historical Tables (2000), Table 1.4.

recorded as a dollar amount in the year in which it is granted. Although the funds may not be spent in the year they are granted, the budget does not record these accounts as budget authority again. Under prescribed circumstances, the unobligated balances of budget authority may be carried over to the following year (*Analytical Perspectives* 2000: 453). The budget authority dollar figures entered in the *Historical Tables* (2000) document are for new authority recommended for the given year and do not include unspent authority from prior years. Section notes to the tables advise that the measurement of budget authority has changed for the special funds, trust funds, and credit programs; and, not all the figures in the dollar-denominated tables have been corrected for these changes. Table 9 is in percentage terms and may still offer some perspective on the relative size of agency budget authority. For example, over the nine-year period from 1991 to 1999, the Treasury holds the largest percentage of new budget authority for those years except for a tie with the SSA (off-budget) account in 1993 at 20.4 percent, and in 1994, when the Treasury dropped below 20.2 percent while the SSA was at 20.6 percent. The only other agencies near this range are "Defense-Military" at its high point of 19.9 percent in 1991, and HHS at its high point of 21.5 percent in 1997.

THE FEDERAL DEBT

"Federal Debt at the End of Year 1940–2005," Table 10, records the gross federal debt and its major components together with their proportions as a share of GDP. In the section notes in the *Historical Tables* (2000) volume, "Gross Federal Debt" contains both the debt held by the public and the government accounts. The "Public" includes individuals, private banks, and insurance companies, the Federal Reserve Bank and foreign central banks. The "Other" category refers to all the foregoing categories except the Federal Reserve Banks and the government accounts. The "Federal Government Accounts" holding federal debt are primarily the trust funds, particularly the civil service and military retirement, Social Security, and Medicare trust funds. Smaller, but substantial amounts are held by other government accounts such as the highway and unemployment trust funds.

The figures have been modified to account for a requantification of the public debt of less than one percent of the recorded value of the debt which occurred in the 1990 budget and affected amounts back to 1956. The revision was made to maintain consistency with the requantification of interest outlays. Most debt held by the public currently reflects sales price plus amortized discount instead of par value. This reporting method differs from that for debt held by government accounts which are issued at par regardless of whether there has been a premium or a discount, except for zero coupon bonds, which are recorded at estimated market price. A closing

Table 9
Percentage Distribution of Budget Authority by Agency

Department or other unit	1991	1992	1993	1994	1995	1996	1997	1998
Legislative Branch	0.2	0.2	0.2	0.2	0.2	0.2	0.2	0.2
The Judiciary	0.2	0.2	0.2	0.2	0.2	0.2	0.2	0.2
Agriculture	4.3	4.5	4.6	4.3	3.8	3.7	3.7	3.4
Commerce	0.2	0.2	0.2	0.2	0.3	0.2	0.2	0.2
Defense—Military	19.9	19.2	18.1	16.4	16.6	16.1	15.7	15.3
Education	2.0	2.0	2.1	1.8	2.1	1.8	2.0	2.1
Energy	1.2	1.2	1.2	1.1	1.0	0.9	0.9	0.9
Health and Human Services	14.5	17.1	17.5	20.1	19.6	20.1	21.5	21.2
Housing and Urban Development	2.0	1.7	1.8	1.7	1.3	1.3	1.0	1.2
Interior	0.5	0.5	0.5	0.5	0.5	0.5	0.5	0.5
Justice	0.6	0.7	0.7	0.7	0.8	1.0	1.1	1.1
Labor	2.6	3.3	3.2	2.5	2.1	2.1	2.0	2.0
State	0.4	0.4	0.4	0.5	0.4	0.4	0.4	0.4
Transportation	2.2	2.5	2.7	2.8	2.5	2.3	2.4	2.6
Treasury	20.1	20.2	20.4	20.2	23.0	23.1	23.1	23.2
Veterans Affairs	2.4	2.3	2.4	2.4	2.5	2.4	2.4	2.5
Corps of Engineers	0.2	0.2	0.3	0.3	0.2	0.2	0.3	0.2
Other Defense—Civil Programs	1.7	1.7	1.8	1.8	1.8	1.8	1.8	1.9
Environmental Protection Agency	0.4	0.4	0.5	0.4	0.4	0.4	0.4	0.4
Executive Office of the President	*	*	*	*	*	*	*	*
Federal Emergency Management Administration	*	0.3	0.2	0.4	0.3	0.3	0.3	0.1
General Services Administration	0.1	*	*	*	*	*	*	*
International Assistance Programs	1.1	0.9	1.7	0.6	1.0	0.6	0.5	0.4
National Aeronautics and Space Administration	1.0	1.0	1.0	1.0	0.9	0.9	0.8	0.8
National Science Foundation	0.2	0.2	0.2	0.2	0.2	0.2	0.2	0.2
Office of Personnel Management	2.7	2.4	2.7	2.6	2.8	2.8	2.7	2.8
Small Business Administration	*	0.1	0.1	0.1	0.1	0.1	0.1	*
Social Security Administration (On-budget)	1.5	1.7	2.0	2.2	2.2	2.0	2.1	2.2
Social Security Administration (Off-budget)	19.4	19.3	20.4	20.6	21.3	21.9	21.9	21.9
Other Independent Agencies (On-budget)	6.0	3.4	1.1	2.1	0.9	0.8	0.8	1.1
Other Independent Agencies (Off-budget)	0.2	0.1	0.2	0.2	0.2	0.2	0.2	0.4
Undistributed offsetting receipts	-7.9	-8.0	-8.1	-8.1	-8.9	-8.5	-9.4	-9.5
(On-budget)	(-6.1)	(-6.0)	(-5.9)	(-5.7)	(-6.4)	(-5.8)	(-6.5)	(-6.3)
(Off-budget)	(-1.9)	(-2.0)	(-2.3)	(-2.3)	(-2.6)	(-2.7)	(-2.9)	(-3.2)
Total budget authority	100.0	100.0	100.0	100.0	100.0	100.0	100.0	100.0

Department or other unit	1999	2000 estimate	2001 estimate	2002 estimate	2003 estimate	2004 estimate	2005 estimate
Legislative Branch	0.2	0.2	0.2	0.2	0.2	0.2	0.1
The Judiciary	0.2	0.2	0.2	0.2	0.2	0.2	0.2
Agriculture	3.8	4.0	3.5	3.4	3.1	3.0	2.9
Commerce	0.3	0.5	0.3	0.3	0.3	0.3	0.3
Defense—Military	15.7	15.5	15.4	15.3	15.1	14.9	14.8
Education	1.9	1.8	2.3	2.3	2.3	2.3	2.3
Energy	0.9	0.9	0.9	0.9	0.9	0.8	0.8
Health and Human Services	20.6	21.9	22.7	23.2	23.9	24.9	25.9
Housing and Urban Development	1.5	0.9	1.8	1.5	1.4	1.4	1.3
Interior	0.5	0.5	0.5	0.5	0.5	0.5	0.4
Justice	1.1	1.1	1.1	1.1	1.1	1.0	1.0
Labor	2.0	1.8	2.1	2.2	2.3	2.3	2.3
State	0.5	0.5	0.4	0.4	0.4	0.4	0.4
Transportation	2.9	2.9	3.1	2.9	2.8	2.8	2.8
Treasury	21.9	21.6	20.7	20.6	20.2	19.7	19.1
Veterans Affairs	2.5	2.6	2.4	2.5	2.6	2.6	2.5
Corps of Engineers	0.2	0.2	0.2	0.2	0.2	0.2	0.1
Other Defense—Civil Programs	1.8	1.8	1.8	1.8	1.8	1.8	1.8
Environmental Protection Agency	0.4	0.4	0.4	0.4	0.4	0.4	0.4
Executive Office of the President	*	*	*	*	*	*	*
Federal Emergency Management Administration	0.2	0.2	0.2	0.2	0.2	0.2	0.2
General Services Administration	*	*	*	*	*	*	*
International Assistance Programs	1.5	0.7	0.7	0.7	0.7	0.6	0.6
National Aeronautics and Space Administration	0.8	0.8	0.7	0.8	0.7	0.7	0.7
National Science Foundation	0.2	0.2	0.2	0.2	0.2	0.2	0.2
Office of Personnel Management	2.7	2.8	2.8	2.9	3.0	3.0	3.1
Small Business Administration	*	*	0.1	0.1	0.1	0.1	0.1
Social Security Administration (On-budget)	2.3	2.5	2.1	2.3	2.4	2.4	2.5
Social Security Administration (Off-budget)	21.4	22.0	22.1	22.6	23.1	23.4	23.7
Other Independent Agencies (On-budget)	0.7	0.8	0.9	0.9	0.9	0.9	0.9
Other Independent Agencies (Off-budget)	0.3	0.3	0.1	0.1	-	-	-
Allowances			-	-	-	-	*
Undistributed offsetting receipts	-9.0	-9.7	-10.0	-10.6	-10.9	-11.2	-11.5
(On-budget)	(-5.6)	(-5.9)	(-6.0)	(-6.2)	(-6.0)	(-5.9)	(-5.9)
(Off-budget)	(-3.3)	(-3.7)	(-4.0)	(-4.5)	(-4.9)	(-5.3)	(-5.6)
Total budget authority	100.0	100.0	100.0	100.0	100.0	100.0	100.0

* 0.05 percent or less.

Source: *Historical Tables* (2000), Table 5.3.

135

Table 10
Federal Debt at the End of the Year, 1940–2005

End of Fiscal Year	In Millions of Dollars					As Percentages of GDP				
	Gross Federal Debt	Less: Held by Federal Government Accounts	Equals: Held by the Public			Gross Federal Debt	Less: Held by Federal Government Accounts	Equals: Held by the Public		
			Total	Federal Reserve System	Other			Total	Federal Reserve System	Other
1940	50,696	7,924	42,772	2,458	40,314	52.5	8.2	44.3	2.5	41.8
1941	57,531	9,308	48,223	2,180	46,043	50.5	8.2	42.3	1.9	40.4
1942	79,200	11,447	67,753	2,640	65,113	54.9	7.9	47.0	1.8	45.2
1943	142,648	14,882	127,766	7,149	120,617	79.2	8.3	71.0	4.0	67.0
1944	204,079	19,283	184,796	14,899	169,897	97.6	9.2	88.4	7.1	81.3
1945	260,123	24,941	235,182	21,792	213,390	117.5	11.3	106.2	9.8	96.4
1946	270,991	29,130	241,861	23,783	218,078	121.6	13.1	108.5	10.7	97.8
1947	257,149	32,810	224,339	21,872	202,467	109.5	14.0	95.5	9.3	86.2
1948	252,031	35,761	216,270	21,366	194,904	98.2	13.9	84.3	8.3	76.0
1949	252,610	38,288	214,322	19,343	194,979	93.0	14.1	78.9	7.1	71.8
1950	256,853	37,830	219,023	18,331	200,692	93.9	13.8	80.1	6.7	73.4
1951	255,288	40,962	214,326	22,982	191,344	79.5	12.7	66.7	7.2	59.6
1952	259,097	44,339	214,758	22,906	191,852	74.3	12.7	61.6	6.6	55.0
1953	265,963	47,580	218,383	24,746	193,637	71.3	12.8	58.5	6.6	51.9
1954	270,812	46,313	224,499	25,037	199,462	71.6	12.3	59.4	6.6	52.8
1955	274,366	47,751	226,616	23,607	203,009	69.4	12.1	57.3	6.0	51.4
1956	272,693	50,537	222,156	23,758	198,398	63.8	11.8	52.0	5.6	46.4
1957	272,252	52,931	219,320	23,035	196,285	60.4	11.7	48.7	5.1	43.6
1958	279,666	53,329	226,336	25,438	200,898	60.7	11.6	49.1	5.5	43.6
1959	287,465	52,764	234,701	26,044	208,657	58.5	10.7	47.7	5.3	42.4
1960	290,525	53,686	236,840	26,523	210,317	55.9	10.3	45.6	5.1	40.5
1961	292,648	54,291	238,357	27,253	211,104	55.1	10.2	44.9	5.1	39.8
1962	302,928	54,918	248,010	29,663	218,347	53.3	9.7	43.6	5.2	38.4
1963	310,324	56,345	253,978	32,027	221,951	51.7	9.4	42.3	5.3	37.0
1964	316,059	59,210	256,849	34,794	222,055	49.2	9.2	40.0	5.4	34.6

Year										
1965	322,318	61,540	260,778	39,100	221,678	46.8	8.9	37.9	5.7	32.2
1966	328,498	64,784	263,714	42,169	221,545	43.4	8.6	34.8	5.6	29.3
1967	340,445	73,819	266,526	46,719	219,907	41.9	9.1	32.8	5.8	27.1
1968	368,685	79,140	289,545	52,230	237,315	42.4	9.1	33.3	6.0	27.3
1969	365,769	87,661	278,108	54,095	224,013	38.5	9.2	29.3	5.7	23.6
1970	380,921	97,723	283,198	57,714	225,484	37.6	9.6	27.9	5.7	22.2
1971	408,176	105,140	303,037	65,518	237,519	37.7	9.7	28.0	6.1	22.0
1972	435,936	113,559	322,377	71,426	250,951	37.0	9.6	27.4	6.1	21.3
1973	466,291	125,381	340,910	75,181	265,729	35.5	9.5	26.0	5.7	20.2
1974	483,893	140,194	343,599	80,648	263,051	33.6	9.7	23.8	5.6	18.2
1975	541,925	147,225	394,700	84,993	309,707	34.8	9.4	25.3	5.5	19.9
1976	628,970	151,566	477,404	94,714	382,690	36.2	8.7	27.5	5.5	22.0
TQ	643,561	148,052	495,509	96,702	398,807	35.0	8.1	27.0	5.3	21.7
1977	706,398	157,294	549,104	105,004	444,100	35.8	8.0	27.8	5.3	22.5
1978	776,602	169,476	607,126	115,480	491,646	35.0	7.6	27.4	5.2	22.2
1979	829,471	189,161	640,310	115,594	524,716	33.1	7.6	25.6	4.6	20.9
1980	909,050	197,118	711,932	120,846	591,086	33.3	7.2	26.1	4.4	21.6
1981	994,845	205,418	789,427	124,466	664,961	32.5	6.7	25.8	4.1	21.7
1982	1,137,345	212,740	924,605	134,497	790,108	35.2	6.6	28.6	4.2	24.5
1983	1,371,710	234,392	1,137,318	155,527	981,791	39.9	6.8	33.0	4.5	28.5
1984	1,564,657	257,611	1,307,046	155,122	1,151,924	40.7	6.7	34.0	4.0	29.9
1985	1,817,521	310,163	1,507,357	169,806	1,337,551	43.9	7.5	36.4	4.1	32.3
1986	2,120,629	379,878	1,740,750	190,855	1,549,895	48.2	8.6	39.6	4.3	35.2
1987	2,346,125	456,203	1,889,922	212,040	1,677,881	50.4	9.8	40.6	4.6	36.1
1988	2,601,307	549,487	2,051,819	229,218	1,822,601	51.9	11.0	40.9	4.6	36.3
1989	2,868,039	677,084	2,190,956	220,088	1,970,868	53.0	12.5	40.5	4.1	36.5
1990	3,206,564	794,733	2,411,831	234,410	2,177,421	55.9	13.8	42.0	4.1	37.9
1991	3,598,485	909,179	2,689,306	258,591	2,430,715	60.7	15.3	45.4	4.4	41.0
1992	4,002,123	1,002,050	3,000,073	296,397	2,703,676	64.3	16.1	48.2	4.8	43.5
1993	4,351,403	1,102,647	3,248,755	325,653	2,923,103	66.3	16.8	49.5	5.0	44.6
1994	4,643,691	1,210,242	3,433,449	355,150	3,078,299	66.8	17.4	49.4	5.1	44.3

Table 10 (continued)

End of Fiscal Year	In Millions of Dollars					As Percentages of GDP				
	Gross Federal Debt	Less: Held by Federal Government Accounts	Equals: Held by the Public			Gross Federal Debt	Less: Held by Federal Government Accounts	Equals: Held by the Public		
			Total	Federal Reserve System	Other			Total	Federal Reserve System	Other
1995	4,921,005	1,316,208	3,604,797	374,114	3,230,683	67.2	18.0	49.2	5.1	44.1
1996	5,181,921	1,447,392	3,734,529	390,924	3,343,605	67.3	18.8	48.5	5.1	43.4
1997	5,369,694	1,596,862	3,772,832	424,507	3,348,324	65.6	19.5	46.1	5.2	40.9
1998	5,478,711	1,757,090	3,721,621	458,131	3,263,490	63.4	20.3	43.1	5.3	37.8
1999	5,606,087	1,973,160	3,632,927	488,865	3,144,062	61.5	21.6	39.9	5.4	34.5
2000 estimate	5,686,338	2,210,478	3,475,860	N/A	N/A	59.4	23.1	36.3	N/A	N/A
2001 estimate	5,768,957	2,463,977	3,304,980	N/A	N/A	57.5	24.5	32.9	N/A	N/A
2002 estimate	5,854,990	2,721,326	3,133,664	N/A	N/A	55.7	25.9	29.8	N/A	N/A
2003 estimate	5,946,792	2,983,602	2,963,190	N/A	N/A	54.1	27.2	27.0	N/A	N/A
2004 estimate	6,033,583	3,252,900	2,780,683	N/A	N/A	52.5	28.3	24.2	N/A	N/A
2005 estimate	6,118,364	3,540,844	2,577,520	N/A	N/A	50.6	29.3	21.3	N/A	N/A

Notes:

N/A = not available.

GDP, percentages of GDP, deflators, and constant dollar amounts for years prior to 1960 are OMB estimates based on detailed historical GDP series for which revised data are not yet available from the Bureau of Economic Analysis. For additional details, see the Special note on GDP and Constant Dollar Amounts in the Introduction to the *Historical Tables* (2000).

Source: Historical Tables (2000), Table 7.1.

sentence in the notes states, "Starting in 1989, total debt held by Government accounts is adjusted for any initial discount on other securities" (*Historical Tables* 2000: 8–9).

In 1960, the gross federal debt was approximately $291 billion or just below $0.3 trillion. The amount of debt did not pass the trillion mark until 1982, at a little over $1.1 trillion. After that time, the debt grew rapidly by $200 to $300 billion annually, until 1990 when it reached $3.2 trillion. At the end of 1999, the gross federal debt totaled $5.6 trillion, which means the debt had risen by almost 20 times its original size over the 40 years since 1960, with the greatest growth occurring during the 1980s. The public's holdings of the debt during the same period dropped from 45.6 percent of GDP to 39.9 percent at the end of 1999. Within those figures, the Federal Reserve Banks held 5.1 percent in 1960 and 5.4 percent of GDP in 1999. The federal debt held by the government accounts was 10.3 percent in 1960 compared to 21.6 percent, or double the size, at the end of 1999.

In the early 1980s, investment by government accounts including the trust funds was about $10 billion annually. There has been a sharp increase in annual investment since that time, due to the expanding economy, the Social Security amendments of 1983, and the creation of the military retirement fund. Investments by government accounts were $160.8 billion in 1998, almost all of which was by the trust funds, $99.3 billion off-budget, and $54.2 billion on-budget. The largest of the trust fund investments were the OASI and DI accounts.

In 1999, investments by government accounts rose to $216.1 billion, and it is estimated to increase to $253.5 billion for 2001. For 1999, trust fund investments were $124.6 billion off-budget, a 25 percent rise from the previous year, and $86.5 billion on-budget, an almost 60 percent rise from the previous year. The "Other" category, or debt held by the public less FRS holdings, amounted to 40.5 percent of GDP at the end of 1960, and dropped to 34.5 percent at the end of 1999 (*Analytical Perspectives* 2000: 265–267, 275–277; *Historical Tables* 2000: 110–111).

CONCLUDING COMMENTS

The most significant change in unified budget totals is the appearance of relatively large surpluses in place of years of huge deficits. It should be emphasized that the surpluses are not in the on-budget, or federal funds segment of the budget except for $724 million in 1999. The surplus since 1983 rests entirely within the off-budget, or trust funds segment, known as the Social Security funds group. Besides the Treasury, the group has had the largest share of new budget authority over the last decade of the twentieth century with prospects of further increases for five years into the twenty-first century. The rising federal debt reflects the mounting investments by the government accounts, of which the Social Security funds are the major portion.

Chapter 7

Summary and Financing of the Federal Budget

Since 1921, the form of the budget has undergone several revisions. In this chapter, the present structure and its method of financing are highlighted. Both the means of financing the deficit and the current concern over the disposal of the surplus are introduced. The role of Treasury debt, agency debt, government accounts, and their relative sizes are examined. In closing, Table 15 provides an overview of the federal government, as recorded in the *United States Government Manual 2000/2001*.

BUDGET PRESENTATION

The *Report of the President's Commission on Budget Concepts* in 1967 originated the idea of a single, unified budget presentation to replace the three competing measures previously in use. The oldest budget was called the administrative budget and, in the 1960s, the consolidated cash budget was introduced. The third budget, known as the National Income and Product Accounts (NIPA), forms the basis for most of the unified budget estimates. The unified budget first appeared in FY 1969 togethcr with an explanation of the major differences among the three budgets. The differences were described in terms of coverage, timing, borrowing treatment, and the extent of netting practices. The President's Commission defined six major purposes of the budget, which it regarded as a financial plan for the coming year. The purposes are to enumerate the president's requests to Congress; to propose the resource allocation that would best serve the nation's goals; to set forth the government's policies for employment, prices, growth, and balance of payments; to serve as a basis for executive management of federal programs; to provide information to the Treasury for financial requirements; and to inform the public of the government's policies and its stewardship of the citizens' monies and resources (Meyer 1989a: 111–115).

The still picture of the budget, as opposed to its movements over time, has had many dramatic changes. The first of these occurred in FY 1969 as a result of the work of the President's Commission that required budget summary totals to enable measurement of the impact of the budget on the economy, appropriations clearly related to expenditures, and financial transactions that revealed the managerial and accountability requirements of government. At that time, there were three main sections listed: (1) The Budget, (2) The Credit Budget, and (3) The Federal Debt. Financial transactions related to the federal debt were not included in the summary table but did appear elsewhere in the budget. During the 1970s, the credit budget was removed but reappeared again in another form in the 1980s. From the FY 1969 period into the FY 1990s, the first item listed in the budget summary statement was the reporting of budget authority.

Although the President's Commission on Budget Concepts had made clear that the executive budget should include proposals for new legislation and appropriations, a basic form of budget authority, and his overall fiscal policy recommendations, the recent budget summaries do not contain a reference to budget authority. The Budget Summary FY 2001 (Table 11) includes outlays separated into discretionary and mandatory programs, total receipts, and the unified budget surplus. Below these items are the president's proposals for the allocation of the surplus to debt reduction, and a memorandum section listing "discretionary outlays net of offsets." The footnote to the memorandum indicates that the 1999 and 2000 figures of $575 and $618 billion, respectively, have been reidentified as mandatory outlays.

Some other changes in the presentation of the budget summary have had to do with (1) the inclusion or exclusion of the ownership of the federal debt in terms of whether by government acounts, the public including the FRS, or others; and (2) the separation of each budget category into on- or off-budget items or, in some years, according to whether the budget items are from the federal funds, trust funds, or intragovernmental transactions.

In FY 1992, the budget document reviewed some alternative presentations of the unified budget currently used: one called the GAO federal budget presentation, which included a comprehensive budget, an operating budget, and a capital budget; one called the California presentation of the federal budget, which had three parts, called "Receipts," "Outlays, Expenses and Investments," and "Surplus/Deficit"; and the last one, called the Sanford presentation of the federal budget, which was particularly concerned with drawing attention to control over the operating budget and to protecting the retirement trust funds (*Budget FY 1992* (1991): Part six, 12, 32, 36, 40). None of the presentations gave consideration to the financing of a deficit or the allocation of a surplus. Over 15 years ago, in an article

Table 11
Budget Summary (in billions of dollars)

	1999 Actual	Estimates										
		2000	2001	2002	2003	2004	2005	2006	2007	2008	2009	2010
Outlays:												
Discretionary:												
Department of Defense	262	278	279	285	294	303	317	318	322	332	341	349
Non-DoD discretionary	313	339	355	366	371	378	384	393	402	412	421	431
Subtotal, discretionary	575	618	634	651	665	681	701	711	724	744	762	781
Mandatory:												
Social Security	387	403	422	443	465	490	516	545	575	608	645	685
Medicare and Medicaid	296	316	342	362	389	426	462	489	535	574	617	661
Means-tested entitlements (except Medicaid)	104	110	111	119	126	131	139	140	141	150	154	160
Other	112	123	117	121	128	136	144	150	157	168	177	187
Subtotal, mandatory	898	952	993	1,046	1,108	1,183	1,260	1,324	1,408	1,500	1,594	1,693
Net interest	230	220	208	199	189	178	164	150	134	118	100	80
Total outlays	1,703	1,790	1,835	1,895	1,963	2,041	2,125	2,185	2,267	2,362	2,456	2,553
Receipts	1,827	1,956	2,019	2,081	2,147	2,236	2,341	2,440	2,559	2,676	2,785	2,917
Unified Budget Surplus	124	167	184	186	185	195	215	256	292	314	329	363
Surplus Allocated for Debt Reduction:												
Social Security solvency lock-box	124	148	160	172	184	195	214	224	239	250	260	272
Medicare solvency transfers			15	13				26	47	57	61	80
Reserve for catastrophic prescription drug coverage						*	2	4	5	7	8	11
On-budget surplus	1	19	9	1	*	*	2	1	1	*	*	*
Total debt reduction	124	167	184	186	185	195	215	256	292	314	329	363
Memorandum:												
Discretionary outlays net of offsets [1]	575	618	626	649	663	679	699	709	723	743	762	780

Notes:

* $500 million or less.

[1] Offsets for 1999 and 2000 have been reclassified as mandatory.

Source: Budget of the United States Government FY 2001 (2000), Table S-3.

in *Public Budgeting and Finance* (1986), the author furnished a table reconciling the budget surplus or deficit and its financing in a way that would permit it to be an integral part of the unified budget (Meyer 1986: 64).

At the beginning of the *Budget FY 2001* on page 2, there is a diagram of "The Federal Government Dollar" and "Budget Totals" that are reproduced as Table 12. Receipts and outlays are illustrated in a pie diagram with each slice of the pie representing the appropriate percentage of the component. In the lower portion of Table 12, total budget receipts and outlays are listed and below "Total unified budget surplus," the identical information that appeared in Table 11 concerning its distribution is indicated. The memorandum section which dealt with discretionary outlays in that table is not present.

BUDGET FINANCING AND DEBT

"Federal Government Financing and Debt" is the title of two tables presented, in different formats, in both the *Budget* document and the *Analytical Perspectives* volume. Table 13 is a copy of the one found in *Analytical Perspectives* (2000). A similar table has been offered in the *Budget* documents ever since the removal, in FY 1972, of budget financing from the "Budget Summary." In the first section of Table 13, "Financing," the 1999 unified budget surplus of $124 billion is entered, followed by several categories listed under the heading "Means of financing other than borrowing from the public." There are another two sections devoted to "Debt Subject to Statutory Limitation, End of Year" and to "Debt Outstanding, End of Year." The new features consist of listings in parentheses after the statement of the surplus in the first section, such as "Social Security solvency lock-box: Off-budget" and "Medicare solvency debt reduction reserve," and further listings after the last section of the table, entitled "Debt Outstanding, End of Year," which details under "Debt securities held as assets by Government accounts" such accounts as "Social Security," Federal employee retirement," and "Other." The Federal Reserve System is not mentioned in the section because it has been assigned, according to footnote 9 of the table, to the final line of the presentation, "Debt securities held as assets by the public." Total assets held by the public were approximately $3.1 trillion at the end of 1999, of which about 0.5 trillion were held by the Federal Reserve Banks (*Budget FY 2001* [2000]: 393, 420–421).

Perhaps the most significant part of the "Federal Government Financing and Debt" Statement is the relatively recent addition to the means of financing category, "Net financing disbursements," which consists of direct loan financing accounts and guaranteed loan financing accounts. Their inclusion is a result of the Federal Credit Reform Act of 1990. The Act distinguished between what is and what is not a cost to the government. Costs to the government for direct loans and loan guarantees are the esti-

Table 12
Budget Totals (in billions of dollars)

	1999 Actual	Estimates											Total 2001–2010
		2000	2001	2002	2003	2004	2005	2006	2007	2008	2009	2010	
Receipts	1,827	1,956	2,019	2,081	2,147	2,236	2,341	2,440	2,559	2,676	2,785	2,917	24,202
Outlays	1,703	1,790	1,835	1,895	1,963	2,041	2,125	2,185	2,267	2,362	2,456	2,553	21,683
Total unified budget surplus	124	167	184	186	185	195	215	256	292	314	329	363	2,519
Debt Reduction:													
Social Security solvency lock-box	124	148	160	172	184	195	214	224	239	250	260	272	2,169
Medicare solvency transfers	....	....	15	13	....	....	....	26	47	57	61	80	299
Reserve for cata-strophic prescription drug coverage	....	....	....	....	....	....	....	4	5	7	8	11	35
On-Budget surplus ...	1	19	9	1	*	*	2	1	1	*	*	*	16
Total debt reduction	124	167	184	186	185	195	215	256	292	314	329	363	2,519

* $500 million or less.

Source: *Budget of the United States Government FY 2001* (2000), Table I-1.

Table 13

Federal Government Financing and Debt[1] (in billions of dollars)

	1999 Actual	Estimate													
		2000	2001	2002	2003	2004	2005	2006	2007	2008	2009	2010	2011	2012	2013
Financing:															
Surplus or deficit (−)	124	167	184	186	185	195	215	256	292	314	329	363	403	443	479
(Social Security solvency lock-box: Off-budget)	124	148	160	172	184	195	214	224	239	250	260	272	280	295	309
(Social Security interest savings transfer)			15	13				30	52	64	69	91	100	118	138
(Medicare solvency debt reduction reserve)													22	30	32
(On-budget)	*	19	9	1	1	*	1	2	1	*	*	*	*	*	*
Means of financing other than borrowing from the public:[2]															
Changes in:[2]															
Treasury operating cash balance	−18	16													
Checks outstanding, deposit funds, etc.[3]	−6	1													
Seigniorage on coins	1	1	2	2	2	2	2	2	2	2	2	2	2	2	2
Less: Social Security equity purchases													−52	−66	−83
Less: Net financing disbursements:															
Direct loan financing accounts	−19	−29	−18	−18	−17	−16	−16	−16	−16	−15	−15	−15	−16	−16	−16
Guaranteed loan financing accounts	5	*	1	1	1	2	2	2	2	2	2	2	3	3	3
Total, means of financing other than borrowing from the public	−36	−9	−13	−15	−14	−12	−12	−12	−12	−12	−11	−11	−63	−78	−95
Total, repayment of publicly held debt	89	157	171	171	170	183	203	243	280	302	318	352	340	365	384
Change in debt held by the public[4]	−89	−157	−171	−171	−170	−183	−203	−243	−280	−302	−318	−352	−340	−365	−384
Debt Subject to Statutory Limitation, End of Year:															
Debt issued by Treasury	5,578	5,658	5,742	5,828	5,921	6,009	6,096	6,185	6,268	6,347	6,424	6,502	6,595	6,693	6,794
Adjustment for Treasury debt not subject to limitation and agency debt subject to limitation[5]	−15	−15	−15	−15	−15	−15	−15	−15	−15	−15	−15	−15	−15	−15	−15
Adjustment for discount and premium[6]	6	6	6	6	6	6	6	6	6	6	6	6	6	6	6

Total, debt subject to statutory limitation [7]	5,568	5,648	5,732	5,819	5,912	5,999	6,086	6,175	6,258	6,337	6,414	6,492	6,585	6,683	6,785
Debt Outstanding, End of Year:															
Gross Federal debt:															
Debt issued by Treasury	5,578	5,658	5,742	5,828	5,921	6,009	6,096	6,185	6,268	6,347	6,424	6,502	6,595	6,693	6,794
Debt issued by other agencies	29	28	27	27	25	24	23	22	20	20	20	20	20	20	20
Total, gross Federal debt	5,606	5,686	5,769	5,855	5,947	6,034	6,118	6,206	6,288	6,367	6,444	6,522	6,615	6,713	6,815
Held by:															
Debt securities held as assets by Government accounts	1,973	2,210	2,464	2,721	2,984	3,253	3,541	3,872	4,234	4,615	5,010	5,440	5,873	6,335	6,821
Social Security	855	1,004	1,164	1,338	1,522	1,717	1,930	2,154	2,392	2,641	2,899	3,170	3,498	3,843	4,206
Federal employee retirement	643	681	717	754	789	824	858	891	922	952	980	1,006	1,034	1,063	1,093
Other	475	525	582	630	672	712	752	828	920	1,023	1,131	1,263	1,341	1,429	1,523
Debt securities held as assets by the public [8]	3,633	3,476	3,305	3,134	2,963	2,781	2,578	2,334	2,054	1,752	1,434	1,082	742	377	*** [9]

Notes:

* $500 million or less.

[1] Almost all Treasury securities held by the public and zero-coupon bonds held by government accounts are measured at sales price plus amortized discount or less amortized premium. Almost all agency debt is measured at face value. Almost all Treasury securities in the government account series are measured at face value less unrealized discount (if any).

[2] A decrease in the Treasury operating cash balance (which is an asset) would be a means of financing a deficit and therefore would have a positive sign. An increase in checks outstanding or deposit fund balances (which are liabilities) would also be a means of financing a deficit and therefore would also have a positive sign.

[3] Besides checks outstanding and deposit funds, includes accrued interest payable on Treasury debt, miscellaneous liability accounts, allocations of special drawing rights, and, as offsets, cash and monetary assets other than the Treasury operating cash balance, miscellaneous asset accounts, and profit on sale of gold.

[4] Includes a $355 million reclassification of debt in 2000. Indian tribal funds that are owned by the Indian tribes and held and managed in a fiduciary capacity by the government on the tribes' behalf were reclassified from trust funds to deposit funds as of 1 October 1999, and their holdings of Treasury securities were accordingly reclassified from debt held by government accounts to debt held by the public.

[5] Consists primarily of Federal Financing Bank debt.

[6] Consists of unamortized discount (less premium) on public issues of Treasury notes and bonds (other than zero-coupon bonds) and unrealized discount on government account series securities.

[7] The statutory debt limit is $5,950 billion.

[8] At the end of 1999, the Federal Reserve Banks held $489 billion of federal securities and the rest of the public held $3,144 billion. Debt held by the Federal Reserve Banks is not estimated for future years.

[9] Total debt will be fully redeemed in 2013. Policy decisions will be required on use of the surplus once debt has been redeemed.

Source: Analytical Perspectives (2000), Table 12–2.

mated subsidy costs of these two items at the time the direct loans or loan guarantees are paid. Any cash flows to and from the public resulting from the loans and guarantees beyond the estimated subsidy costs, which are considered budget outlays, are nonbudgetary in nature and therefore are treated as "net financing disbursements." The classification includes the net cash flows of the financing accounts which record the transactions with the public and the intragovernmental transactions. In FY 1999, direct loan financing accounts reduced the size of the surplus by $19 billion while the guaranteed loan financing accounts added $5 billion. *Analytical Perspectives* (2000) states that these accounts, previously, had little effect on borrowing requirements until the mid-1990s. The major cause of the increase in the growth of this financing category is the direct student loan program. The major way that the federal government finances a deficit as opposed to a surplus has been by borrowing from the public. For the last decade, the cumulative deficit was $1.34 trillion and the amount of debt held by the public increased by $1.44 trillion. The difference between the two figures is ascribed to the other means of financing methods, such as changes in cash balances of the Treasury, checks outstanding, seignorage, or when the face value of minted coins exceeds the costs of their production including their metal content, and net financing disbursements (*Analytical Perspectives* 2000: 272–274). To gain a clearer insight into the government's effect on the economy through the financing of the deficit or disposal of the surplus, it is helpful to refer to materials furnished by the Treasury Department on the subject of the federal debt.

The Bureau of the Public Debt (BPD) manages the federal debt as an entity in the Treasury Department. In March 2000, the "Schedules of Federal Debt" for FY 1998 and 1999 were audited by the GAO. In a statement to the Commissioner of the Bureau of the Public Debt, David M. Walker, Comptroller General of the United States, expressed the following opinion:

The Schedules of Federal Debt including the accompanying notes present fairly, in all material respects, in conformity with generally accepted accounting principles, the balances as of September 30, 1999, 1998, and 1997, for Federal Debt managed by BPD, the related Accrued Interest Payables and Net unamortized Discounts and Premiums, and the related increases and decreases for the fiscal years ended September 30, 1999 and 1998. (GAO 2000b: 7–8)

Nevertheless, the GAO found that the Schedules of Federal Debt for FY 1999 and 1998 contained deficiencies involving computer controls, and that the audit did not consider compliance with laws, regulations, and internal controls in all respects. Table 14, with accompanying notes, compares the Schedules of Federal Debt for FY 1999 and 1998 to the balance as of FY 1997. The balance held by the public in FY 1997 diminished over the next two years by more than $50 billion by FY 1998, and more than

Table 14
Schedules of Federal Debt and Notes

Schedules of Federal Debt Managed by the Bureau of the Public Debt for the Fiscal Years Ended September 30, 1999 and 1998 (dollars in millions)

	Federal Debt					
	Held by the Public			Held by Federal Entities		
	Principal (Note 2)	Accrued Interest Payable	Net Unamortized Discounts	Principal (Note 3)	Accrued Interest Payable	Net Unamortized Premiums/ (Discounts)
Balance as of September 30, 1997	$3,814,687	$46,052	($70,252)	$1,583,459	$28,924	$12,215
Increases						
Borrowings from the Public	2,127,992		(34,338)			
Net Increase in Amounts Borrowed from Federal Entities				166,512		(6,877)
Accrued Interest (Note 4)		205,215			120,858	
Total Increases	2,127,992	205,215	(34,338)	166,512	120,858	(6,877)
Decreases						
Repayments of Debt Held by the Public	2,181,457					
Interest Paid		205,837			119,268	
Net Amortization (Note 4)			(37,870)			611
Total Decreases	2,181,457	205,837	(37,870)	0	119,268	611
Balance as of September 30, 1998	$3,761,222	$45,430	($66,720)	$1,749,971	$30,514	$4,727
Increases						
Borrowings from the Public	2,159,683		(29,695)			
Net Increase in Amounts Borrowed from Federal Entities				222,920		(4,278)
Accrued Interest (Note 4)		196,448			127,517	
Total Increases	2,159,683	196,448	(29,695)	222,920	127,517	(4,278)
Decreases						
Repayments of Debt Held by the Public	2,252,525					
Interest Paid		199,290			125,243	
Net Amortization (Note 4)			(33,619)			2,048
Total Decreases	2,252,525	199,290	(33,619)	0	125,243	2,048
Balance as of September 30, 1999	$3,668,380	$42,588	($62,796)	$1,972,891	$32,788	($1,599)

The accompanying notes are an integral part of these schedules.

Table 14 (continued)

Notes to the Schedules of Federal Debt Managed by the Bureau of the Public Debt for the Fiscal Years Ended September 30, 1999 and 1998 (dollars in millions)

Note 1. Significant Accounting Policies

Basis of Presentation

The Schedules of Federal Debt Managed by the Bureau of the Public Debt have been prepared to report fiscal year 1999 and 1998 balances and activity relating to monies borrowed from the public and federal entities to fund the U.S. government's operations. All fiscal year end balances reported on the Schedules of Federal Debt are not covered by budgetary resources.

Reporting Entity

The Constitution empowers Congress to borrow money on the credit of the United States. Congress has authorized the Secretary of the Treasury to borrow monies to operate the federal government. Within Treasury, BPD is responsible for issuing Treasury securities in accordance with such authority and to account for the resulting debt. Title 31 U.S.C. authorizes BPD, an organizational entity within the Fiscal Service of the Department of the Treasury, to prescribe the debt instruments and otherwise limit and restrict the amount and composition of the debt. In addition, BPD has been given the responsibility to issue Treasury securities to trust funds for trust fund receipts not needed for current benefits and expenses. BPD issues and redeems Treasury securities for the rust funds based on data provided by program agencies and other Treasury entities.

Basis of Accounting

The schedules were prepared in conformity with generally accepted accounting principles and from BPD's automated accounting system, Public Debt Accounting and Reporting System. Interest costs are recorded as expenses when incurred, instead of when paid. Certain Treasury securities are issued at a discount or premium. These discounts and premiums are amortized over the term of the security using the effective interest method for zero-coupon bonds and the straight line method, which is not materially different from the effective interest method, for the other securities. The Department of the Treasury also issues inflation-indexed securities. Inflation-indexed securities accrue principal over the life of the security based on the Consumer Price Index for all Urban Consumers.

Budgetary Authority

Permanent, indefinite appropriations are available for the payment of interest on the federal debt and on the redemption of Treasury securities.

Note 2. Federal Debt Held by the Public

As of September 30, 1999 and 1998, Federal Debt held by the Public consisted of the following:

	1999		1998	
	Amount	Average Interest Rates	Amount	Average Interest Rates
Marketable:				
Treasury Bills	$653,165	4.9%	$637,648	5.2%
Treasury Notes	1,896,427	6.0%	2,051,046	6.2%
Treasury Bonds	667,359	8.4%	625,675	8.6%
Total Marketable	$3,216,951		$3,314,369	
Nonmarketable	$451,429	6.1%	$446,853	6.2%
Total Federal Debt Held by the Public	$3,668,380		$3,761,222	

Table 14 (continued)

Treasury issues marketable bills at a discount and pays the par amount of the security upon maturity. The average interest rate on a Treasury bill represents the average effective yield on the security. Treasury bills are issued with a term of 1 year or less.

Treasury issues marketable notes and bonds as long term securities that pay semi-annual interest based on the security's stated interest rate. These securities are issued at either par value or at an amount that reflects a discount or a premium. The average interest rate on marketable notes and bonds represents the stated interest rate adjusted by any discount or premium. Treasury notes are issued with a term of 2–10 years and Treasury bonds are issued with a term of more than 10 years. As of September 30, 1999, Treasury marketable notes included $67,589 million of inflation-indexed notes and Treasury marketable bonds included $24,776 million of inflation-indexed bonds. As of September 30, 1998, Treasury marketable notes included $41,863 million of inflation-indexed notes and Treasury marketable bonds included $16,960 million of inflation-indexed bonds.

As of September 30, 1999, nonmarketable securities primarily consisted of $186,333 million in U.S. Savings Securities, $168,091 million in securities issued to State and Local Governments, $30,970 million in Foreign Series Securities, and $29,995 million in Domestic Series Securities. As of September 30, 1998, nonmarketable securities primarily consisted of $186,006 million in U.S. Savings Securities, $164,431 million in securities issued to State and Local Governments, $35,079 million in Foreign Series Securities, and $29,995 million in Domestic Series Securities. Treasury issues nonmarketable securities at either par value or at an amount that reflects a discount or a premium. The average interest rate on the nonmarketable securities represents the weighted effective yield. Nonmarketable securities are issued with a term of on demand to more than 10 years.

Government Account Series (GAS) securities are nonmarketable securities issued to federal entities. Federal Debt Held by the Public includes GAS securities issued to certain federal entities. One example is the GAS security held by the Thrift Savings Fund. Federal employees and retirees who have individual accounts own the GAS securities held by the fund. For this reason, the fund is considered part of the Federal Debt Held by the Public rather than Federal Debt Held by Federal Entities. Also, the GAS securities held by the Thrift Savings Fund consist of overnight investments redeemed one business day after their issue. The net increase in amounts borrowed from the fund during fiscal years 1999 and 1998 are included in the respective Borrowings from the Public amounts reported on the Schedules of Federal Debt.

Federal Debt Held by the Public includes federal debt held outside of the U.S. government by individuals, corporations, Federal Reserve Banks (FRB), state and local governments, and foreign governments and central banks. The FRB owned $515 billion and $478 billion of Federal Debt Held by the Public as of September 30, 1999 and 1998, respectively. These securities are held in the FRB System Open Market Account (SOMA) for the purpose of conducting monetary policy.

Note 3. Federal Debt Held by Federal Entities

As of September 30, 1999 and 1998, Federal Debt Held by Federal Entities is owed to the following:

		1999	1998
SSA:	Federal Old-Age and Survivors Insurance Trust Fund	$762,226	$653,282
OPM:	Civil Service Retirement and Disability Fund	465,640*	431,757*
HHS:	Federal Hospital Insurance Trust Fund	153,767	118,250
DOD:	Military Retirement Fund	141,274	133,843
SSA:	Federal Disability Insurance Trust Fund	92,666*	76,996*
DOL:	Unemployment Trust Fund	77,358	70,641*
FDIC:	The Bank Insurance Fund	28,359	27,445
DOT:	Highway Trust Fund	28,083	17,926
HHS:	Federal Supplementary Medical Insurance Trust Fund	26,528	39,502
RRB:	Railroad Retirement Account	22,347	19,764
OPM:	Employees' Life Insurance Fund	20,755	19,377
DOE:	Nuclear Waste Disposal Fund	15,195	11,169
HUD:	FHA—Liquidating Account	14,942	14,344
DOT:	Airport & Airway Trust Fund	12,414	8,550
Treasury:	Exchange Stabilization Fund	12,382	15,981
VA:	National Service Life Insurance Fund	11,954	12,008

Table 14 (continued)

		1999	1998
FDIC:	Savings Association Insurance Fund (SAIF)	10,144	9,602
DOS:	Foreign Service Retirement & Disability Fund	10,131	9,550
Other Programs and Funds		66,726	59,984
Total Federal Debt Held by Federal Entities		$1,972,891	$1,749,971

* These accounts include marketable Treasury securities as well as GAS securities as follows:

	GAS Securities	Marketable Treasury Securities	Total
As of September 30, 1999:			
Civil Service Retirement and Disability Fund	$464,561	$1,079	$465,640
Federal Disability Insurance Trust Fund	92,622	44	92,666
As of September 30, 1998:			
Civil Service Retirement and Disability Fund	$430,595	$1,162	$431,757
Federal Disability Insurance Trust Fund	76,947	49	76,996
Unemployment Trust Fund	70,598	43	70,641

Social Security Administration (SSA); Office of Personnel Management (OPM); Department of Health and Human Services (HHS); Department of Defense (DOD); Department of Labor (DOL); Federal Deposit Insurance Corporation (FDIC); Department of Transportation (DOT); Railroad Retirement Board (RRB); Department of Energy (DOE); Department of Housing and Urban Development (HUD); Department of the Treasury (Treasury); Department of Veterans Affairs (VA); Department of State (DOS).

Federal Debt Held by Federal Entities primarily consists of GAS securities. Treasury issues GAS securities at either par value or at an amount that reflects a discount or a premium. The average interest rates for fiscal years 1999 and 1998 were 6.8 percent and 7.1 percent, respectively. GAS securities are issued with a term of on demand to 30 years.

Note 4. Interest Expense

Interest expense on Federal Debt Managed by BPD for fiscal years 1999 and 1998 consisted of the following:

	1999	1998
Federal Debt Held by the Public		
Accrued Interest	$196,448	$205,215
Net Amortization of Premiums and Discounts	33,619	37,870
Total Interest Expense on Federal Debt Held by the Public	230,067	243,085
Federal Debt Held by Federal Entities		
Accrued Interest	127,517	120,858
Net Amortization of Premiums and Discounts	(2,048)	(611)
Total Interest Expense on Federal Debt Held by Federal Entities	125,469	120,247
Total Interest Expense on Federal Debt Managed by BPD	$355,536	$363,332

Note 5. Fund Balance With Treasury

	As of September 30, 1999	As of September 30, 1998 pro forma (unaudited)	As of September 30, 1998 actual
Appropriated Funds Obligated	$117	$209	$45,652

Table 14 (continued)

Prior to fiscal year 1999, interest accruals on Federal Debt Held by the Public were charged over the life of the security to the Interest on Public Debt appropriation. These amounts were included in BPD's Fund Balance With Treasury (FBWT), a non-entity, intragovernmental account, until the semi-annual interest payments were disbursed. Effective October 1, 1998, interest accruals are no longer charged to the interest on Public Debt appropriation. Instead, the interest is charged to the appropriation when paid. Therefore, the interest accruals are no longer included in BPD's FBWT. The pro forma amount of appropriated funds obligated as of September 30, 1998, represents the FBWT amount had this change in operating procedure been effective in fiscal year 1998.

The FBWT and other debt related accounts are not included on the schedule of Federal Debt and are presented for informational purposes.

Note 6. Other Debt Related Balances

As of September 30, 1999 and 1998, other debt related balances consisted of the following:

	1999	1998
Accounts Receivable from Overpayments	$7	$6
Advances Received for Purchases of Federal Debt	(24)	(123)
Other Miscellaneous Balances	(91)	(82)
Total Other Debt Related Balances	($108)	($199)

Note 7. Subsequent Event

On January 19, 2000, the Department of the Treasury issued rules in final form pursuant to 31CFR Part 375 setting out the terms and conditions by which outstanding, unmatured marketable Treasury securities may be redeemed through Treasury buying back the securities. This authority to buy back securities will enable Treasury to better manage financing needs, promote more efficient capital markets, and may lower financing costs for taxpayers. As of January 28, 2000, no outstanding, unmatured marketable Treasury securities had been redeemed through such authority.

Source: GAO (2000b: 13–18).

$90 billion by FY 1999. The balance of accrued interest payable on 30 September 1997 was approximately $46 billion; it dropped to slightly more than $45 billion in FY 1998; and it went down further to about $43 billion as of 30 September 1999. However, Note 4 explains that total interest expense on federal debt managed by BPD in FY 1998 was $363 billion, of which $242 billion was for federal debt held by the public. In FY 1999, total interest expense was about $356 billion, of which $230 billion was interest expense for federal debt held by the public. As for debt held by the federal entities, the balance on principal was approximately $1.58 trillion on 30 September 1997; it grew to almost $1.75 trillion by 30 September 1998, and by the end of FY 1999, or 30 September 1999, it was almost $1.97 trillion. Accrued interest on federal debt held by federal entities, according to Note 4, was about $120 billion at the end of FY 1998, and about $125 billion at the end of FY 1999. Table 14 reports figures for total increases of accrued interest paid for the year ending 30 September 1998 of over $205 billion, and of over $196 billion for the year ending 30 September 1999. An additional $3 billion paid in that year relates to net amortization adjustments contained in Note 4. With a gross federal debt at the end of FY 1999 of $5.6 trillion, there are substantial financial and fiscal impacts on the economy. These impacts arise not simply from the sheer size of the debt, but from other related sources. The federal debt's (1) maturity structure, (2) types of securities, (3) ownership, (4) market yields, and (5) average interest rates are some of the major factors affecting private sector liquidity and financial market operations in general. Investigating the role of these five factors in generating strong and vital financial markets is a necessary and significant contribution to achieving budget objectives.

In the *Treasury Bulletin* (Office of the Secretary of the Treasury, 2000), produced and published by the Financial Management Service of the Department of the Treasury, information on the aspects of the debt that directly and indirectly affect financial market operations are given.

1. For example, in Table FD-5, "Maturity Distribution and Average Length of Marketable Interest-Bearing Public Debt held by Private Investors," the average length of the debt is described as 5 years, 9 months, at the end of FY 1999. The average length was lowest in December 1975, when it dropped to 2 years, 5 months, and highest in May 1991, when it was 6 years, 4 months.

2. The government issues interest-bearing marketable and nonmarketable Treasury securities. Table FD-2 lists under the first category: Treasury bills, notes, bonds, inflation-indexed notes and bonds, Federal Financing Bank, and the nonmarketable total. The second half of the table lists nonmarketable securities, which include U.S. savings securities, foreign series, government account issues, state and local government series, domestic series, and other. The largest category of interest-bearing public debt at the end of FY 1999 was the government account series totaling $2.0 trillion.

3. U.S. Treasury securities are widely owned here and abroad. In addition to Federal Reserve Banks and government accounts, which include OASI, Federal Employees Retirement Fund, and the Federal Hospital Insurance Trust Fund as the largest in the group (totaling just under half of the $2.0 trillion in the government account series at the end of FY 1999), there are other large holders of the federal debt. They consist of commercial banks, savings institutions, and credit unions reported under depository institutions; U.S. Saving Bonds reported at current accrual value; private, state, and local governments' pension funds; insurance companies; mutual funds; state and local governments; foreign and international; and other investors including individuals, GSEs, brokers and dealers, bank personal trusts and estates, corporate and noncorporate businesses, and other investors. The total public debt is reported at face value at the end of December 1999, in the pages of the *U.S. Treasury Monthly Statement of Public Debt*, as almost $5.8 trillion. Of that figure, almost half, or $2.5 trillion, is held by the government accounts and the Federal Reserve Banks. The third largest owners are foreign and international for a total of approximately $1.3

trillion at the end of December 1999. In the table reporting "Total Liabilities by Country," on page 65, the Latin American and Caribbean nations' position is the largest, totaling almost $603 billion, with the British West Indies representing more than half of the total at $332 billion. There are additional tables in the *Treasury Bulletin* (Office of the Secretary of the Treasury 2000) and on the Treasury International Capital (TIC) reporting system web site on current and historical data concerning these transactions and other capital movements.

4. In the same issue of the *Treasury Bulletin* there is a table featuring Treasury market bid yields at constant maturities for bills, notes, and bonds, and a second table showing average yields of long-term Treasury, corporate, and municipal bonds. The long-term average yield for Treasury securities is the 30-year constant maturity yield, which was 6.35 percent on average for the month of December 1999 (Office of the Secretary of the Treasury 2000: 23–26, 63–67).

5. According to the "Federal Debt Managed by the Bureau of the Public Debt," Table 14, Note 2, average interest rates for FY 1999 for each type of Treasury security are: bills—4.9 percent, notes—6.0 percent, bonds—8.4 percent, and nonmarketable debt—6.1 percent (GAO 2000b: 15). Foreign holdings of the federal debt have increased as a proportion of total federal debt, particularly since the late 1980s. In FY 1988, foreign holdings were almost $346 billion, or 16.9 percent of a total federal debt of $2.052 trillion held by the public. In FY 1999, foreign holdings were $1.281 trillion or 35.3 percent of total federal debt of $3.633 trillion held by the public.

In FY 1999, interest on the total federal debt held by the public was $234.9 billion, which does not include interest received by trust funds, agency debt, or offsets for interest on public debt received by government revolving funds and special funds. The budget documents are not clear as to the budget treatment of interest for the trust funds or their totals. At one point, net interest is said to exclude trust fund interest, but later, after explaining that OASI and DI are excluded from the budget, the two following sentences appear: "Social Security, however, is a Federal program. Thus, the net interest of the Federal Government as a whole includes the off-budget interest earnings" (*Budget* 2000: 285–286). Interest on foreign holdings of federal debt coupled with that of the GSEs, curiously, was $97.2 billion, or 39.5 percent of total interest paid on federal debt held by the public (*Analytical Perspectives* 2000: 275–280).

FEDERAL DEBT AND THE BUDGET SURPLUS

The two principal purposes of debt issuance are to finance the deficit and for government accounts, the majority of which are trust funds that accumulate surpluses. The public debt is the name for all federal debt issued by the Treasury; agency debt is a small portion of federal debt issued by other government agencies.

Since 1988 there has been a change in the way debt held by the public is measured. Up to that time, it was face, or par value, the principal amount due at maturity, that was used in budget calculations, except in the case of savings bonds. Since 1988, debt held by the public has been calculated at its sales price initially, then afterwards, plus or minus the amortized discount or premium. Agency debt, however, continues to be recorded at face value except for zero-coupon certificates. Although agency debt in the budget refers to government agencies on-budget, primarily, in the securities market it includes, also, the debt of the GSEs and certain government securities. According to the budget documents for FY 2001, at the end of 1999, actual Treasury debt outstanding was $5.6 trillion, agency debt was $29 billion, and GSE net borrowing outstanding was over $1.2 trillion.

Of the $5.6 trillion of Treasury outstanding debt, $3.6 trillion was held by the public, and about $0.5 trillion of that was held by the FRS, which is considered part of the public holdings. Of the balance of $2 trillion held by the government accounts, the largest component is the SSA accounts, OASI and DI, which held approximately $0.9 trillion of Treasury debt (Table 13; *Analytical Perspectives* 2000: 238, 272). The *Analytical Perspectives* (2000) volume states, on page 270: "By law, Trust fund surpluses must be invested in Federal securities." On page 272, it is stated that

Social security which comprises almost all of the off-budget totals, accounted for nearly all the unified budget surplus in 1999. It is estimated to have large and rising surpluses throughout the projection period, continuing to account for a major part of the estimated budget surpluses. This will be used to repay the publicly held debt, which decreases from $3,633 billion at the end of 1999 to $1,082 billion at the end of 2010 and is fully repaid in 2013.

In fact, on page 269, it is reported that in both 1998 and 1999, the unified budget surpluses of $69 billion and $124 billion enabled repayment of the debt held by the public of $51 billion in 1998 and $89 billion in 1999. Because the trust funds have annual surpluses, the surpluses are loaned to the Treasury and the government does not have to borrow as much from the public. In the government's consolidated financial statements, these transactions are netted out because they are intragovernmental. The Treasury does not have to pay back this debt when it is necessary for the federal entities to turn in their Treasury securities. Any interest earned on the securities may be used by the federal entities for outlays or to purchase more Treasury securities. The GAO, in its financial audit of the *1999 Financial Report of the United States Government* (2000d), comments on the surplus in the trust fund accounts. On page 37, it states that the surplus is invested in Treasury securities and the Treasury uses the cash to meet its current needs. The report adds that as these are intragovernmental transactions, the $2 trillion of investments and liabilities at 30 September 1999 are netted out in the attached financial statements. When expected shortfalls in the trust funds occur, the funds will need to redeem their investments in Treasury securities. The redemptions by government will need to be funded by future surpluses (if available), reduction in spending programs, higher taxes, or more borrowing from the public.

AGENCY DEBT AND THE GOVERNMENT ACCOUNTS

At the end of 1999, agency debt was $29 billion, one percent of federal debt in the hands of the public. The largest component of debt outstanding was the Tennessee Valley Authority (TVA) share of $26.4 billion. Of the GSEs debt of $1.2 trillion, the largest component of its debt outstanding was the FHLMC. In turn, the FHLMC had portfolio programs outstanding debt of slightly over $341 billion and mortgage-backed securities (MBS) outstanding debt of slightly less than $500 billion.

The amount of annual borrowing by agencies from the public has been lowered considerably by the existence of the FFB, an entity housed in the Treasury Department. It was created in 1974 as a financial intermediary to expedite improved financial arrangements for obligations issued, guaranteed, or sold by federal agencies; its borrowing is outside the general statutory limit on federal debt. The FFB can purchase agency debt and either finance the purchases by borrowing from the treasury, or by swapping its agency debt holdings for Treasury securities, as it did to a large extent in 1996. A great deal of accounting knowhow is required to avoid the problem of double counting for the various exchanges.

The largest investment of government accounts in the federal debt are the holdings of the two Social Security Trust funds; their contribution was 61 percent in 1999. There are large investments made, also, by the Civil Service Retirement and Disability Trust Fund and the Military Retirement Trust Fund; their contributions were 13 percent and 3 percent, respectively, in 1999. Other holdings include the Hospital Insurance Fund and the Unemployment Trust Fund.

There have been two reclassifications from debt held by the government accounts to debt held by the public. They are deposit funds which entail, in some cases, the holding of money by government as an agent for others, such as withholding state income taxes from federal workers' wages. The case of the government account "Outer Continental Shelf" receipts was in dispute as to ownership. Presently, it has been reassigned to debt held by the public rather than to the government accounts. The change was made retroactive to 1977; as of 30 September 1999, the amount transferred was approximately $1.7 billion. The other deposit fund is the "Indian Tribal Funds," which are owned by the Indian tribes and are managed and held by the government in a fiduciary capacity. They were reclassified from on-budget trust funds to deposit funds on 1 October 1999. They became a part of debt held by the public instead of debt held by government accounts. The amount involved was $355 million.

THE GOVERNMENT OF THE UNITED STATES

The government of the United States, Table 15, is an organization chart beginning with the Constitution and ending with the 57 independent entities and government corporations listed in the *United States Government Manual 2000/2001* (Office of the Federal Register 2000).

CONCLUDING COMMENTS

The unified budget is meant to be a comprehensive budget that consolidates the federal funds and the trust funds and, therefore, comprises the on- and off-budget activities of the federal government. In fact, they are not identified in the Budget Summary nor do they include all programs, such as the GSEs. Perhaps the most glaring omission is the neglect in separating receipts by fund type but, at the same time, splitting outlays into "discretionary" and "mandatory." A recurring problem is finding the appropriate expression for the costs of credit programs. Eliminating cash flows beyond estimated subsidy costs of loan programs because they are nonbudgetary items does not remove the need to finance them. Similarly, arguing that interest earned on securities held by federal entities is different from interest earned on debt held by the public does not remove the need for its financing. Changing definitions for valuation of federal debt in a nonuniform pattern and changing the composition of the federal debt from external to internal debt may have larger ramifications than analysts have implied.

Table 15
The Government of the United States

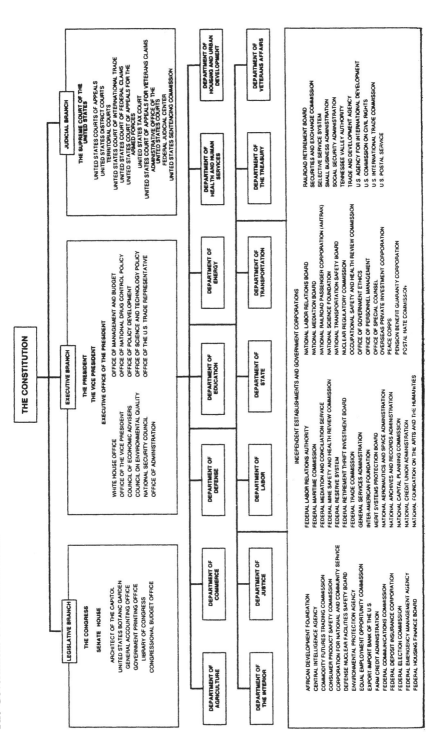

Source: Office of the Federal Register (1999: 22).

Part IV

Budget Reporting and Control

Chapter 8

Budget Authority, Capital Budgeting, and Impoundment

There are important, ongoing issues associated with the budget and the budget process, three of which are the subjects of this chapter. Budget authority, the first issue, is the quintessence of budgeting. There is no federal budget without the granting of budget authority. This chapter describes the various types and their recently evolved limitations as legislated in the Budget Enforcement Act (BEA) of 1990 and 1997. The relationship between budget authority and budget outlays is explained. The second issue, capital budgeting, has dimensions less clearly identified. Alternative definitions and principles are offered here, together with arguments for, and the rejections of capital budgeting by two presidential commissions. Impoundment, the last issue of this chapter, has diminished in significance since the passage of the Congressional Budget and Impoundment Control Act of 1974. Congress has accepted presidential proposals for deferrals recently, and the sizes of both deferrals and recissions proposed have decreased from former years.

AUTHORIZATION

Budget authority is the largest single category in the unified budget. It is the second step after authorization in the budget process. Rules of the House and the Senate of the U.S. Congress make a clear distinction between the authorization process and the appropriations process. Authorizations are the substantive policy instrument which initiates government activities, while appropriations, a major form of budget authority, are the means of financing these activities. The purpose of separating authorization from appropriation is associated with the avoidance of two possibilities: (1) the delay in supply of funds to government if there should be controversy over the legislation, and (2) the inclusion of undesirable legislation with the appropriations known to be necessary for government operation. In addition, the separation is a means of furthering integration of the expenditure process, in the sense that spending decisions would be limited to the appropriations procedure.

In the 1980s, the rules of both Houses were disregarded as a tendency to merge the authorization and appropriations process occurred. Sometimes the authorization phase was skipped entirely, and other times legislation was inserted into appropriations bills. Still other cases, such as for defense, have two distinct processes for authorization and appropriations but they duplicated consideration of many of the same issues (Meyer 1989b: 2–3, 13; Schick 1987: 12, 50).

TYPES OF BUDGET AUTHORITY AND BUDGET FUNDS

Budget authority is the authority provided by law for the federal government to incur financial obligations that will result in present or future outlays. Budget authority includes the credit subsidy cost of direct loan and loan guarantee programs. There are four types of budget authority listed in *Analytical Perspectives* (2000): appropriations, borrowing, contract, and spending from offsetting collections. Three types of budget authority were listed in the 1980s: appropriations, contract, and authority to spend debt receipts (Meyer 1989b: 124). Another type of budget authority has been in use: reappropriations. These are provisions of law that extend the availability of unobligated amounts that have already expired or may expire. Ordinarily, budget authority provided by legislation remains available until spent.

Appropriations are the most common form of budget authority and, if they are annual, can be used only during the fiscal year to which the Act applies. However, an Act may provide that budget authority for a particular purpose be available over a longer period, or indefinitely, or as specified. In other words, appropriations may be one year, multiple year, no year, current, indefinite, permanent, supplemental, or advance. If budget authority is not obligated in the year it becomes available and there are no limitations on timing, it may be carried forward as the account's unobligated balance. An obligated balance is budget authority that has been obligated but not paid. The condition will occur most frequently in the case of budget authority (mainly provided in permanent law) that permits agencies to make obligations in advance of separate appropriations of the cash for payment.

Borrowing authority is provided most of the time in permanent laws. It permits agencies to incur obligations on condition they borrow funds, usually from the Treasury's general fund, to make payments. The fourth and last type of budget authority, spending from offsetting collections, is usually provided in permanent law also. In this case, agencies are allowed to credit offsetting collections to an expenditure account; they then may make obligations and pay for them by using the offsetting collections. Offsetting collections and receipts are deducted from gross budget authority (*Analytical Perspectives* 2000: 453–454; Meyer 1989b: 125). The BEA classifies budget authority as discretionary or mandatory. Discretionary budget authority is granted in annual appropriations acts while mandatory authority is granted by authorizing legislation with certain programs provided in annual appropriations acts (*Analytical Perspectives* 2000: 454–455).

Contract authority is provided primarily in permanent laws. An agency can incur an obligation in advance of an appropriation of the money for payment as in anticipation of the collection of receipts that can be used for payment.

Offsetting collections or offsetting receipts are two methods for recording monies collected by government agencies. In one case, they are deducted from gross outlays to arrive at net outlay figures. Alternatively, they may be recorded as receipts, which are compared in total to outlays after deduction of offsetting collections and receipts, in calculating the deficit or surplus. Receipts consist mainly of individual and corporate income taxes and the social insurance taxes. Offsetting collections and receipts result from either market-oriented activities with the public or from intragovernmental transactions. The market-oriented activities range from the sale of postage stamps to admission fees to recreation areas. Budget treatment calls for subtracting these items from gross budget authority and outlays.

Intragovernmental transactions arise, for example, when the General Services Administration rents office space to another federal agency. The payment of rent is an offsetting collection and is deducted from gross budget authority and outlays. In both types of offsetting collections and receipts, fiscal budget totals measure the transactions of the government with the public. Most offsetting collections are credited to expenditure accounts; offsetting receipts, in contrast, are those credited to general fund, special fund, or trust fund receipts accounts. They do not offset budget authority and outlays at the account level but, rather, at the agency or subfunction level, except for undistributed offsetting receipts. There are three types of offsetting receipts: proprietary receipts from the public, intragovernmental transactions, and offsetting governmental receipts. The first two types contain some undistributed offsetting receipts, which are deducted from government-wide totals for budget authority and outlays. In FY 2001, they are estimated at $45.6 billion (*Analytical Perspectives* 2000: 452–453; *Budget* 2000: 291).

Offsetting receipts are part of income for the federal funds and the trust funds. These are the two major funds in the budget. The federal funds represent the larger part of the budget and its main financing component is called the "general fund." General funds are used to carry out the general purposes of government and are not restricted to a specific program. Federal funds include other components, such as the "special funds" and the "revolving funds." Trust funds, however, consist of funds that are established by law as "trust" funds. However, similar to the special funds and the revolving funds, their spending is for specific purposes and from earmarked collections. The major trust funds include OASI, the Federal Hospital Insurance Fund, and the Highway Fund. By far, the OASI fund is the most important with receipts of $447.0 billion and outlays of $337 billion, resulting in a surplus of $109.1 billion as recorded in the *United States Government Annual Report Fiscal Year 1999* (U.S. Treasury n.d.). The next largest is the Federal Hospital Insurance Fund: receipts were $153 billion, outlays were $131.5 billion, resulting in a surplus of $21.5 billion (U.S. Treasury n.d.: 15).

The Treasury report for FY 1999 contained a section on the "Revolving Fund Activity by Department." The public enterprise revolving funds are authorized in law to finance a continuing cycle of operations. The cycle includes outlays which produce receipts and the receipts then become available for outlays without any action by Congress. The major revolving funds are found in HUD and the USDA, while the balance are in independent agency accounts including the U.S. Postal Service, the TVA, and the FDIC. The largest revolving fund is the U.S. Postal Service which generated $64.1 billion in gross outlays and $63.1 billion in gross receipts for fiscal 1999 (U.S. Treasury n.d.: 17).

In testimony before the Committee on Rules, House of Representatives, Susan J. Irving, Associate Director, Accounting and Information Management Division of the GAO, gave additional information about the trust funds. There are, in most Budget Summary tables, according to Irving, only 12 major trust funds listed. Actually, in FY 1997, there were over 110 individual trust funds. These trust funds are not like private trust funds. The government trust funds are owned by the government and the government can, by enacting legislation, change the purposes of the trust fund or change the amounts of the fund's collections or payments. There is no difference between special funds and trust funds, except the use of the word "trust" in the original legislation. Both represent internal accounting methods employed to follow the collection and use of funds earmarked for specific purposes. Irving remarks that GAO located about 100 special accounts in an analysis of OMB's receipt accounts.

SPENDING LIMITS OR "CAPS"

The fact that an account is a trust fund or a special fund does not reveal whether spending is subject to any limitations or if it is controlled through the appropriations process. For the information concerning its designation as mandatory or discretionary, it is necessary to go back to the original legislation because the status of the account depends on the nature of the activity funded. Social Security and Medicare are direct spending or mandatory programs with permanent appropriations. Most trust and special fund spending comes from permanent appropriations which constitute almost 95 percent, and over 80 percent, respectively, of their total spending. Except for Social Security, which is subject to special rules, these programs must submit to PAYGO rules.

In opposition, discretionary spending is limited to caps whether it originates from the federal funds or the trust funds. Recently, a new way around the rules has appeared with the creation of guaranteed funding levels in transportation accounts as part of the discretionary spending limits. Effectively, it would cause these funds to have what amounts to a permanent appropriation similar to most trust funds (Irving 1999: 7–8). Permanent appropriations are the budget authority type for those programs known as entitlements. According to Joseph White, author of the chapter called "Budgeting for Entitlements," (White 1999) the deficits of the 1980s and 1990s have been blamed on entitlement programs. The Bipartisan Commission on Entitlements and Tax Reform, in 1995, expressed the opinion that they might cause huge deficits in the future. Others have warned of coming catastrophes if entitlement program growth is not curtailed.

The term "entitlement" appears to have become a budgeting term as a result of its use by Justice William Brennan of the Supreme Court in 1969. In his written statement about benefits in the Aid to Families with Dependent Children (AFDC) program, he argued that they were a legal entitlement for individuals eligible to receive them. In 1993, the GAO, in its *A Glossary of Terms Used in the Budget Process*, defined entitlement authority as permitting payments including loans and grants to be made to any individual or government if the law provides that the U.S. government is obligated to make the payments because they meet the legal requirements. The foregoing applies if budget authority has not been provided in advance by appropriations acts to the individual or government (GAO 1993a: 44).

Over the years, entitlement programs have been known by other names, such as uncontrollable spending, mandatory spending, and direct spending. In current use are "mandatory" and "direct" spending, which are referred to in most recent budget legislation, including the BEA 1990 and its amendment. One nagging problem of entitlements is that they are rather awkwardly situated in the annual budget process. Entitlement programs should not be changed each year for both political and technical reasons. In the effort to make them part of the annual budget process, they have prevented the passage of reconciliation measures. In addition, the use of multiyear budgeting for entitlements has not benefited the discretionary side of budgeting. It has led, according to White, to the adoption of long-term caps on appropriations. Policy changes do not have to be specified to enforce these caps, so that forecasting savings in this way is simpler than legislating entitlement changes. Since 1995, reduction in discretionary spending targets has been the way to achieve budgeting goals (GAO White 1999: 679–680, 695–696).

In FY 1999, the CBO estimated that discretionary spending would represent one-third of total outlays. With the present statutory caps, these outlays were expected to remain practically unchanged between FY 1999 and 2002. However, the caps, and therefore the constraints on the budget, have changed since the BEA first created them in 1990. The original caps for defense, domestic, and international discretionary spending lasted from FY 1991 through 1993. In FY 1994 and 1995, a single discretionary cap was used for each year. For FY 1995 onward, caps were extended and new categories created. The BEA 1997 rewrote the cap structure for FY 1996 through 2002 with different categorical arrangements in each of the years. Besides, the Transportation Equity Act for the 21st Century (TEA-21) established two more outlay caps for highway and mass transit programs for 1999 through 2003, and specified annual guaranteed minimum spending levels for certain programs. The limits on overall discretionary spending are very tight; separate caps within discretionary programs limits trade-offs among them, and guaranteed minimum funding levels limits the range of trade-offs even further, remarks Irving. In addition, the guarantee ensures that activity from competition with others for resources is cut off, turning it into a permanent appropriation within the discretionary spending side of the budget. In FY 1998, there were permanent appropriations amounting to about 66 percent of total spending. The types of funds containing permanent appropriations can appear in any of the federal funds, which include the "general fund," "special funds," and the "public enterprise funds." It is the other type of fund, the trust fund, which uses the most permanent appropriations (Irving 1999: 2–7).

BUDGET AUTHORITY; BUDGET OUTLAYS

New budget authority for more than half of all outlays comes from permanent appropriations. The balance is provided annually through 13 appropriations acts. Permanent appropriations are the type of budget authority available to most trust funds, interest on the public debt, and spending from offsetting collections credited to appropriations or fund accounts.

For FY 2001, for example, new authority recommended to be spent in that year is approximately $1.5 trillion. However, outlays are estimated to be $1.8 trillion, so that the difference of 0.3 trillion comes from unspent authority of prior years. Total new budget authority recommended for FY 2001 is actually almost $1.9 trillion, or about 0.4 trillion above the amount to be spent in FY 2001. The additional 0.4 trillion is budget authority to be spent in future years. Finally, there is unspent authority enacted in prior years amounting to $950 billion, or almost 1.0 trillion, of which $338 billion will be spent in 2001 and $600 billion in future years (*Analytical Perspectives* 2000: 373–374). All of these interrelationships between budget authority and budget outlays in the past, the present, and the future, make the budget document complex and difficult to interpret.

With more and more accounts in the budget funded through permanent appropriations or permanent-like appropriations, such as guaranteed funding, the process of budgeting is no longer a process of adjustment of inner details against outer totals. Instead, budgeting loses its ability to seek efficient means to satisfy government objectives. In its place, budget targets are set with no boundaries on the cost or resource side to constrain overly ambitious budget goals. The conflict involves more than numbers. It is over the incompatibility of trying to set long- and short-range goals utilizing one set of rules within an annual budget setting.

In 1989, at a conference of the Eastern Economic Association in Baltimore, the author presented the paper "From Budget Authority to Deficit: The Federal Budget Maze," which indicated the need for a reorganization of the budget process in a time sense. If the annual budget decision-making procedure could focus on spending for the coming fiscal year alone, the short range, attention would be directed to program totals and budget totals for that year. Then, if programs furnished under permanent appropriations along with budget totals for future years were considered in a separate process in which long-range objectives were the main agenda, more emphasis on program priorities would be possible. The dual process would allow for more than one range of estimates in long-term, macroeconomic forecasts while permitting the annual budget to retain the mutual adjustment necessary for allocative efficiency (Meyer 1989b: 17–18; GAO/White 1999: 695–696).

CAPITAL BUDGETING; DEFINITIONS; PRINCIPLES

Since the 1950s the budget documents have reported on federal investment outlays, meaning outlays that yield long-term benefits independently of current outlays. These investment outlays include physical investment, research, education, development, training, as well as grants to state and local governments for highways, education, and other investments labeled "direct federal programs." The investment outlays in this category are owned by the federal government and consist of defense items and certain office buildings for general purposes. Grants received by individuals or private organizations, and higher education loans to person or capital grants to Amtrak are listed among these federal programs.

Part I, "Description of Federal Investment" in *Analytical Perspectives* (2000), suggests a variety of definitions of investment other than the one currently employed that could be used for other purposes. They are:

1. Investment means government-owned physical assets only.
2. Investment means improving economic growth and national productivity and, therefore, national defense assets and the like are excluded.
3. Investment means increasing the efficiency of federal operations and so would consist of items such as computer systems.
4. Investment means "social investment" also, so that in addition to the current budget definition, programs of maternal health and substance abuse treatment would be covered.

It is stated that the definition of investment in use by the federal government is consistent with that portrayed in budget documents since 1940. There are two technical problems of classification involving grants to state and local governments and the avoidance of double counting of investment outlays, which are explained. In Part I, also, a fuller description of investment outlays and other matters are presented.

In the Appendix to Part II, which deals with "Planning, Budgeting, and Acquisition of Capital Assets," the administration describes the principles for acquisition of capital assets that it is planning to use. These principles incorporated four considerations: planning, benefits and costs, risk management, and financing aspects. The first three considerations are explained in detail, demonstrating typical economic efficiency criteria. Under benefits and costs, for example, would be the statement that capital assets proposed for funding should project a future return greater than or equal to an alternative employment of accessible public resources. The last consideration, financial aspects, calls for "useful segments" to be funded with advance or regular appropriations. Procurement of the asset is to be financed separately from the planning segments, generally speaking. Finally, capital acquisition accounts containing all assets of the agency should be set up, along with other procedures to handle lumpiness or problems of indivisibility within capital investment projects (*Analytical Perspectives* 2000: 145–165).

In Part IV, "Alternative Capital Budget and Capital Expenditure Presentations," there is the statement that other industrial nations have a more systematic analysis of investment and operating expenditures in their budget than the United States. Of the European countries, Greece, Ireland, Luxembourg, and Portugal have distinct separation between current and capital budgeting. However, a 1993 survey by the CBO found only two industrial nations, Chile and New Zealand, that incorporate depreciation of capital assets into their budgets, although the United Kingdom plans to budget on an accrual basis and include depreciation beginning with its budget for 2001–2002.

The World Bank, in its *Public Expenditure Management Handbook* (1998), blames dual budgeting for being based on the mistaken premise that government capital expenditures are more productive than current expenditures. The separation of capital and operating budgets leads to the capital budget being the more desired place for agencies to plan their expenditures. When that happens, expenditure proposals are no longer associated with policy priorities. The GAO has used similar reasoning for rejecting budgeting for capital with depreciation. In studies done in 1993 and 1995, the GAO stated that depreciation would mean loss of budgetary control because only a fraction of the total cost of an investment is appropriated when annual depreciation is applied (*Analytical Perspectives* 2000: 171–177).

Five general principles that are considered important to the capital decision-making process are outlined in the statement of Paul L. Posner, Director of Budget Issues in the Accounting and Information Management Division of the GAO, before the President's Commission in March 1998:

1. Capital decision making should have organizational goals integrated into the process.
2. An investment approach should be employed to choose and evaluate assets.
3. The funding of capital projects requires attention to both managerial flexibility and budget control.
4. Optimizing project success needs development of appropriate management techniques.
5. Outcomes should be assessed and relevant results and information should be inserted into future decision-making processes (Posner 1998: 12–13).

ARGUMENTS FOR CAPITAL BUDGETING

In the 1990s, the discussion of capital budgeting and changes in the budget procedures to accommodate it were the subject of a Hearing before the Legislative and National Security Subcommittee of the Committee on Government Operations, House of Representatives, on 23 July 1992, on the topic *Investing in America: Proposed Changes in the Federal Budget Process* (1993). Capital spending discussion was addressed to infrastructure, namely, spending on buildings improving roads, bridges, sewers, and other physical capital. It was said that these are the types of spending that create jobs and promote economic growth. All of the participants in the second session of the 102nd Congress on this date, and they included congressional representatives from Arkansas, Michigan, New York, Utah, and West Virginia, confined their statements or writings primarily to three topics: infrastructure, the fact that the government budget obscures the importance of capital spending, and that concentration on deficit reduction had added to the problem. Two of the participants referred to the importance of human capital and the need for its inclusion in a capital budget. In fact, the congressional representative from Utah remarked that investment in human capital is most significant, as was demonstrated by the GI bill. We are in a different world now, he claimed, where the key issue is to prevail in world competition and that we can only do with the aid of information and information services. Nothing is as important as educating young people, in his viewpoint, and we are not doing it as well as others are. Capital investment must include education, research, and development (*Investing in America* 1993: 14–15).

Another Hearing on capital budgeting took place in the House of Representatives, three years later, 2 March 1995. The last page of the printed Hearing on *Capital Budgeting* (1995) before the Subcommittee on Government Management, Information, and Technology of the Committee on Government Reform and Oversight contained the "Prepared statement of the National Society of Professional Engineers" (NSPE). It said that the society is deeply troubled by the present methods of planning and financing the U.S. infrastructure. Funds for new construction and maintenance of existing assets are limited and the process of obtaining the funds complicated and disorganized. The society recommended the adoption of a capital budget that would include aggregate capital investments required, estimates of operations and maintenance needed, priority rankings and sources of financing, relation of annual capital expenditures to the nation's long-range goals, and a five-year investment plan.

NSPE represents 70,000 engineers in the United States and abroad, was founded in 1934, and represents all technical disciplines and areas of engineering practice, including construction, education, and government. The society considered the adoption of a capital budget as a high priority item that would ensure the proper use of trust fund accounts, aid government in establishing infrastructure priorities, and inspire public confidence in budgeting and budgeting procedures (*Capital Budgeting* 1995: 128).

At the meeting of the Subcommittee on Government Management, Information and Technology on 2 March 1995, the chairman of the full committee, the Committee on Government Reform and Oversight, William B. Clinger, Jr., of Pennsylvania, addressed the members, staff, and clerk of the subcommittee, 12 in all, on the subject of capital budgeting. Clinger explained why he has supported the introduction of a capital budget at the federal level for a long time. Among the features he mentioned is the possibility of improved investment decision making for the nation's crumbling physical assets, assigning the burden of payment for the assets to those who will reap the benefits through the use of debt to finance them, and removing bias in the treatment of capital programs by eliminating "front end loading of capital costs."

Bud Shuster, a congressional representative from Pennsylvania, takes a different view in his written statement in support of capital budgeting. He finds the current budget process has failed to recognize "the economic value of infrastructure investments and their unique funding mechanisms." Shuster argues that shifting spending toward infrastructure investments would have lowered the deficit and that economic studies have shown that infrastructure spending increases private sector productivity and the ability of the economy to furnish new jobs. In addition, it fosters export-based growth in an increasingly competitive world framework, transportation, and core infrastructure such as airports, water and sewer systems, bridges and roads, which are critical to economic health. Compared to all the G-7 countries, the United States had the lowest public infrastructure investments from 1978 to 1990.

Shuster claims that, in the case of the Highway Trust fund, the Aviation Trust fund, the Inland Waterways Trust fund and the Harbour Maintenance Trust fund, the government has permitted large cash balances to accumulate. These balances have been built up, says Shuster, to hold down spending out of those funds and thereby conceal the size of the operating deficit. Actually, the PAYGO programs are artificially reduced to enable spending in the "general fund" programs, the basic reason for the deficit. He finds that the fiduciary responsibility of government for the trust funds has been violated. To counteract the budgetary treatment of these funds, Shuster and the leadership of the Transportation and Infrastructure Committee introduced a bill to make the transportation trust funds off-budget and other measures to correct this offense against the American taxpayer.

Norman Y. Mineta, congressional representative from California, said it differently. Budgetary affairs of the federal government need the organization that state governments and private business employ. When the government borrows for current expenses now, it is requiring future taxpayers to pay for government's expenses today. With a capital budget, policy makers would need to decide whether the investment is worth borrowing to finance. Infrastructure translates into productivity and competitiveness. The separation of operating and capital budgeting would indicate to the public that the first should be paid for today, and that the second might be more equitably financed by borrowing so future taxpayers could share the burden.

In his written statement, Robert E. Wise, Jr., congressional representative from West Virginia, made similar comments. He expressed dismay "that the federal government's unified budget makes no distinction between money spent on investments and money spent for consumption." Government programs, such as health benefits, foreign aid, federal salaries, and highways, are paid for by borrowing and taxes and are recorded in the same way. But, borrowing for current expenses is not justifiable while that for infrastructure is. In the long run, infrastructure raises the wealth of the nation and its capability for economic growth (*Capital Budgeting* 1995: 1–18).

REJECTION OF CAPITAL BUDGETING AND ALTERNATIVE RECOMMENDATIONS

Executive Order No. 13037 of 3 March 1997, establishes the Commission to Study Capital Budgeting, which is to be bipartisan and composed of 20 members appointed by the president. The president selects two co-chairs from among the members. The president requires the Commission to report back on four items:

1. Capital budget practices of foreign governments, state governments, local governments, and private sectors in the United States.
2. Appropriate definitions of capital of all types, including the distinction between physical and human capital.
3. The role and measurement of depreciation in a capital budget and a federal capital budget.
4. Implications of a federal capital budget for macroeconomic stability and for choices between capital and other means of obtaining public objectives (USC Supplement III 3 March 1997: 1215).

In a letter to the president on 1 February 1999, reproduced in the *Report of the President's Commission to Study Capital Budgeting* (1999), the co-chairs of the Commission, Kathleen Brown and Jon S. Corzine, state that their research has shown that the present budget process does not allow government decision makers to adequately view the long-run consequences of their decisions. Misallocation among capital expenditures and improper maintenance of existing assets is the result. The letter states:

In this report, we propose a series of recommendations that we believe would improve each of the component parts of the budget process: *setting priorities* currently and for the long run, *making budget decision* in the current year, *reporting on those decisions*, and subsequently *evaluating them* in order to make improvements in future years. We do not propose, however, the current adoption of a formal capital budget, as defined and discussed in the report. (*Report of the President's Commission* 1999: iii)

The Commission report recommends 11 ways in which the setting of priorities among all programs could be facilitated:

1. Five-year strategic plans instead of the three-year ones required now for federal agencies under the Government Performance and Results Act. These plans should be integrated with the overall performance plans, should have standardized formats, and should be evaluated for the purpose of government-wide planning. Both strategic and annual budgets should be related to the life cycles of their capital assets.
2. All major government programs should be subjected to benefit-cost analysis.

The Commission recommends the following to improve annual budget decision making.

3. All capital projects should be fully funded before the work begins.

4. Experimentation for specified agencies with separate appropriations for capital acquisition funds (CAFs). Once federally owned capital assets are acquired, the CAFs would rent their facilities to various agency programs and charge them for the service. In this way, the cost of using capital assets in all programs of the agency is assessed.

5. The scoring rules for leasing which enable a better decision between leasing and constructing or purchasing a facility should be observed.

6. Capital-related trust funds, such as highways, need disclosure of information about the use of earmarked taxes or fees. They are presently insulated from the competition for resources occurring in the rest of the budget and, therefore, the possibility of bias toward investment in the public sector may be present.

7. Incentives are needed to motivate agencies to manage assets efficiently. The Commission made recommendations concerning improvements in the way the budget decisions are presented to the public and policy makers:

8. The annual budget year and the following four years should show spending plans for the categories: investment, operating expenditures, transfers to individuals, and interest.

9. Financial statements and reporting about the composition and condition of federally owned or managed assets should be summarized in the annual budget.

10. Standardized methods for estimating deferred maintenance and the condition of existing assets need to be further developed.

The Commission recommended as its final contribution to an improved budget process:

11. Better evaluation of past budgetary decisions through the use of a federal report card. Information on the rates of return of major investment projects might be included and, in addition, presented in the annual budget. The Commission sees the executive branch as the one to put these recommendations to work but, at the same time, active congressional cooperation would be necessary to make it work (*Report of the President's Commission* 1999: 3–8).

In examining the methods of capital budgeting, the Commission studied several versions of a capital budget. In one version, the balance of the total budget is dependent, in whole or in part, on capital expenditures. A second version is one in which capital expenditures are financed, in whole or in part, by borrowing. A single decision is made about the amount to be spent on capital and that determines the amount to be borrowed. The second definition of a capital budget is analyzed as being the equivalent of a separate "cap" on capital expenditures or, alternatively, a method in which capital depreciation becomes an integral part of the budget process and includes a move toward accrual-based accounting procedures. Other versions of a capital budget are briefly mentioned and consist of separate operating and capital budgets, or a specific constraint upon the growth of debt similar to that recently adopted in the United Kingdom.

The report concedes that it is not possible to objectively evaluate the present budget process as to whether it favors capital spending or not. But, the Commission states firmly that the process has flaws and it believes the recommendations offered are the appropriate ways to correct them. The Commission could not settle for one definition of capital or investment. They argued that different purposes by government and firms inspired different definitions for each term. The first definition offered is that capital should be looked at according to function. This definition, in order to be satisfied, would have to have benefits extend beyond the fiscal year, and then spending as it occurs would be considered as investment and the asset created by the spending would be considered as capital.

Under the above definition, spending includes physical and human capital along with intangible assets such as research, development, and copyrights. Statements made that the expenditures should include improving social welfare or raising long-term growth rates are too theoretical, claims the report. For practical purposes, more specific definitions are required, such as those spelled out by the Generally Accepted Accounting Principles (GAAP), even though they have possible shortcomings.

Another definition offered in the debate over what is investment or capital refers to who owns it, the private or the public sector. In the case of the public sector, government spending benefits the public. If it benefits a large group of consumers, it is a public good because as the commission explains, "no private person or firm can capture all of their benefits" and, for evaluation reasons, measurement is in both monetary and nonmonetary terms. The commission distinguishes this expenditure from that in the private sector by indicating that returns go to individuals or firms and are measured primarily in monetary terms.

A third definition makes the distinction between capital owned by the federal government and national capital. The latter is a more inclusive phrase extending to all government spending with long-term benefits whether or not owned by the federal government. The GAO, in its 1993 *Budget Issues: Incorporating an Investment Component in the Budget*, identified a variation of national capital meant to consist of public investments that look forward to improving the public sector's long-run productivity. Education, housing, and infrastructure would be included but government-owned buildings, land, and weapon systems would not.

A fourth definition distinguishes between direct government spending to produce capital and private and public spending encouraged by government policies. The Commission deliberated on the subject of depreciation for many forms of capital spending whose value is reduced over time through use. According to a GAO report in 1995, no government budget presently accounts for depreciation of infrastructure (*Report of the President's Com-*

mission 1999: 9–12, 43). None of the studies mentioned dealt with the topic of how to measure the appreciation of human capital and physical capital. Neither the private nor the public sectors have developed consistent methods to demonstrate in accounting statements, that, for example, education and training may cause the value of human capital to increase just as technological improvements added to existing capital may accomplish a similar result for physical capital.

IMPOUNDMENT

The Congressional Budget and Impoundment Control Act of 1974 altered provisions of the Antideficiency Act of 1906 (Statutes at Large 34, pt. 1), which gave the president the right to withhold funds from spending. In the 1974 Act, withholding or impoundment of funds were classified as deferrals or rescissions. The deferral type, if not objected to by any congressional resolution, may stand until the end of the fiscal year. But, the funds must be made available for spending purposes within the fiscal year to which they apply. There were $4.8 billion in deferrals proposed by the president in 1998 and $1.7 billion proposed by him in 1999. Congress accepted all the deferrals in both years. Initially, defferals could be for any reason but, currently, they can be for contingencies or to achieve savings through greater efficiency or because of changes in requirements. Deferrals cannot be made for policy reasons. Rescissions are a complete cancellation of the original intent of Congress to spend. Therefore, the cancellation must be approved by the Congress within 45 days of continuous session, or the funds must be released for spending purposes. Congressionally approved rescissions in the 1970s and 1980s were larger than they have been recently. The GAO furnished figures on proposed and enacted rescissions for the years 1974 to 1993 that are cited in Allen Schick's *The Federal Budget* (1994a: 176). Amounts rescinded with congressional approval ranged from almost $11 billion in 1981 to a low of $2 million in 1989. There were years of no rescissions but two of these were years that no rescissions were proposed by the president, 1988 and 1993, while the others were proposals of $1 billion or less in 1974, 1983, and 1990. In 1998, there were proposed rescissions of $25 million and Congress agreed to rescissions of $17 million. In 1999, proposed rescissions were $35 million and Congress agreed to rescissions of $17 million as in the prior year. Since the enactment of the Impoundment Control Act, Congress has rescinded almost one-third of the total amount that presidents have proposed for rescissions. The Government-Wide Rescission Consolidated Appropriations Act, 2000, which is reported by individual account in *Analytical Perspectives* (2000), totals approximately $2.4 billion. The largest rescission appears in the Department of Defense for $1.05 billion. The Act contained certain specifications about the limitations placed on the rescissions, two of which are that no activity, program, or project of any entity of the federal government can be reduced by more than 15 percent, and no reduction is to be made in the military personnel accounts. The other two limitations concern how to apportion the rescissions that apply to the Defense accounts and the need for reports from the OMB about the allocation of all rescissions by accounts (*Analytical Perspectives* 1999: 398; *Analytical Perspectives* 2000: 381–397, 450; Meyer 1989b: 131–132).

CONCLUDING COMMENTS

Budget authority no longer has a position in the Budget Summary, to which it is entitled as the source of budget outlays. The various types of budget authority should be listed so that the categories of permanent appropriations and authority to spend offsetting collections are clearly visible. When budgets were smaller, netting practices may have appeared to be minor considerations, but with greater focus on the trust funds and market-oriented activities of government, there is more reason to clarify their roles. Capital budgeting's time has come. It is no longer possible to claim that ignorance or faulty estimates for depreciation, for instance, prevent its use. A great deal has been learned from unsuccessful experiences with the credit budget. Impoundment procedures have served their initial purpose. Perhaps it is appropriate to lessen the paperwork involved.

Chapter 9

Current Services Budget, Tax Expenditures Budget, and Off-Budget Federal Entities and Activities

The special budget issues contained in this chapter consist, primarily, of two particularly active ones. The chapter begins with consideration of the Current Services budget, which is vital to the formulation of budget estimates. The next issue is Tax Expenditures, which make a substantial contribution to the achievement of national goals but, to what extent is difficult to measure. The discussion of Off-Budget Federal Entities and Activities includes Credit, Deposit Funds, and Regulation. This chapter's main concentration is focused on the Off-Budget entities known as the Social Security Trust fund and the Government Sponsored Enterprises (GSEs). Both of these federal entities are being studied by government agencies and reforms have been recommended, mainly addressed to present and/or future financial rearrangements.

CURRENT SERVICES

The current services concept was a development of a provision in the Congressional Budget and Impoundment Control Act of 1974. There has been controversy in the years following the Act concerning the uniformity of the application of the concepts, the underlying policies used to construct the baseline, as it is called, and competition from alternative baselines projected by the CBO and the G-R-H estimates. The current services baseline has the purpose of establishing the sums of budget authority, outlays, receipts, and deficits or surpluses that would occur without any changes in existing laws. Three of its major uses are: (1) as a starting point for formulating the annual budget, (2) as a way to compare the relative magnitude of proposed changes, and (3) as a device to discover possible problems for government fiscal policy. In addition, under the BEA, it serves as the basis for the determination of sequestered amounts for the mandatory accounts and the level of funding remaining after sequestration. The standard definition of the current services baseline applies to direct spending and receipts, or those items controlled by authorizing legislation, such as the major entitlement programs. A different estimating rule is used for discretionary spending, or that spending provided during the annual appropriations process. For discretionary spending, the current services baseline is equal to the enacted 2000 appropriations for 2000. After that, for 2001 to 2005, the 2000 level is adjusted for inflation.

The economic assumptions underlying the current services estimates are extensive and involve the specific situations of each program, all of which are not reported. In general, the starting point is the economic assumptions of the executive budget, assuming the executive's budget is adopted. These assumptions are discussed in the first chapter of *Analytical Perspectives* (2000). In chapter 14, "Current services Estimates," additional tables provide a table summary of the assumptions found in chapter 1, including estimates for FY 1999 through 2005 of GDP in current and real chained terms of 1996 dollars, along with estimates for inflation, unemployment, and interest rates for the same period. Other tables and text offer: projection of beneficiaries in the major benefit programs, impacts of regulations and expiring authorizations, and other assumptions. Tables are furnished of the current services receipts by source, of current services outlays by agency and function, and budget authority by agency, function, category, and program. There is no additonal description of the methods of computation for these estimates. In the late 1980s, there was considerable discussion about them by the OMB, the CBO, and the GAO (*Analytical Perspectives* 2000: 3–15, 297–340, 460; Meyer 1989a: 134–135).

TAX EXPENDITURES

Tax expenditures are revenue losses due to special provisions of the tax law which provide credits, deductions, deferrals, exclusions, exemptions, or special tax rates. Instead of tax expenditures, other policies could be established for reaching federal goals, such as spending or regulatory programs. The purposes of tax expenditures include encouragement of certain activities, improvement in equity aspects, and to lower any distortions the tax system might introduce.

According to Bruce F. Davie, a financial economist in the Treasury Department's Office of Tax Analysis, the first U.S. tax expenditure was used to encourage the production of wool and, therefore, sheep were excluded from the base of the property tax. The term "tax expenditure" was made popular in the late 1960s by Stanley Surrey, the Assistant Secretary for Tax Policy, in the Treasury Department. In the 1970s, the administration agreed to have the Treasury staff work with the Joint Committee on Taxation staff to produce ongoing estimates of tax expenditures. Further pressure from Congress resulted in the passage of the Congressional Budget and Impoundment Control Act of 1974, which contained the mandate for a tax expenditure list and related information to be part of the executive budget presentation.

There are two sources of annual estimates for tax expenditures: one by the Treasury Department published as part of the budget, and the other produced by the Joint Committee on Taxation. They both forecast tax expenditures for five years ahead, but they differ with respect to the economic forecasts that are used. The congressional committee employs a macroeconomic forecast developed by the CBO, while the Treasury prefers the administration's projection of future outlays and receipts.

For computing tax expenditures, three methods are used: revenue loss, present value, and outlay equivalent. In order to determine whether a tax expenditure is a preferential exception to some "normal" tax structure and to determine the size of the tax expenditure, a basic tax structure must be selected. Two baseline concepts are used: the normal tax baseline and the reference tax law baseline. The normal tax baseline is used by the Joint Committee on Taxation and is based on a comprehensive income tax. Income, under this method, is the sum of consumption and the change in net wealth over a given time period, the Haig-Simons definition. The reference tax law baseline has been used by the administration since 1983; it calls for a comprehensive income tax base also, but is somewhat nearer to existing law. Most of the time, the two baseline methods arrive at similar conclusions.

Under the revenue loss method of determining the value of a given tax expenditure, the estimates attempt to measure the increase in federal revenues that would result from repealing the special provisions. In practice, there are several reasons why the measure is not accurate. Two reasons are: incentives may change economic behavior of individuals without the tax expenditure, and tax expenditures are interdependent. The largest revenue losses in the income tax are (1) net exclusion of pension contributions and earnings, which include employer plans, estimated at over $92 billion; and (2) the exclusion of employer contributions for medical insurance premiums and medical care, estimated at over $80 billion for 2001 (*Analytical Perspectives* 2000: 117).

The present value approach is used in cases where tax expenditures involve long-term effects, such as deferrals of tax payments into the future. In the table of the "Present Value of Selected Tax Expenditures for Activity in Calendar Year 1999" on page 119 of *Analytical Perspectives* (2000), the largest item is "Exclusion of pension contributions-employer plans," at over $95 billion. The second largest item is "accelerated depreciation of machinery and equipment," at over $32 billion.

The third method, outlay equivalent, is the amount of outlay necessary to give the taxpayer the same after-tax income as would be obtained through the tax preference. The administration uses this approach to compare a direct federal outlay with the "price" of a tax expenditure. This type of tax expenditure appears in the budget within each functional category to which it applies, and there is a separate listing of outlay equivalent tax expenditures in the summary tables, as required by the 1974 Act.

With the passage of the Government Performance and Results Act of 1993, tax expenditures were realized to be a contributing factor to the achievement of agencies' performance objectives. Pilot studies were attempted but statistics were not available for the thorough analyses necessary. The Treasury, the OMB, and the other agencies are working to improve the quantity and quality of data on individual economic behavior and the tax laws over time to enable better measurement of the contributions of tax expenditures to national goals (*Analytical Perspectives* 2000: 107–125; Davie 1999: 277–306; Meyer 1989a: 133, 135–137).

OFF-BUDGET FEDERAL ENTITIES AND ACTIVITIES

The unified budget concept has been applied since the FY 1969 budget. It had been recommended by the President's Commission on Budget Concepts in 1967, and required all government programs and transactions of the federal sector with the public to be part of the budget. Since 1971, this requirement has not been observed because of legislation providing for the exclusion of one or more entities. The off-budget federal entities currently consist of the Social Security Trust funds: OASI and DI, and the U.S. Postal Service fund. In the late 1980s, at least nine federal entities were off-budget, including the Export-Import Bank, the U.S. Postal Service fund, and the FFB.

The nonbudgetary activities of the federal government include transactions of credit programs other than costs. Costs of credit programs which refer to direct loans or guarantees of a private loan made by the federal government are included in the budget. However, their cash transactions are recorded in financing accounts and the transactions of these financing accounts, other than the costs that are part of the credit program are excluded from the budget. Nevertheless, the financing accounts change the requirements for borrowing or debt repayment.

Some of the other off-budget entities and activities mentioned in *Analytical Perspectives* (2000) are the Deposit Funds, Tax Expenditures, and Regulation. The Deposit Funds, such as the Thrift Savings fund, the largest deposit fund, is a defined contribution retirement plan. The assets of the plan belong to employees and are held by the government in a fiduciary capacity, so they are excluded from the budget reporting. The administrative costs and any transactions with budgetary accounts are included in the budget.

Tax expenditures or revenue losses that arise from special exclusions, exemptions, or deductions and other provisions that are observed by comparing the tax law with a baseline are excluded. However, they are separately listed in the *Analytical Perspectives* volume of the budget document annually, as well as identified by function together with expenditures in the budget and, again, at the end of the detailed functional tables presentation of the budget. Another off-budget activity of the federal government is regulation. It has effects similar to budget outlays but it is not recorded as such. The effects occur when government requires the private sector to make outlays for items such as pollution control. Although there are no recorded costs for regulation in the budget, the OMB published a report in 1997 on the costs and benefits of federal regulation. There is an annual document entitled *The Regulatory Plan and the Unified Agenda of Federal Regulatory and Deregulatory Actions*. The latest edition of this work appeared in October 1999; it was printed in the *Federal Register* on 22 November 1999 (*Analytical Perspectives* 2000: 375–377).

The most important off-budget entities are the Social Security Trust funds and the privately owned GSFs. The remaining pages of the chapter are devoted to some major issues of each of these operations.

OFF-BUDGET ISSUES OF SOCIAL SECURITY

The Social Security Act was signed in August of 1935. The act created the program known as Old Age and Survivors Insurance (OASI) and a federal/state system of unemployment insurance. In addition, the law established federal matching grants-in-aid to states to aid them in assisting the elderly poor, children, and the blind. Monthly payments of benefits began in 1940. In 1956, major changes were made entailing the introduction of Disability Insurance (DI). In 1965, Medicare and Medicaid were added. In the 1970s, the Black Lung program for miners and their survivors was adopted, the Social Security Administration (SSA) came into being, and cost-of-living increases were implemented. Taxing of up to one-half of benefits for wealthier individuals was specified in amendments passed in 1983.

Retirement, disability, and Medicare benefits are paid from equal contributions paid by employer and employee to the Social Security program. Since 1990, 7.65 percent of the employee's paycheck is deducted for the program, and an equal amount is matched by the employer. The self-employed must pay both shares, for a total of 15.3 percent. On 1 January 2001, the taxable earnings base for the payroll tax increased from $76,200 to $80,100, and there are scheduled increases up to $93,900 on 1 January 2005. Medicare taxes ignore the earnings base limit and continue at a rate of 1.45 percent each for employer and employee, and 2.9 percent for the self-employed for all earnings above that amount (*Analytical Perspectives* 2000: 47; Wright 1999: 169–170).

According to Mary Jo Bane, Commissioner of the New York State Department of Social Services at the time she wrote "Overview: Social Policy,"
there are two periods in our history when social policy was of paramount
importance. The first was in the 1930s, when the Social Security Act was
passed, and the second was in the 1960s when the mission of social investment was proclaimed. The legislation of both social insurance and social investment programs entailed the creation of new procedures and new
agencies and managers or administrative leadership. The list of programs
has expanded over the years to consist of OASI and DI, often combined
into OASDI, Medicare including Hospital Insurance (Part A) and Medical
Insurance (Part B), Supplemental Security Income (SSI), Black Lung program, Medicaid, Food Stamps, Aid to Families with Dependent Children
(AFDC), special nutrition programs, housing subsidies, housing for the
homeless, Head Start, poverty income guidelines, unemployment compensation, workers' compensation, permanent partial disability compensation,
veterans' benefits, medical programs, housing and loan programs, and other
veterans' programs.

Overall federal social policy is conducted by HHS, HUD, and Department of Labor. There are state and local agencies, not-for-profit and private
contractors who work with the federal departments. The primary role of
the federal government is to provide leadership for the many programs and
to offer financial support and federal regulations for their provision (Bane
1992: 375–376; Wright 1999: 169–177).

To furnish some indication of the magnitude of social insurance programs, the SSA released a booklet entitled *Fast Facts and Figures about
Social Security* in 1998. The booklet states that 48 million people received
OASDI and/or SSI payments in December 1997, that Social Security was
the largest single source of income for older individuals representing 40
percent of total income in 1996, and that OASDI and/or SSI prevented 1.4
million children from living in poverty in 1996 (Social Security Administration 1998: 6, 30, 35).

Recently, as a result of forecasts that predict projected revenues of Social
Security funds will fall short of expenditures within the next two decades,
there has been a surge of reform proposals. On 25 March 1999, David M.
Walker, Comptroller General of the United States, set forth criteria for
choosing among the wide array of proposals seeking to improve the financial outlook for Social Security. In testimony given before the Subcommittee
on Social Security, Committee on Ways and Means, House of Representatives, Walker recommends three policy criteria that policy makers should
utilize in making their choice.

1. The degree to which lasting financial soundness would be achieved and the effect
   of the proposal on the U.S. budget and the economy.

2. The priority ranking chosen between the income adequacy objective with respect to level and certainty of payments, and the personal equity objective with respect to rates of return on contributions.

3. The speed with which changes can be put into action, supervised, and made understandable to the public.

The major focus of most proposals is on the first criterion. These proposals suggest some combination of higher receipts and/or lower payments to gain financial soundness.

The Comptroller General views Social Security and its components (Social Security, personal savings, and both private and public employer-sponsored pensions) as the basis of the retirement income in the United States. Social Security is the foundation on which the other components build. A major reason for the decline in poverty rates for the elderly has been the existence of Social Security. However, only 20 percent of Social Security beneficiaries rely on it as their only source of retirement income. It is the future of Social Security that is in jeopardy, according to Walker, not its present financial position. The long-range forecast of the 1998 Trustees' Report says that by 2032, if nothing is changed, the trust funds would be entirely depleted (see Table 1). In that year, annual tax income to both funds is forecast to cover 71 percent of program costs. The major factor accounting for this forecast, states Walker, is the projection of demographic trends. The proportion of the population on the receiving end continues to rise compared to the proportion on the contributing end. In other words, the retiree/worker ratio is rising, especially because of the life expectancy factor (Walker 1999: 1–9).

The Board of Trustees of the OASI Trust funds, who are responsible for the *1999 Annual Report* of these two programs, was established under the Social Security Act to supervise their financial operations. There are six members, two of whom are appointed by the president and confirmed by the Senate for four-year terms. The other four are the Commissioner of Social Security, the Secretary of Health and Human Services, the Secretary of Labor, and the Secretary of the Treasury, who is the Managing Trustee. One of the duties of the Board, according to the Social Security Act, is to present to Congress each year a report on the actuarial and financial position of OASI and DI Trust funds. The 1999 report is the fifty-ninth annual one fulfilling that obligation. As there have been changes in the computation of the CPI, the values underlying the report's three basic assumptions were changed from 1998:

1. The CPI inflation rate was lowered to 3.3 percent from 3.5 percent.
2. The projected nominal interest rate earned on trust fund assets remained at 6.3 percent, so that the intermediate inflation-adjusted interest rate assumption was raised to 3.0 percent from 2.8 percent in line with the lower CPI assumption.

3. The intermediate unemployment rate assumption was lowered to 5.5 percent from 6.0 percent.

The demographic assumptions are only slightly different from the 1998 report. These factors include unchanged mortality rates, but life expectancy and fertility rates are higher.

Short-range and long-range actuarial estimates are offered in the report. For the short range, the primary measure of the funds' financial soundness, or adequacy, is the "trust fund ratio," or the ratio of trust fund assets at the start of the year to payments during the year. In the next 10 years (the short range), OASI and DI funds, both separately and together, pass the short-range test for financial adequacy. In the next 75 years (the long range), the assets of OASI and DI Trust funds are estimated to be exhausted by 2034 (two years later than forecast in 1998) under present law and based on the intermediate cost assumptions, one of three sets of assumptions used. The DI Trust fund will be exhausted several years earlier than the OASI fund and, as it has been fluctuating, the report recommends that it be tracked closely (Trustees Report 1999: 1015). Walker has commented that cash deficits will begin to appear in the Social Security program by 2013 (Walker 1999: 5).

The various proposals suggested to correct the financial problems involve increasing the payroll tax, raising the taxation of benefits, changing the benefit formula, raising the retirement ages, changing dependent benefits, and reducing the inflation adjustment. Some of the proposals recommend that the government be permitted to purchase equities along with Treasury securities while other proposals would allow individuals to invest some part of their own contributions. Changes in the financing of increased returns are recommended as well.

In view of the large number of alternative reforms, a fourth criterion could be added to the Comptroller General's list: the costs of the transition and the costs of the end product compared to continuation of the present system. No matter which proposal might be adopted, there will be costs of restructuring, administering, implementing, and educating the public. If a system of individual accounts were initiated, the costs of administering the system would depend on how much choice individuals would have, how they would receive retirement benefits, and what type and level of customer service were furnished (GAO 1999g: 1–15; Trustees Report 1999: 1–15; Walker 1999: 1–22). The GAO has undertaken several studies on the various aspects of Social Security reform and proposals offered. Two of them are described below.

One study is concerned with *Social Security Capital Markets and Educational Issues Associated with Individual Accounts* (GAO 1999f). The main results of the study find that the effect on capital markets will be determined by (1) the means of funding the assets, (2) the assets in which the funds are invested, and (3) the savings behavior of the participants. For most proposals, the source of funding is either the payroll taxes or general fund revenues. The financial effect would mean large flows of capital from the Treasury debt market to private capital markets, the amount of national savings might change, and, arguably, returns received and risks taken by participants would increase relative to the current program. It would be advisable to offer an educational program, based on choices offered individuals, to provide information and explain how to guard against misinformation (GAO 1999F: 1–63).

Another study, *Social Security Reform Implementation Issues for Individual Accounts*, raises significant considerations concerning the efficient operation of these programs. Choices involve: centralization or decentralization of administration and bookkeeping, the degree of control exercised by individuals over their investments, and the options available for payment of retirement benefits (GAO 1999g: 3). The same Board of Trustees that oversees the Social Security programs supervises the operations of the Medicare programs. In a summary report of both programs, further details of the status and future performance of both trust funds are indicated. *A Summary of the 1999 Annual Reports* (Boards of Trustees 1999), states that the future performance of both funds is expected to improve and the dates on which the funds are forecast to be short of money needed to give full benefits is moved forward. The projection for the Hospital Insurance (HI) Trust fund, which covers hospital costs, is that it will be able to pay all benefits up to 2015, or seven years earlier than specified in the 1998 report. The projection for Supplementary Medical Insurance (SMI) Trust fund, which covers outpatient expenses including physicians' bills, remains the same, well financed into the indefinite future. Outlays in the program, however, have increased 41 percent in the last five years. The reason they are covered is because present law provides the annual financing needed to pay the following year's forecast costs. Nevertheless, as medical costs rise, the financing problems become more complex than they do for Social Security.

The outlook for the trust funds is built on the actuarial balance over a 75-year period. To determine the actuarial balance, subtract yearly costs from yearly income, state the result as a percentage of taxable payroll, and summarize the outcome over the 75-year forecast period. Using the intermediate assumptions, the following figures are the actuarial deficits as a percentage of taxable payroll for each fund offered in this combined report: OASI 1.7 percent, DI 0.36 percent, and HI 1.46 percent. Another interpretation for these numbers is that if this percentage were added to the current-law income rate in each of the next 75 years, or subtracted from the cost rate in each year, actuarial balance would be achieved in each of the funds.

As the Comptroller General remarks in his report of 25 March 1999, this measure of solvency is short-lived. If forecast revenues equal forecast outlays over the 75-year time period, as this computation requires, the system is in actuarial balance. But, the following year, the actuarial period changes, as it did between 1998 and 1999, and a year of surplus may be substituted for a year of deficit, or the reverse. In addition to the uncertainty involved, there is the need to recognize that deficits appear before assets are depleted in the trust funds, and that changes in economic or demographic conditions affect the outlook also. Walker would prefer a solution for lasting solvency that does not require periodic returns to the same issue. For that to happen, the method of financing the system is the most significant factor together with the need for a healthy, growing economy (Boards of Trustees 1999: 1–7; Walker 1999: 9–11).

OFF-BUDGET ISSUES OF GOVERNMENT SPONSORED ENTERPRISES

Beginning in the 1990s, there have been more intensive inquiries by Congress into the forms and functions of the GSEs and their relationship to federal programs and activities. In the late 1980s, interim steps had been introduced to limit GSE operations (Meyer 1989a: 40). The GSEs consist of five financial institutions chartered by the federal government to act in the public's behalf to expedite the flow of funds to housing, higher education, and agriculture: the FHLMC, the FNMA, the FHLB, the SLMA, and the FCS. Together, these institutions receive special benefits and congressional support for their purposes so that investors in their obligations consider them to bear an implicit federal guarantee. At the end of 1990, outstanding obligations totaled $980 billion, according to a study by the CBO, *Controlling the Risks of Government Sponsored Enterprises*, reported in April 1991.

Senator Kohl, in his opening statement to the Subcommittee on Governmental Information and Regulation, Committee on Governmental Affairs of the Senate, was concerned with the risks the GSEs pose for taxpayers. He emphasized that the implicit federal guarantee of GSEs is a serious matter for the government and the taxpayers. That fact has been proven already by the $4 billion bail-out of the FCS in 1987. In his statement given on 18 July 1991, Senator Kohl continues by pointing out the guarantee effectively eliminates the market discipline over the risks these enterprises may take. Stockholders of GSEs, such as Freddie Mac and Fannie Mae, receive substantial earnings on their investments but the government guarantees the possible losses. Senator Kohl likens the system to the one that caused the Savings and Loan (S&L) disaster and the current banking crisis. Only the GSEs contain more potential risk than the S&Ls because the number involved is one trillion dollars. After this introduction, Senator Kohl announced the agenda for the day's Hearing. There are two compet-

ing proposals concerning regulation of GSEs to be discussed. One is au-
thored by the Treasury and consists of improving existing regulation within
parent agencies, and the other is recommended by the GAO, which would
create a new superagency regulator.

Robert D. Reischauer, Director of CBO, commented upon both proposals. He spoke of HUD's weak supervision of Fannie Mae and Freddie Mac.
Reischauer suggested that one way of getting better supervision would be
to follow the Treasury recommendation of setting up an independent supervisory agency within HUD. The relationship of the presidentially appointed director of the new agency and the Secretary of HUD could be
similar to that of the Secretary of the Treasury and the Comptroller of the
Currency. This step would effectively separate the two GSEs from HUD's
other activities and raise the chances that the government would be pro-
tected from foolish risk-taking moves by the GSEs. The OMB and the GAO
could serve, also, to monitor performance.

The second option offered by the GAO and some private analysts, continues Reischauer, would establish an entirely new independent supervisory
agency over all the GSEs. The agency would have greater responsibility and
broader interests than in the other arrangement and could work more directly to protect the interests of the general taxpayer. The agency would be
made accountable, in the final analysis, for any losses the five enterprises
might cause the government to suffer in the future. An important aspect of
this arrangement is making sure that the agency develops sufficient expertise in housing, higher education, and agriculture, to be able to supervise
all the GSEs in an effective manner. If it could do so, the director of the
CBO recommends the GAO proposal of a single agency to supervise all the
GSEs as the superior choice. Reischauer claims it is the one with the best
chance of success at minimizing the risk of any GSEs' manipulation of
supervisory procedures at the cost of sound and safe policies (*Various Proposals* 1991: 37–65).

The recommendations of the GAO were:

1. Establish an independent federal enterprise regulatory board which would in-
   clude a presidentially appointed chair, the Secretary of the Treasury, and the
   Chairman of the FRS as voting members; and the Secretaries of Agriculture,
   Education, and HUD as nonvoting members.

2. Vest authority in the board that would direct it to establish rules, to monitor
   performance, and to enforce the rules in the event of noncompliance.

3. Furnish risk-based capital requirements for the GSEs (*Various Proposals* 1991:
   2–3)

The CBO took a second look at the GSEs in 1996. Their viewpoint
shifted to an overall assessment of the costs and benefits of Freddie Mac
and Fannie Mae, specifically. In order to do so, they studied the initial

reasons the two superagencies came into existence. There were no housing GSEs until 1968, when Fannie Mae was converted from a federal agency to a GSE; Freddie Mac was chartered in 1970. The problem, at that time, was the shortage of funds for lending on home mortgages and the accompanying high interest rates, particularly in the West and the South. Even the existence of a GSE lender for thrift institutions, the FHLB, did not sufficiently ease the situation. Attracting deposits to areas of chronic shortages so that loanable funds would increase was limited, and the effect was exaggerated by the presence of the Federal Reserve's Regulation Q on interest rates. The Regulation Q ceilings on interest rates prevented savers from obtaining rates equivalent to those obtainable on Treasury and other securities. The process of disintermediation or outflows of funds from mortgage markets to capital markets to capture higher returns occurred periodically. It tended to increase cyclical tendencies in housing markets nationwide.

With the creation of Freddie Mac and Fannie Mae, and their ability to acquire funds directly from bond markets without interest rate or geographic limits, mortgages from primary lenders were now available. In short, the creation of the housing GSEs integrated national capital markets and retail mortgage markets. However, the integration resulted in higher average mortgage interest rates along with the greater access to mortgage funds. It resulted, also, in segmenting the resale or secondary market for mortgages according to size, credit quality, and the public or private nature of the intermediary.

Another aspect of the risk factor of GSEs concerns their funding strategies. They sell both their own debt securities in capital markets or they issue mortgage-backed securities (MBSs). The debt securities are a more risk-prone method than MBSs. The reason is, mainly, because the GSEs can take advantage of interest rate spreads in the various markets. For example, the GSE can use debt with short maturity to buy and retain long-term fixed rate mortgages. Ordinarily, short-term interest rates are lower than long-term interest rates, so the return on the asset held exceeds the cost of the short-term liability. Obviously, the risk is that short-term rates will rise and wipe out the advantage. Even with a long-term liability, there is the interest rate risk that rates will drop.

Nonetheless, Fannie Mae opted for the debt strategy of using short maturities to finance purchases of long-term mortgages. Alternatively, Freddie Mac used acquired mortgages bundled into pools and resold guaranteed claims on them in the form of MBSs, calling them "participation certificates." In addition, Freddie Mac often swapped MBSs to the mortgage lender for the underlying mortgages.

Fannie Mae's gamble with short-term debt securities did not work out and, in the early 1980s, the market value of her mortgages was $10 million less than her liabilities. Fortunately, interest rates went down and Fannie

Mae's position improved. From that point on, both Fannie Mae and Freddie Mac used MBSs and debt funding, or as it is called, portfolio lending. The latter has a profit margin of at least four times more than the MBS method. The FHLB has made use of the portfolio lending approach as well. Interest rate risk is controlled by management in the two GSEs by hedging with the use of long-term callable debt. Freddie Mac and Fannie Mae use other methods, such as short sale of Treasury securities, currency and interest rate swaps, and derivatives. All of these techniques tend to mask the extent of interest rate exposure to management and the government.

During the period from 1991 to 1995, debt finance portfolio investment increased for Fannie Mae and Freddie Mac. Considering the mortgage portfolio as a percentage of MBSs outstanding, Fannie Mae began the period with 36 percent, and by 1965 it was at 49 percent. Freddie Mac began at 7 percent in 1991, and by 1995 it was more than three times higher at 23 percent (CBO 1996: 1–8).

Other GSEs have been investigated particularly with respect to risk taking. According to a letter dated 31 August 1999, written by Thomas J. McCool, Director, Financial Institutions and Markets Issues, General Government Division of GAO, he is responding to a request to summarize past reports and recommendations. The capital structure of the system is important to Congress because of its current consideration of changes in that structure and its regulator, the Federal Housing and Finance Board (FHFB).

The letter states that the GAO continues to support, as it has since May 1991, the introduction of risk-based capital requirements together with a leverage ratio consisting of a minimum capital-to-asset ratio for the FHLB system. One basic benefit would be the elimination of government daily oversight by providing a specific guide for risk taking within the system. With 12 federally chartered, privately owned banks in the FHLB system, a huge burden would be lifted from the government's shoulders. The FHLB system has been most useful since its inception in 1932 for extending mortgage credit. It does this action by making "loans," read advances, to member institutions that turn around and lend the funds to home buyers for mortgages. Advances are secured by anything from Treasury securities, deposits at an FHLB, to home mortgage loans. The member institutions improve their liquidity position in this manner, and have access to national capital markets. As of 30 June 1999, there were $330 billion in advances extended by the FHLBs to member institutions. In addition, the system had $148 billion in investments and $25 billion in capital. The FHLB System, at the time, was composed of 7,101 member institutions, which included commercial banks, thrifts, credit unions, and insurance companies. The use of risk-based standards and the leverage ratio is now even more important for the system, comments Thomas McCool. Along with new activities and enlargement of the system comes the possibility of increased risk taking. Together, the two recommendations could accommodate the risk problem but, also, system capital must become more permanent in order to provide the appropriate amount of protection in the event of unforeseen losses. Presently, the system has both voluntary and mandatory membership arrangements. The voluntary members may withdraw on six months' notice. GAO recommends one of two ways of increasing the permanence of the system's capital: either extend the withdrawal notice period, the time for repayment after a member institution makes notification of withdrawal, from six months to at least one year; or set new capital requirements for minimum retained earnings in each FHLB. Retained earnings are funds that are not paid out to members so that FHLBs would have a source of permanent capital (McCool 1999: 1–7).

In 1996, the Treasury Department furnished a report on the subject of possible termination of the government sponsorship of Freddie Mac and Fannie Mae. The study was one of four done for the same purpose by HUD, CBO, and GAO. The Treasury study finds that the United States has the strongest housing finance market in the world and that Fannie Mae and Freddie Mac have played significant roles in adding liquidity to the secondary market for home mortgages. They have, in addition, expanded the opportunities for low and moderate income families to purchase homes. In a letter to the Committee on Banking and Financial Services of the House dated 11 July 1996 accompanying the report, Deputy Secretary Lawrence Summers spoke for the Treasury by saying that "the Treasury believes it is too early to consider ending or changing the government's sponsorship of Fannie Mae and Freddie Mac" (Summers/Treasury 1996: 1–2).

However, according to the summary of the Treasury report, there are considerable benefits to the two GSEs from government sponsorship. It is estimated that the reduced operating and borrowing costs of the two GSEs, resulting from their status, allow them benefits amounting to approximately $6 billion a year. The estimate for the benefits that Fannie Mae and Freddie Mac provide in reduced mortgage costs and in access to mortgages that would not have been available without them is stated to be about $4 billion annually in total savings to consumers. The difference of $2 billion is assumed to be gained by GSE stockholders as retained pretax income. The Treasury mentions that these estimates are similar to those reported in 1996 by the CBO and the GAO (*Analytical Perspectives* 2000: chs. 8, 12; Summers/Treasury 1996: 1–11).

In the report that the CBO prepared in 1996, on the same subject of the possible privatization of Freddie Mac and Fannie Mae, the source for the investigations is given. The Federal Housing Enterprise Safety and Soundness Act of 1992, section 1355, required the Secretary of the Treasury, the Secretary of HUD, the Comptroller General, and the Director of the CBO to make investigations to learn if the two GSEs could function as entirely private enterprises without federal sponsorship. The Act required study of the costs resulting from privatization, including cost of capital, home ownership, secondary market competition, capital requirements, and other factors. Additional information was requested by the Home Banking Committee's Subcommittee on Capital Markets concerning the use of an analytical setting and policy choices for widening the difference between public benefits and costs. In preparing the report, the committee specified that three scenarios be used for comparing benefits and costs: (1) to remain as is, (2) to alter the responsibilities of the two GSEs, and (3) to privatize them.

GSEs had provided greater accessibility to mortgage credit for home buyers during nearly 30 years before this report. Funds are obtained from the bond markets and mortgages are acquired from local lenders. Thus, the GSEs deal in two markets, at least, and enable home buyers to reach the nation's savings pool for financing mortgages. Oversight of these operations is done by periodic evaluations of policies by the Congress. Oversight is necessary on the basis of size alone, as the market values of the two GSEs exceed that of Citicorp and Wells Fargo together. As of September 1999, Fannie Mae and Freddie Mac had $2.0 trillion outstanding in purchased or guaranteed mortgages.

In spite of the fact that the GSEs are owned by shareholders as private corporations, the federal sponsorship of Freddie Mac and Fannie Mae means the government has given an implicit guarantee to obligations of these enterprises. Besides, they enjoy special privileges that other private organizations do not obtain, such as exemptions from state and local taxes and from the registration requirements of the SEC. The report claims that in 1995, 40 percent of the earnings of Freddie Mac and Fannie Mae were a result of the advantages of federal sponsorship. The study measures the credit enhancement subsidies to the two GSEs, implied by the sponsorship and the several advantages offered, at $6.5 billion annually, as of May 1996. Of this figure, $4.4 billion benefits home buyers. The outcome, outlined in the CBO study, is that the GSEs use up almost $1.00 for each $2.00 of aid to home buyers. In conclusion, the CBO asks the question of whether the increased home ownership achieved by the two enterprises is of greater value than the subsidy cost (*Analytical Perspectives* 2000: 195; CBO 1996: i–xv; Meyer 1989a: 40). The question behind the question is: given that increased home ownership is a national goal, is there a more efficient and effective way to achieve that goal?

CONCLUDING COMMENTS

The unsystematic treatment of the current services baseline and its reliance upon a proposed executive budget curbs its usefulness. There is a similar difficulty with the employment of the tax expenditures concept. Commitment to one viewpoint in each case for use in the budget documents would not preclude mentioning another viewpoint when the circumstances warrant it. As for projected Social Security revenues falling short of expenditures within 20 years, that information should be studied with the awareness that no one forecasted the budget surpluses given a one-year lead time. Adequate financing of the Social Security and Medicare programs should be the object no matter what the state of the economy. Supervising the GSEs in their current massive proportions would appear to be more costly than it is worth. After careful attention to transition problems, turn them loose and let the market do the supervising. Regulations, subsidies, and a host of other instruments could be used, if desired, to encourage attainment of national goals for housing, higher education, and agriculture.

Chapter 10

Perspectives on Deficits and Surpluses

Deficits were a large and expected annual event in U.S. budgets for many years. Their economic impacts and the debt management techniques that they required were generally well understood. The budget stance has changed to surpluses. New information must be collected and new procedures must be developed to meet the changed situation. This chapter contains: clues to the origins of deficits and surpluses, some information concerning the contribution of tax policy to surpluses, and contradictory evidence about the U.S. external balance of payments. The final section of the chapter is devoted to a discussion of the development of new debt management techniques to deal with a diminishing federal debt held by the public.

BACKGROUND ON DEFICITS

In *The Federal Budget: Politics, Policy, Process* (1994a), Allen Schick claims that the huge federal deficits were on everyone's mind in the administration during the 1980s and 1990s. In the early 1990s, the deficit was blamed on the nation's economic woes, the high cost of health care, conflicts between the president and Congress, and between politicians and their constituents. Taxes had remained at slightly over 18 percent of GDP since the 1960s; however, by the early 1990s there were many more programs that the same revenue had to cover: Medicare, Medicaid, supplementary social insurance, food stamps, income tax credits, education, and others (Schick 1994a: 1–5).

In 1981, there was a huge tax reduction and several tax increases occurred over the period from 1982 to 1990. Altogether, the revenue base rose about one percent of GDP and large deficits were projected, as before, into the twenty-first century. Discretionary spending, or outlays controllable through the congressional appropriations process, accounted for 35 percent of total outlays (GAO 1993: 42).

In another work in which Allen Schick collaborated with John F. Cogan and Timothy J. Muris (Cogan, Muris, and Schick 1994), a chapter entitled "The Dispersion of Spending Authority and Federal Budget Deficits" by John F. Cogan investigates the contribution to federal budget deficits that the congressional budget process has made since World War II. It is his contention that there were two institutional changes during the 1930s that were most responsible for the unbalanced budgets. One was the shift in both houses of Congress from a centralized committee structure to a decentralized one with respect to jurisdiction over expenditures and general fund revenues. Accountability for the total level of spending was no longer traceable to any one committee under the decentralized structure. No one committee had any reason to limit its spending under these circumstances. As a result, expenditures rose faster than general revenues and deficits appeared.

The second change was the introduction of the trust funds. The trust funds are financed by their own earmarked taxes and include Social Security and Medicare Hospital Insurance. Trust fund revenues are placed in the hands of the tax-writing committees and they have been encouraged to switch from general fund revenues to trust fund revenues.

With these two institutional changes, general fund revenues declined and expenditures rose in relation to GNP. Total budget deficits increased along with the rising general fund expenditures (Cogan, Muris, and Schick 1994: 16–35).

By 1996, the problem of deficits was drawing a great deal of attention. Joseph J. Cordes remarked that in recent budget debates, it is no longer the spending side which holds legislators' attention, rather it is the question of how the spending is to be financed. The new outlook tended to limit the flexibility of budget makers as they realized that past decisions had committed budget resources to other goals. Some of these prior commitments continue to include income transfers and entitlement programs, growing interest payments on the rising national debt, contingent liabilities such as loan and loan guarantee programs, and earmarked tax revenues which are treated in the same manner as the payroll tax deduction assigned to the Social Security Trust funds. One final source of prior commitment may arise from indexation of taxes or of spending for inflation. The Social Security benefits system incorporates the concept that allows benefits to rise annually based on the increase in the price level or similar measure.

In the U.S. budget, the single largest prior commitment is the entitlement programs. They make payments on the basis of criteria written in the law. Social Security and Medicare programs provide income and health benefits to the aged and represent 60 percent of all entitlement spending. Another

20 percent is accounted for by entitlement programs based on economic need or means including Medicaid, SSI, AFDC, Food Stamps, and the Earned Income Tax Credit (EIC). The 20 percent remaining is for programs supporting specific populations such as farmers and veterans.

Other prior commitments in the budget are net interest or the difference between what the government must pay out for its outstanding debt less interest received by government on loans and cash balances, deposit insurance, and offsetting receipts. Deposit insurance consists of payments that financial institutions make to finance the $100,000 guarantee on individual deposits by government if the institution should become insolvent. Offsetting receipts are negative spending and are collected by government and credited to separate accounts. Proprietary receipts, payments for specific government services, are one type of offsetting receipts (Cordes 1996: 95–116).

Allen Schick has argued that the development of the characteristics mentioned hinge, in part, on the fact that budget policies are built from assumptions about the future direction of the main components of national economic behavior. These assumptions must reflect, also, the fact that the current national budget will have a mutual impact. There is a continual back-and-forth exchange between the budget and the economy. Therefore, forecasts about the size of the budget, its composition, trends in employment, interest rates, or whatever, must integrate these reciprocal effects.

Any errors in reporting economic conditions currently, or in forecasting them for the future, magnify the errors of budget estimates as they are projected to later years. The magnified effect will be larger the greater the difference in the projected economic conditions and the ones which actually occur. Added to the technical problems is the perennial one which leads to manipulation of the estimates for political advantage.

Schick claims that during the years from 1982 to 1990, there was a strong causation between the size of budget deficits and the rate of economic growth. The period was one of slow economic growth and it was associated with large deficits. In spite of frequent efforts to reduce the deficit by altering spending and taxing laws up until 1994, there was little sign of improvement in its size.

The lesson to be learned, according to Schick, is that trying to control the deficit alone is not enough. The economy must grow fast enough to allow the extra revenues from rising incomes to exceed the automatic rises in expenditures, presumably from the entitlement programs. An additional problem in closing a deficit gap is deciding which deficit it is that needs to be controlled. Any deficit represents the difference between what is spent and what is collected in revenues. The two categories will disagree in amount depending, in the case of the federal budget, on whether the discussion concerns (1) the consolidated deficit, (2) the on-budget deficit, (3) the Federal funds deficit, (4) the operating deficit, or (5) the structural deficit (Schick 1994a: 27–30).

1. The consolidated deficit, called the unified budget deficit in the budget documents, has been the basis for the budget presentation and budget analyses since the FY 1969 budget. The *Report of the President's Commission on Budget Concepts* in October 1967 specified that the budget should include all federal fiscal activities except for those items needing special treatment. Initially, an expenditure and a loan account were to appear in the unified budget. The expenditure account has remained; the loan account was dropped beginning with the FY 1974 budget. The FY 2001 unified budget totals consist of on- and off-budget entities but not direct or guaranteed loans, contingent liabilities such as deposit insurance or GSEs, or pension guarantees.

2. The on-budget deficit is the unified budget deficit minus the budget balance of the Social Security Trust funds and the U.S. Postal Service.

3. The federal funds deficit gets its name from its comprehensive nature of including the general, special, public enterprise, and intragovernmental funds but not those designated as trust funds. Trust funds are specified in the law as a type of account for receipts earmarked for special purposes and used for the spending of these receipts.

4. The operating deficit deals only with the difference between current expenditures and receipts. It does not include physical capital investment such as buildings or highways. Up until the present time, the federal government does not have a separate capital budget, but the matter has been constantly under review. One of the most recent studies is the *Report of the President's Commission to Study Capital Budgeting* issued in February 1999.

5. The structural deficit, or balance, is the deficit or surplus remaining after the balance is calculated for what it would be if the unemployment were at the long-run "nonaccelerating inflation rate of unemployment" (NAIRU) less that portion due to cyclical factors such as when the economy is operating above potential. At the time of the transmission of the budget documents for FY 2001, or February 2000, the long-run NAIRU was assumed to be consistent with a 5.2 percent unemployment rate. The structural balance is used as an analytical tool for viewing the stance of fiscal policy because the structural balance will remain after the economy returns to its long-run operating levels. In 1999, the adjusted structural surplus was $44.3 billion, or approximately 36 percent of the unified budget surplus of $124.4 billion reported in the FY 2001 budget (*Analytical Perspectives* 2000: 6, 13).

The calculation of each of these budget balances is highly dependent on methods used for revenue estimation. Alan J. Auerbach commented on the difficulties of arriving at accurate figures in the *National Tax Journal* (December 1993). Revenue estimation, explains Auerbach, is performed each time a legislative proposal is made. It is done by economists at the Joint Committee on Taxation (JCT) and the Office of Tax Analysis (OTA) at the Treasury Department. The estimates are usually calculated for a period of five years.

Recently, the importance of revenue estimation has increased because of the increase in budget control measures. The BEA of 1990 requires that if a proposal results in a loss of tax revenue, it must be compensated by a gain that raises tax revenue by the same amount.

Revenue estimates made by government estimators, according to Auerbach, are usually performed hurriedly with little research, data, or information on the range of error. Furthermore, the policy responses of government that will offset changes in revenue and the baseline specified must be implicit in the estimation. Therefore, a whole body of asumptions underlie any given estimates. Another problem is raised by conventions such as indirect taxes being included in GNP while direct taxes are not, and that a five-year budget "window" is the method of gauging a proposal's revenue effects. The budget window permits revenue to be counted again after the expiration of that time when compared to the baseline from which the tax had been excluded.

Other ambiguities in the use of revenue estimates arise when they are assumed to tell us by how much the budget deficit will change. The information yields no clue as to what the final burden will be on taxpayers at different income levels, nor does it imply any particular set of macroeconomic effects. For example, it is often argued that reducing the deficit will lower interest rates.

The yearly budget deficit, or a five-year deficit prediction, are not reliable because of the ever-present possibility of moving the numbers around from year to year to suit whatever policy choice leaves the least revenue loss in the budget year being considered.

Auerbach insists that to calculate the fiscal impact of a policy, one must know the present value of generated positive or negative revenues and who bears the burden of the policy. Calculations of the distribution of the burden could be found by the method of generational accounts. "A generational account equals the present value of taxes, not of transfers, that each generation can expect to pay in the future, based on current policy" (Auerbach 1993: 522). The main objection to the use of generational accounting is the uncertainty involved in forecasting revenues for the distant future.

Some other questions which arise in arriving at more accurate revenue estimates are: how to account for behavioral or other feedback effects for distributional effects, for the incidence of the corporate income tax, for the difference between the burden of taxes and their level: and how to determine the appropriate length of time for the study of tax incidence (Auerbach 1993: 519–526). In another paper, which was written to appear as the *National Tax Journal*'s "Beck Memorial Paper," Auerbach considers the performance of the CBO and the OMB as government revenue fore-casters. He finds that forecast errors are so large in the period from 1986 to 1999 that it is impossible to determine if there is any existing bias. The forecasts demonstrate serial correlation and their use in the budget process completely ignores the uncertainty inherent in the point estimates furnished by the two agencies (Auerbach 1999: 433–438).

BACKGROUND ON SURPLUSES

For FY 2001, the administration was no longer concerned with a deficit gap. Even before the start of the year 2000, the federal budget had under-gone a sudden reversal. "The Dawning of a New Era" in *Setting National Priorities The 2000 Election and Beyond* contained relevant estimates by Robert D. Reischauer in which he comments that after nearly three decades of deficits, the overall federal budget is in surplus. There have been two years of surpluses, 1998 and 1999, in the government's on-budget accounts together with the off-budget accounts consisting of Social Security and the U.S. Postal Service (Reischauer 1999: 1–3).

One of the several reasons for the amazing turnaround is the impressive growth of the economy. Other reasons stated in the *Economic Report of the President Transmitted to Congress February 2000* (Council of Eco-nomic Advisers 2000) include rising productivity, the lowest core inflation rate since 1965, the lowest unemployment rate since 1969, and a 20-million-job increase in payroll employment since January 1993. Much of the favorable data is a result of rapid technological change and investment in plant and equipment, especially computers and information technology. Other technological revolutions have occurred in medicine, biology, and materials science (Council of Economic Advisers 2000: 21–30).

The Council of Economic Advisers and the former director of the CBO from 1989 to 1995, Robert D. Reischauer, agree that fiscal discipline on the part of Congress and the president was another reason for the appear-ance of surpluses. In 1990, 1993, and 1997, deficit reduction legislation was passed and the president signed the acts. The laws enacted provided for various amounts of tax increases and spending reductions. In the BEA of 1990, the caps on discretionary spending permitted future deficits to be avoided. In the event of unforeseen events, the BEA called for automatic adjustment to the spending caps and the PAYGO scorecard, a kind of tally sheet, if Congress and the president indicated an emergency situation. Ac-cording to a report to the Chairman, Committee on the Budget of the House of Representatives in April 1999, this provision was exercised in FY 1991, at the time of Operation Desert Storm. Total emergency budget au-thority in that year was almost $46 billion, the highest amount of the decade. Again in 1992, emergency budget authority totaled more than $16 billion; in 1994, almost $14 billion; and in 1999, almost $26 billion (GAO 1999a: 23–24). The 1993 and 1997 Acts were extended to cover FY 1996 to 1998, and 1999 to 2002. The extension referred to discretionary spending caps, the PAYGO scorecard, and slightly modified procedures concerning these mechanisms.

The contribution of the vibrant economy affected the budget in another way. As GDP increased, its composition changed such that corporate profits and wages and salaries became a larger proportion of the total. As these are relatively highly taxed parts of the national income, it boosted government revenues while government spending for unemployment insurance and welfare dropped. Other contributing factors to the size of the surplus were: the large income gains to the wealthy meant larger tax revenues to the government than would have prevailed if income gains had been equally distributed; tax payments on realized capital gains rose with the rising stock market; import prices dropped as economic weakness abroad occurred and helped to keep down domestic prices; and the growth of Medicare and Medicaid spending slowed down sharply. There is one other factor to account for the two budget surpluses, if the actual budget figures for 1999 that are not available until the FY 2002 documents confirm it, and that is good fortune or serendipity. Both OMB and CBO have forecast surpluses for the next decade totaling almost $3 trillion. Reischauer claims that the budgets could register this figure if average rates of unemployment, inflation, interest, and economic growth are close to those assumed. The assumptions are reasonable, he says, because CBO and OMB and the consensus view of private sector forecasters are in agreement. Nevertheless, at the 26–27 June 2001 meeting of the FOMC, it was observed that unemployment had risen, industrial output had dropped sharply, economic activity had grown very little (if at all), prices were rising at a relatively moderate pace, and interest rates were generally lower in accord with frequent open market actions to reduce the federal funds rate (*Federal Reserve Bulletin* 2001b: 1–9). A general overview of FOMC meetings and how policy directives are developed is found in Ann-Marie Meulendyke's *U.S. Monetary Policy and Financial Markets* (1998: 121–138).

Assumptions about spending and taxing policies appear less reasonable. Discretionary spending has been held down by the spending caps, and after they expire in 2002, it is expected that they will grow at the rate of inflation. Reishauer finds this "highly unrealistic." Nevertheless, beginning in 1998, the focus of fiscal policy shifted to the need to save Social Security as the priority item in the president's budget. The president's budget message in the *Budget of the United States Government FY 1999* (1998) includes the paragraph:

More specifically, I believe that the Administration and Congress should not spend a budget surplus for any reason until we have a solution to the long-term financing challenge facing Social Security. With that in mind, my budget proposes a reserve for the projected surpluses for 1999 and beyond. (*Budget* 1998: 3)

Congress offered several proposals in response, frequently referred to as lock-box proposals, an old-fashioned phrase for safe deposit box. The new consensus in government, in Reischauer's opinion, is that deficits should be avoided in the budget accounts and that surpluses occurring in the off-budget account of Social Security should be used to reduce the public debt.

After 30 years of deficits, the issues that were formerly at the top of the list for the federal government, such as personal economic security, income equity, cold war security, and welfare assistance programs have dropped in ranking. They have been replaced by education, health insurance, and the leading issue, how to save Social Security and Medicare from financial insolvency. As for the forecast surpluses and what to do with them, Reischauer views the debate as actually one concerning the right size and range of government and its activities (GAO 1999a: 23–24; Reischauer 1999: 1–16).

One of the aspects of considering surpluses in the federal budget is the need to clarify whether the recommendation is addressing possible surpluses on-budget, off-budget, or both. Alan Greenspan, Chairman of the Board of Governors of the Federal Reserve System, made the distinction in a statement published in the *Federal Reserve Bulletin* (May 2000). Greenspan believes that saving the surpluses is the best way to encourage additional productivity improvements. The increases in saving will enable private sector investment to continue, and thus increase productivity. How we save the surpluses is another matter. It has been proposed, more than once, that the on-budget surplus be transferred to the Social Security Trust funds. The commission that Greenspan chaired in 1983 strongly opposed the idea. One of the objections was that the Social Security system is a social insurance program and completely distinct from ordinary government spending programs.

Actually, the Social Security system and Medicare (Part A) have some similar characteristics to a private insurance program. One of them is that they both are intended to be in long-term balance. However, the standard adopted for the two government programs is that taxes and other income should cover benefits for 75 years. Private pension plans, on the other hand, require full funding in perpetuity.

The public and private insurance plans differ on the basis of benefit payments to beneficiaries. For the private sector insurance plans, individuals receive benefits according to their contributions plus earnings on the contributions over time. Social Security beneficiaries receive a much higher rate of return. Although the average recipient receives benefits equal to 42 percent of an average year's earnings, low-income workers receive a higher fraction because the system is designed to benefit them. Furthermore, automatic increases in benefits occur annually according to the percentage rise of the CPI (Wright 1999: 169).

Even though Social Security programs differ from private insurance programs, many individuals believe that the link between payroll taxes used to finance Social Security programs and benefits should not be broken because then the program would become more of a welfare plan than it currently is. The pressure to reform Social Security would not be as strong were the link to be broken. Medicaid and Medicare (Part B) are financed by general revenues and, therefore, there is much less pressure to change them.

In any event, says Greenspan, use of budget surpluses from general revenues to fund Social Security should be preceded by consideration of other benefit reforms: extending the age of full retirement benefit entitlement and indexing it to longevity, changing the benefit calculation bend points, and revising the annual cost of living increase so that it is a more accurate measure. A study of the Medicare (Part A) program would probably reveal ways to structure it more efficiently, also, before turning to the use of general revenues. In Greenspan's opinion, it is the level of future resources which is most important, not its distribution between future workers and retirees. He claims the way to raise that level is to allow any future budget surpluses to be used to reduce the public debt (Greenspan 2000: 318–320).

CONTRIBUTIONS OF TAX POLICY TO SURPLUSES

Federal revenues for FY 1998 rose to over 20 percent of GDP even though tax cuts were instituted in 1997. In fact, there were five years in which revenue growth exceeded GDP growth and, therefore, made a large contribution to the government's surplus. This information was furnished by Richard A. Kasten, David J. Weiner, and G. Thomas Woodward in an article entitled "What Made Receipts Boom and When Will They Go Bust?" which appeared in the *National Tax Journal*'s symposium issue in 1999.

The article continues that neither the CBO nor other government forecasters predicted the size of receipts for the fiscal years 1996 and 1997. The economy kept expanding, although it was thought that capacity levels had been reached in 1996. Both unemployment and inflation were low. However, it was not because of exceptional cyclical performance of the economy that receipts were underestimated; it was because predictions of the intake from the individual income tax were too low.

For one thing, taxpayers determine their tax liability on a calendar year basis and tax receipts are estimated on a fiscal year basis. The result is that parts of taxpayers' receipts go into different years' collections. It may even affect more than two fiscal years, remembering that collections are made quarterly; final payments and refunds of withheld taxes occur after the end of the tax year, some others occur long after they are due; and still more are not included at all, such as returns filed by fiduciaries and trusts.

Individual income tax liability increased from 7.69 percent to 9.09 percent of GDP between 1994 and 1997. These figures were reported by Kasten, Weiner, and Woodward, independently of their work with the CBO, in 1999. The figures were based on their calculations of tax liability in 1997 if the percentage of GDP had remained unchanged from the 1994 level. They find a difference of $113.3 billion, which they decomposed into four categories:

1. Differences in growth rates of taxable personal income (TPY) and gross domestic product (GDP),
2. Differences in growth rates of TPY and adjusted gross deductions,
3. Differences in growth rates of adjusted gross income (AGI) and itemized deductions, and
4. Changes in the effective tax rates.

All of the effects move in the same direction. More than half of the $113.3 billion difference is accounted for by the differential growth rates of GDP, TPY, AGI, and itemized deductions, while the balance is considered to result from the rise in the average effective tax rate. The rise occurred because of higher real incomes, the fact that sources of income taxes at higher rates grew faster than other forms and, thus, the increased skewness in the distribution of income, together with the other factors, led to the greater tax liability generated.

As to when the boom will go bust, Kasten, Weiner, and Woodward observe that even a good macroeconomic forecast cannot capture all of the possibilities. However, the verdict is that the boom may have reached its limit because corporate profits have slowed substantially (Kasten, Weiner, and Woodward 1999: 339–347).

The fact that such large errors in forecasting tax receipts have happened has led to additional studies concerning the issue. One report by Ann D. Parcell of the Office of Tax Analysis in the Treasury Department explains the underlying difficulties. Parcell states that forecasts of tax receipts are made primarily for three reasons: (1) official estimates of annual budget deficits or surpluses which incorporate the existing tax law, spending rules, and comprehensive guidelines; (2) guidance functions for those concerned with the federal cash flow and the federal debt; and (3) modeling information for the private sector and state governments' own estimates of macroeconomic activity (Parcell 1999).

Forecasting tax liability is the first step in predicting individual tax receipts, explains Parcell. A microsimulation model to forecast 1997 returns was based on a 1995 Statistics of Income Sample (SOI) of approximately 118,000 tax returns weighted to reflect the income of the tax filers. Tax liability must be forecast annually for the entire budget. The macroeconomic predictions of the president's latest budget are used to weight the base SOI file in the microsimulation model. In each of the forecast years, the information yields income, population, itemized deduction growth, and the path for inflation.

Tax returns contain precise information on the factors but the data are usually several years old due to lags in processing the tax returns. In recent years, there has been a move to use tax collections liability from the most recent collections data rather than tax return liability. Then, collections liability is grown by the growth in liability from the tax return–based microsimulation model. Finally, the forecast of receipts is arrived at by gauging the cash flow of the forecast liability across fiscal years.

In recent years, writes Parcell, there have been receipt surges and it has been very difficult to separate short- and long-term effects of the surges on revenue forecasts. Some of the sharp increases have been attributed to capital gains realizations in 1995, 1996, and 1997, and the trend toward performance-based compensation, which raised the effective tax rate rapidly.

Another problem associated with the recent surges is that it has contributed to a change in the composition of receipts. Net tax collections, which are composed of estimated taxes, withheld taxes, final payments, and refunds, are the elements used to predict tax receipts before the returns become available. But, according to Parcell, the composition of the tax payments has changed drastically in the 1990s decade due to many factors, including modification of the rules concerning timing of the payments. Other changes consist of additional marginal tax brackets (The Omnibus Budget and Reconciliation Act of 1993) an increase in the alternative minimum taxable income (AMTI), permanent extension of the phaseout of personal exemptions and the limitation on itemized deductions (PEP and PEASE). Later, the maximum amount of Social Security benefits for inclusion in AGI was raised to 85 percent from 50 percent. In 1997, The Tax Relief Act of 1997 cut taxes and lowered the tax rates on long-term capital gains. These and other modifications of tax laws resulted in large changes in the forms of payments as a percent of net liability during the surge period.

The big problem, therefore, with forecasting tax receipts has been to try to separate the temporary from permanent components of increased receipts and to study the effects of increased receipts on the forms of payment that compose the collections data (Parcell 1999: 325–338).

EXTERNAL DEFICITS AND SURPLUSES

In the book, *Global Engagement: How American Companies Really Compete in the Global Economy* (2000), Joseph P. Quinlan writes that the United States has consistently run surpluses in service exports while running a chronic deficit in goods exports with the rest of the world. Service exports include:

1. Travel or receipts earned from foreigners traveling in the United States,
2. Passenger fares received by U.S. operators for transporting foreigners,
3. Other transportation including freight and port services,
4. Royalties and fees or receipts and payments on intellectual property rights, and
5. Other private services exports which consist of education and financial services exports.

Travel and other private services exports dominate the group of five, and represent two-thirds of total service exports in 1999.

The international trade sector of the United States is relatively small, representing less than 12 percent of total U.S. output in 1998. The significant area of exposure to the rest of the world is not in trade, but rather in foreign direct investment and associated sales. U.S. exports amounted to $933 billion in 1998 while sales of U.S. overseas affiliates were more than $2.4 trillion in the same year. The sales were approximately one-third of the GDP of the United States in 1998.

"America's trade deficit is a misleading indicator of how U.S. firms really stack up in the global market place and is therefore a dangerous variable shaping bilateral and multilateral relationships with other nations" (Quinlan 2000: xii). In 1999, the U.S. trade gap in goods and services was at a record $265 billion. At the same time, there were over 23,000 U.S. foreign affiliates and their combined total output exceeds the output of most nations. In manufacturing alone, U.S. foreign affiliates employ 4.6 million workers abroad. Foreign affiliate sales of goods and services are more than two and a half times total U.S. exports annually. Quinlan argues that trade figures are an inaccurate measure of global commerce because affiliate sales are not counted as exports and U.S.-based foreign affiliate sales are not counted in imports (Quinlan 2000: xi–xiv, 19–20, 192–195). There have been other errors in the record of the nation's international transactions reported more than a decade ago. One of the more important ones was incorrect evaluation of transactions so that the sums of credit and debit items were not equal. Throughout the 1980s, there was an unmeasured money inflow in the U.S. statistics amounting to approximately $20 billion annually. It has been attributed to secret money inflows from foreigners seeking a safe place for their funds. A second major discrepancy arose from unreported or undervalued service exports (Caves, Frankel, and Jones 1990: 360).

The information on the inaccuracies of balance of payments accounting may explain the lack of recent studies in this area. Formerly, budget deficits and trade deficits encouraged speculation on their relationships to interest rates, exchange rates, capital flows, and national savings. With the present U.S. internal budget surplus, but with the remaining external balance of payments deficit, new analyses and data are needed.

BUDGET BALANCES, DEBT, AND DEBT MANAGEMENT

Ever since 1982, the U.S. unified budget deficits had been high, ranging from a low of $128 billion in 1982 to a high of $290 billion in 1992. Deficits did not dip below the 1982 level until the 1996 deficit of almost $108 billion (see Table 8). Most of the improvement in the unified budget deficit, when it occurred, resulted from the growing surplus in the Social Security accounts. The surplus resulted from an increased payroll tax that was meant to raise national saving.

Over the same period, the debt held by the public, gross federal debt less debt held by government accounts, rose from over $924 billion in 1982 to $3 trillion in 1992, over three times its original size in one decade (see Table 10). In other words, debt held by the public has risen substantially more than the increase in the deficit over the period. In addition, as a percentage of GDP, debt held by the public was 28.6 percent but, by the end of the period, in 1992, it had risen to 48.2 percent. Public debt reached its peak as a fraction of GDP in 1993 at 49.2 percent, stayed at approximately that fraction through 1996, and then began to drop to its 1999 level of 39.9 percent of GDP at the end of the year. Debt held by the federal government accounts rose from 6.6 percent of GDP in 1982 to 21.6 percent by the end of 1999. A good portion of this rise was due to the increasing surpluses in the Social Security accounts that are bound by law to invest the excess funds in government securities.

Gary Gensler, Undersecretary of Domestic Finance at the Department of the Treasury, is proud of the longest series of improvements in U.S. history (seven consecutive years) in reducing budget deficits, since the peak 1992 deficit of $290 billion. By 1999, federal debt held by the public had been forecast to rise to $5.4 trillion and, instead, it reached $3.6 trillion. As Treasury debt diminishes and becomes a smaller share of the economy, it becomes, also, a smaller share of capital markets. Outstanding debt of the Treasury in U.S. markets was over 33 percent in 1994; it was less than 25 percent in 2000. Treasury debt managers must seek new ways to fulfill their goals of promoting efficient capital markets, using least-cost financing methods, and ensuring the availability of adequate cash balances at any time. There are several ways that the Treasury has dealt with the declining debt and the need to refund maturing debt with smaller amounts of new debt: (1) by modifying the types of securities offered, (2) by changing issue sizes, and (3) by varying the frequency of auction schedules. As these adjustments continue, the Treasury will have to consider how to issue enough longer-term debt without an undue lengthening of the maturity structure.

Currently, the long-term financing level, with 10-year and 30-year debt, results in an average maturity of Treasury debt of approximately 5 years and 9 months. If the long-term financing level were maintained, the average maturity of the debt would be eight years by 2004. As longer-term debt means higher interest payments, the taxpayer would bear the additional costs.

Gensler writes that the Treasury adopted two new rules that will alleviate the problem. One rule permits the Treasury to reopen benchmark securities within one year of issuance. With this new debt management tool, the Treasury will be able to maintain the size and liquidity of these securities. The second rule will permit the Treasury to conduct debt buybacks. There are three advantages to the procedure: (1) debt buybacks can be used as a cash management tool; they can absorb excess cash when incoming tax revenues are highest; (2) they can permit larger, more liquid auction sizes for the benchmark securities; and (3) debt buybacks can be geared to specific maturities to be repurchased so that maturity structure of the debt is maintained at the desired level.

As the Treasury debt continues to decline, the role of Treasury securities in global capital markets will diminish. It has happened already as Euro-dollar futures are traded more actively than Treasury bills for hedging purposes in the short term. In the investment grade bond market, the role of Treasury securities as a pricing benchmark has been reduced in comparison to the value of other high-grade corporate bonds. Gensler claims that these changes are small in contrast to the benefits of reducing the nation's debt. More of the nation's savings will move into housing and business investment rather than government bonds. Interest rates will be under less pressure, and therefore borrowing costs for individuals and business alike will be lower (Gensler 2000: 83–85).

CONCLUDING COMMENTS

Calculation of the size of deficits or surpluses is an improbable, if not impossible, matter. The information is rarely accurate, meaningful, or reliable. At best, estimates of any kind give a general idea of the order of magnitude; at worst, they indicate the wrong direction. One of the ongoing dilemmas is separating cyclical from secular trends. The findings are applicable to the Social Security quandary. The trust fund is running large surpluses but the present focus is on how to save Social Security from future financial tragedy. The solution may be closer to the "full funding in perpetuity" notion of the private sector than the present 75-year actuarial concept used. The measurement of the external budget deficits may encounter greater acceptance and practicality with the inclusion of U.S. foreign affiliates and their associated sales here and abroad. Debt management, if forecast surpluses materialize, will become a larger task for the Treasury as it tries to maintain desired maturity levels and healthy capital markets at the same time.

Part V

The U.S. Budget in an International Setting

Chapter 11

Megamacroeconomics and International Finance

The budget of the U.S. government interacts with the domestic economy and the world economy. The interaction of world economies occurs through the movements of goods, services, labor, capital, technology, and information. This chapter is concerned with the interaction of economies in terms of capital and information. To that end, the first section on international economic integration involves money, banks, and financial markets. The next section deals with understanding the causes of recent world financial crises. Finally, in order to build a strong and vigorous global financial system, supervisory bodies and regulations are discussed and enhanced information channels are indicated.

INTERNATIONAL ECONOMIC INTEGRATION

Although Robert Mundell (2000) claims that the basis of U.S. macroeconomic policy was primarily directed to the domestic scene until the decade of the 1960s, it would appear that the dating is somewhat premature. There has not been sufficient attention paid to the magnitude and rapidity of international capital flows. According to Mundell, until the 1960s, the basis of macroeconomic policy in the United States was primarily that of a closed economy. Internal balance was the main concern and the balance of payments was of little interest in setting monetary and fiscal policy. Then, writes Mundell, the 1970s were 10 years of inflation, the 1980s were 10 years of correction, and the 1990s were 10 years of relative stability. Furthermore, the economic performance of the 1990s compares favorably with that of the first 10 years of the century, but it has two drawbacks: it lacks a global currency and it suffers from frequent fluctuations in exchange rates. Three islands of stability have been established by the dollar, the yen, and the euro, but this does not change the two drawbacks that remain. Mundell considers the international monetary system today as inferior to that with which the century began (Mundell 2000: 327–340).

There is certainly evidence supporting Mundell's statement. Lawrence A. Summers, appointed Secretary of the Treasury in 1999, explains some of the problems in his Distinguished Lecture of Economics in Government, which appeared in the *Journal of Economic Perspectives* (1999). He writes that probably the largest and most important difference between globalization in the late twentieth century and that of the nineteenth century is that international economic integration affected the activities of government more in 1999 than it did a century ago. Governments do more now. They tax more, regulate more, and are obligated to maintain macroeconomic and financial stability. But today they are no longer insulated against exchange rate fluctuations or domestic or international politics and markets. Summers sees the challenge to policy makers to be their success at combining the three goals of: greater economic integration, public economic management, and national sovereignty. He recommends that integration be pursued initially in those areas of least conflict, such as for air safety standards and bank capital requirements. Second, the use of persuasion in achieving better public economic management rather than reducing sovereignty rights. He applauds the codes of good practice for fiscal and monetary transparency and financial supervision that have been suggested recently. Third, global integration may proceed from subglobal levels. The European Union is only one example of this approach.

The questions of method become more important, states Summers, as the financial disturbances occur nationally and internationally. They have led to a preoccupation on the part of political leaders with reform of the international financial architecture. The debate has ranged from those who want some sort of insurance and lender-of-last-resort mechanisms on an international scale to prevent crises, to those who claim that this would do more harm than good on the basis of moral hazard arguments. Another group is concerned with the integration of national capital markets and excessive capital flows, which is a particular problem for the emerging nations. Finally, there are some who would prefer more regulations and control of the resources in the hands of global institutions. The last approach would have the enormous difficulty of getting nations to permit their money or their banks to be controlled by supranational institutions. The "European Economic and Monetary Union may be the exception that proves the rule about the challenges of integrating national monies" (Summers 1999: 13).

Summers sees reforms underway which make use of these various approaches. In the United States, it began with generally accepted accounting principles (GAAP). Extending the approach, says Summers, to a global scale and employing transparency and effective systems of corporate governance and property rights might be an appropriate path for the global economy. Other steps in this direction are the IMF's Special Data Dissemination Standards entailing greater transparency of official data; the Core Principles of the Basle Committee and the International Organization of Securities Commissions; the present development of similar principles of corporate governance by the OECD. All of these improvements may help to prevent crises, but national policies play an important role as well. Internationally, the IMF has met the increased flows of global capital by creating in 1997 the Supplemental Reserve Facility at the initiative of Japan and the United States. With the facility, there is IMF lending under different sets of conditions, higher volumes, shorter time spans, and at premium rates of interest. In 1998, 40 percent of IMF lending fell in this category. The IMF has a contingent credit line for countries who suffer from "market contagion," which will use similar conditions.

The option of dollarization on a subglobal level has occurred to several Latin American countries. El Salvador's decision to adopt the U.S. dollar as its currency in December 2000 was greeted with support by the IMF and the U.S. Treasury Department. However, the move must be approved by the Central American nation's Congress. Economists claim that the move may result in domestic financial stability but with the loss of an independent monetary policy. For the United States, it may mean benefits to domestic business, but it might mean greater obligations to support the dollarized countries.

Summers concludes with the recommendation that it is the United States who should take the lead in establishing international economic integration. There have been obstacles to this step in the 1990s. The U.S. support of the World Bank has declined; arrears with the IMF continue, and the increase in IMF funding was difficult to achieve. The greatest barrier to international economic integration in the United States, claims Summers, is the belief that it interferes with government's ability to benefit the citizen (Summers 1999: 1–18).

The *Economic Report of the President February 1999* (Council of Economic Advisers 1999) made some statements concerning financial globalization. The complete report, together with statistical tables of over 450 pages, was submitted by the Council Chair, Janet L. Yellen, and members Jeffrey A. Frankel and Rebecca M. Blank, in accordance with the provisions of the Employment Act of 1946, as amended by the Full Employment and Balanced Growth Act of 1978. The report states that financial globalization in the 1990s has meant the European continent has sought to integrate beyond that accomplished by the initial European Common Market of the 1940s. The European Economic and Monetary Union (EMU) sought to integrate more closely by creating a single monetary unit, the euro. Only

11 of the 15 members of the European Union wanted to join and were found to have the strict fiscal and monetary conditions necessary to participate in the venture. The euro was introduced on 1 January 1999 and the European Central Bank took over control of monetary policy in the 11 countries. National monies now circulate as "nondecimal denominations" and are locked into the euro at permanent conversion rates. The national monies are scheduled to be out of circulation altogether by 2002.

Up until the year 2001, the U.S. dollar continued to be a key currency. The following is a list of the advantages of being a key currency:

1. Convenience for U.S. citizens who deal in dollars.
2. Increased business for U.S. banks and other financial institutions because of the comparative advantage of dealing in dollars.
3. Seignorage. Others hold dollars abroad and the United States has the use of their money without paying interest. Using the interest rate on Treasury bills multiplied by foreign dollar holdings of $265 billion in mid-1998, seignorage would equal $13 billion annually, according to the *Economic Report* of 1999.
4. Power and prestige.
5. Ability to borrow in international markets with U.S. dollars and to finance the current account deficit in the same way.

The disadvantages are:

1. Instability of demand for dollar currency and greater difficulty in controlling U.S. money stocks.
2. Increase in average demand for dollars tends to raise the dollar exchange rate and reduce the competitiveness of U.S. exports.

The United States is larger than the 11 countries of the EMU, but if Denmark, Greece, Sweden, and the United Kingdom join them, the two currency areas would be very close in size. The report points out that the long-run well-being of a country does not depend on its money being used as an international currency. Economic welfare is determined by a country's ability to produce goods and services in response to demand, to increase real income and consumption opportunities at home, and to employ sound economic policies (Council of Economic Advisers 1999: 299–305).

The *Economic Report of the President February 2000* (Council of Economic Advisers 2000) named the policies that would enhance the prosperity and welfare of the United States in the world economy. The policies are (1) encourage a skilled and adaptable labor force, (2) construct an economic system in which innovation is rewarded, and (3) build a financial system which is strong and vigorous (p. 37).

INTERNATIONAL FINANCIAL CRISES

One of the most recent international financial crises occurred in Asia. Timothy Lane (1999) stated the problems succinctly in *Finance and Development*. The main ingredients of the Asian crisis in the countries affected were: (1) lack of adequate hedging on the part of institutions who borrowed in foreign currencies, (2) assets were long term while a great deal of debt was short term, (3) prices in equity and real estate markets had strong rises before the crisis, and (4) credit was frequently poorly allocated.

The financial system was weak before the crisis because of inept supervision and regulation. The crisis was affected as it continued by market contagion while neither official financing of the IMF nor the central bank's international reserve positions were adequate. On the fiscal side, policy responses did not adapt well to changing macroeconomic conditions and questions arose about the optimal pace and sequencing of reforms that were introduced. Lawrence A. Summers, Secretary of the Treasury at the time, has studied several international crises that occurred during the 1990s and gives his assessment of the global financial happenings in the *American Economic Review* (Summers 2000). He writes, financial intermediation represents 7 percent of GNP. The six major financial crises during the 1990s were in Mexico, 1995; Indonesia, South Korea, and Thailand, 1997–1998; Russia, 1998; and Brazil, 1998–1999. The similar elements of each crisis were a large decline in real output, an extreme swing in the current account, and a large real depreciation. Summers believes that the underpinning for decisions to withdraw capital from a country rest on a change in investors' sentiments as the economic fundamentals of the country weaken. In turn, international contagion may come about via several routes (i.e., common primary goods price shocks, transfer of price and income shocks through trade linkages and financial linkages, competitors' devaluation, market illiquidity, investors' irrationality in transferring perceptions, and expectations about one country to another).

From Summers' study of the six countries and their crises, he concludes with four commonalities:

1. Financial and banking sector weaknesses were evident;
2. Monetary policy did not support fixed exchange rate regimes;
3. Inadequate monetary, fiscal, and international policies; and
4. Large, short-term government or private sector liabilities appeared in national balance sheets.

Summers claims that the single most important innovation affecting the U.S. capital market was the adoption of GAAP. The transparency inherent in the GAAP encourages efficient market responses to change, and it promotes stability. It is a useful means of fostering self-regulation (Summers 2000: 7–13).

In the same issue of the *American Economic Review*, Bong-Chan Kho, Ding Lee, and René M. Stulz discuss "U.S. Banks, Crises and Bailouts: From Mexico to LTCM." They state that the stability of the global financial system in the 1990s has been recognized suddenly to be highly dependent on the happenings in emerging markets. The information became clear with the huge bailouts conducted for Mexico, Korea, and Brazil, who each received $40 billion in aid. Indonesia, Russia, and Thailand received aid somewhere between $10 and $40 billion each (Kho, Lee, and Stulz 2000: 28–31).

The Council of Economic Advisers, in its 1999 *Economic Report*, appeared to agree but stressed inadequate financial practices in some countries and the economic weakness of a major world nation, Japan. Financial liberalization in industrial and developing economies has encouraged greater capital flows among countries. The report emphasizes that there has been a dramatic expansion of international financial markets in the volume of trading in foreign exchange. The Bank for International Settlements (BIS), a central banker's bank, released preliminary figures on foreign exchange trading in the 1990s for 46 foreign exchange markets. Between April 1995 and April 1998, trading in foreign exchange in current dollar terms grew 26 percent. During the period from 1992 to 1995, it had grown by 45 percent. Foreign exchange trading is almost 60 times as large as trading in goods and services. Per day, the volume of foreign exchange trading in 1999 was $1.5 trillion while the volume of exports of goods and services was almost $25 billion per day.

Trading tends to occur in a few major centers. The largest volume of foreign exchange transactions takes place in London with its share of world turnover at 32 percent and average daily volume of $637 billion. New York is the major center in the Western Hemisphere with 18 percent of world turnover or about $351 billion per day. Tokyo is the major center for Asia, although Singapore is very close behind. Tokyo has 8 percent of world transactions with daily transactions of $149 billion; Singapore handles daily transactions of $139 billion. The trading is mainly in derivatives rather than spot trading. It is done by professional traders at banks and financial institutions. Very little of the trading involves importers or exporters of goods and services (Council of Economic Advisers 1999: 224).

Currency and debt crises in the past, such as in the Latin American countries in the 1980s, suffered from characteristics of a large public debt, large public deficits, slow economic growth, and low investment and saving rates. On the contrary, in Asia, these macroeconomic imbalances did not exist, although the Asian countries did have some severe structural distortions and institutional weaknesses. According to the CEA, some economists claimed the crisis was an irrational event, something like a panic attack which was abetted by hot money and jittery international investors.

Among the bad financial practices prevalent in Asia at the time were connected lending, corrupt credit practices, weak regulation, and supervision of banking systems. The belief that government would bail out financial institutions in trouble engendered moral hazard. If economic participants are covered by some form of insurance, they tend to pursue riskier behavior than otherwise (Council of Economic Advisers 1999: 238).

Then there was a lending boom, and overinvestment occurred in some sectors, especially in real estate. In individual countries, there was growth of nonbank finance companies who borrowed excessively, extraordinary investment in large conglomerates, and credit directed to privileged companies and sectors, often in foreign currency terms. As investment rose, so did current account deficits which were financed by short-term foreign currency denominated in unhedged liabilities by the banking system. The combined problems of exchange rates linked to the dollars as the dollar appreciated, relatively fixed exchange rates, a slowdown in export growth, and stagnation of the Japanese economy contributed along with other factors to the Asian crisis in 1997.

There was a sharp reversal of capital flows to the area to a net outflow of $1 billion for the year for five countries: Indonesia, Korea, Malaysia, Phillipines, and Thailand, after inflows of $90 billion per year. The change represented approximately 10 percent of the total GDPs of the Asian countries. In that same year, the IMF, the World Bank, the Asian Development Bank, and the G-7 countries took action to curb any further spread of the financial crisis. Financial stabilization packages were recommended and the IMF insisted on major economic reforms, including restructuring of the banking system, fiscal discipline, and high interest rates to stem capital outflows and other currency problems as a condition for its lending of funds (Council of Economic Advisers 1999: 237–245).

The restrictions were modified as the occasion arose, and some financial stability was evident by 1998. Nevertheless, there has been sharp criticism of the IMF approach to the Asian crisis. Some of these are: (1) it intrudes into domestic affairs not within the sphere of macroeconomic issues, (2) its requirements with respect to high interest rates stifles growth, (3) overly strict rules concerning fiscal policy that insist on little or no budget deficits, and (4) the rescue packages induce moral hazard.

Unfortunately, the Asian crisis was made worse by the economic weakness of of the world's second largest economy, Japan. Banking problems, large-scale lending to other Asian economies, high consumption taxes, decline in exports, all contributed to its domestic difficulties and, in turn, to the rest of the Asian region (Council of Economic Advisers 1999: 245–249).

A GLOBAL FINANCIAL SYSTEM

The "new international financial architecture" was the name given to reforms proposed under U.S. leadership to reconstruct the international financial system and reduce the possibility of future crises. There was a meeting in Washington of the group of 22 nations (G-22) on 16 April 1998, which resulted in a report calling for greater transparency on the part of the private sector, national, and international institutions. Countries must provide sufficient information to all concerned about financial and macroeconomic conditions prevailing (Council of Economic Advisers 1999: 267–270).

Officials of other national financial entities have commented on the global financial situation. Hans Tietmeyer, president of Deutsche Bundesbank from 1993 to 1999, has stressed that action is needed to improve assessment of global vulnerabilities with the aid of better information channels for those involved directly as well as for national and international regulatory bodies. More attention should be given to in-house risk management together with the establishment, as called for, of international standards and practices. The improvements to the world financial system that are required, according to Tietmeyer, consist of greater efforts to identify possible vulnerabilities in national and international financial systems, development of better procedures and standards for financial stability of major institutions and authorities, closer integration of emerging markets into the systems, and the maintenance of a continuous flow of information among all parties concerned with financial stability (Tietmeyer 1999: 20–23).

In June 2000, the four largest banks in the world (by total assets) were: (1) Fuji/Industrial Bank of Japan (IBJ)/Dai-Ichi Kangyo Bank (DKB), (2) Sanwa/Ashai/Tokai, (3) Sumitomo/Sakura, and (4) Deutsche Bank. The largest U.S. bank, Citigroup, Inc., is seventh on the list. Recent years have seen the consolidation of banks within and across national borders as industrial countries moved into emerging market countries. There have been developments in technology, particularly Internet banking; alliances between major banks and telecommunication conglomerates; and the universalization of banking, which continues to blur the limits of banking and nonbanking financial services. The repeal of the Glass-Steagall Act in 1999, which separated commercial from investment banks and restricted banks' participation in equity financing, is part of the trend. These developments bring up issues with respect to supervisory policy. Issues that concern the appropriate management of risk; the liquidity support, if any, for distressed banks or relevant markets; and the supervisory body for banks with worldwide operations must be considered.

The Basle Committee on Banking Supervision's 1988 capital adequacy recommendations are deficient in dealing with these matters and a number of solutions have been proposed, but none are completely satisfactory. International agencies including the Basle Committee, the IMF, the World Bank, and the Bank for International Settlements have attempted to aid and complement the work of national agencies in dealing with financial sectors at home and abroad. They have begun developing guidelines, standards, and institutions to address cross-country institutional problems. The IMF and the World Bank have set up the Financial Stability Assessment Process (FSAP), which investigates the stability of financial sectors in member countries that have volunteered to participate. In addition, the Basle Core Principles for Effective Banking Supervision have served as an important basis for the search for improved worldwide banking supervision. Another agency, created in 1999, the Financial Stability Forum, composed of national and international agencies, is dedicated to disseminating information and furthering international cooperation through general supervision and observation to achieve international financial stability. The various agencies will need to discuss the issues of deposit insurance and lender-of-last-resort arrangements.

Curzo Giannini has written about the lender-of-last-resort function as it operated in the nineteenth century. At the time of Walter Bagehot in the 1800s there was the gold standard, severe restrictions on the currency supply; and London, the financial center of the world, contained a small, tightly knit group of financial institutions. The Bagehot doctrine, therefore, called for getting rid of any institution in poor financial health and lending generously to any institution which could furnish good collateral and pay a penalty rate (Giannini 1999: 24–27).

In the same issue of *Finance and Development* Alexander Swoboda comments that the key issues in reform of the international monetary and financial system begin with exchange rates in both industrial and developing countries. The present international currencies—the dollar, the yen, and the euro—have all been subject to a high degree of volatility. Other issues concern the boom-bust nature of capital flows to developing nations, the instability of capital flows generally, and the massive adjustments in current accounts necessary in the face of financial crises. The final issue discussed at the IMF's Research Department's Conference in May 1999 had to do with the role of the IMF in furnishing finances and advice (Swoboda 1999: 2–4). In May 2000, Michael Woodford expressed still another aspect of the problems with respect to the policies of central bankers. Some central banks have adopted procedures in which they concentrate unduly upon forward-looking policies based solely on the present state of the world. They make inflation forecasts with an economic model that generates conditional future paths for target variables, and then they evaluate them according to some selected criteria. On the contrary, Woodford claims, optimal monetary policy must take history into account (Woodford 2000: 100–104).

The original core principles developed by the Basle Committee for Banking Supervision were formulated in 1988 for the use of its members. The Committee had been established by the central bank governors of the Group of 10 countries in 1975. The countries include G-7: Canada, France, Germany, Italy, Japan, United Kingdom, and the United States; plus Belgium, Netherlands, Sweden, and Switzerland. Actually, there are 11 countries rather than 10. Luxembourg has participated in their meetings, which usually take place at the Bank for International Settlements in Basle, Switzerland, where the committees' secretariat is located.

There are 25 basic principles for an effective supervisory system. They fall into seven classifications, namely, preconditions for effective banking supervision, prudential requirements and regulations, procedures of banking supervision, structure and licensing, information requirements, formal supervisory powers, and cross-border banking. The core principles, as stated in the initial document and explained in a compendium that is to be updated periodically, are meant to be minimum requirements. In July 1999, another consultative document was issued describing some ways that the agreement might be improved. The suggested framework stressed three aspects of supervision: developing better calculations of capital adequacy, establishing a process of supervisory review, and greater use of market discipline (Karacadag and Taylor 2000: 50–53). Other individuals concerned with the improvement of the world financial structure argue that the institutions involved should not be limited to banks. Martin Mayer conveys the message in a brief prepared for the Jerome Levy Institute of Bard College in 1999. He writes, the Asian crisis has revealed that there is a shift in the world financial system to capital markets and away from banks. In the United States, approximately 20 percent of commercial lending is funded by banks while, in emerging markets, the figures are probably closer to 80 percent. It is likely that in Europe, banks are still the most important commercial lenders. In the future, markets will take over in countries besides the United States as it is recognized that they are more efficient in their pricing. In the market, all information is rapidly translated into price without costly research and calculation necessary for bank operations. Mayer recommends several regulations to stem future crises, such as collective action of central banks to adopt reserve requirements to limit off-shore deposit creation; capital requirements for trading in derivatives; and continuously maintained margins on each contract.

Moreover, Mayer suggests that authorities will need to observe certain conditions at the outset: (1) laws enable markets to function, not the reverse; (2) supervisors will be better able to oversee lenders than borrowers through capital and margin requirements, and soon, together with international standards for accounting and banking supervision; (3) in addition to transparency rules and fair dealing, supervisors should furnish guidelines for banks' self-testing of their financial condition; and (4) governments should insist on private sector preparedness for possible financial crises (Mayer 1999: 41–46).

The U.S. government has been deeply concerned with the concepts involved and the actual structure of a new international financial system. In 1998, Congress established the International Financial Institution Advisor Commission (IFIAC) as part of legislation authorizing $18 billion of additional U.S. funding for the IMF. The purpose of the commission was to recommend future U.S. policy toward seven international institutions: the African Development Bank, the Asian Development Bank, the Bank for International Settlements, the Inter-American Development Bank, the World Bank Group, the IMF and the WTO.

In the report of the Commission, it finds fault with the present system of crisis management. The actions of the IMF are singled out along with the World Bank as particularly in need of improvement. The IMF's "system of short term crisis management is too costly, its responses too slow, its advice often incorrect, and its efforts to influence policy and practice too intrusive" (IFIAC 2000: 5–6).

The Commission recommends that performance of all seven institutions would improve if each institution had formulated a narrower, clear-cut set of objectives. Furthermore, their operations should be changed to lessen the opportunity for corruption in receiving countries. The Commission report proceeds to identify suggestions specific to each institution.

With respect to the IMF, the Commission strongly states that it should not lend for long-term development assistance or for long-term structural transformation. It should confine its operations to serve as "quasi lender of last resort to emerging countries" with all lending operations limited to provision of short-term funds. There could be preconditions for the lending to establish financial soundness and, in this way, there would be no need "for detailed conditionality that has burdened IMF programs in recent years and made such programs unwieldy, highly conflictive, time consuming to negotiate, and often ineffectual" (IFIAC 2000: 7). Conditionality, according to the *Routledge Dictionary of Economics* (Rutherford 1992), is lending to a debtor on condition that the loan be used for a specific purpose so that there is less risk of default in servicing the loan (p. 88).

The World Bank and the Development Banks receive even sharper criticism in the report. Their offices and their work tend to duplicate one another in various cities and open the door to potential conflict in the regions. Further, the World Bank claims to give assistance to those countries most in need because of poverty and inadequate private sector resources. A statement in the report declares that 11 countries that enjoy substantial access to private sector assistance receive 70 percent of World Bank nonaid resources.

The several recommendations for the World Bank Group include greater emphasis on performance and project evaluation for the World Bank, and greater emphasis on technical assistance and encouragement of an increased flow of private sector resources to emerging countries for the Development Banks. As their common goal should be to reduce poverty, their individual financial efforts should be directed to the 80 or 90 poorest countries of the world that do not have access to capital markets (IFIAC 2000: 10). All of the international organizations discussed in the IFIAC report, also known as the Meltzer Commission report, are included in the United Nations system either directly or through cooperative agreements.

CONCLUDING COMMENTS

Adoption of the dollar as another nation's currency, in addition to its service as an international currency, is hazardous. The United States is strong economically but such actions by other countries impinge on its continued good health. It is a pity that the United States has not made a stronger commitment to participation in the activities of the United Nations. Nations acting in concert can maintain sovereignty by observing each other's individual rights. Too much reliance upon rules and regulations for capital requirements, for example, without an open forum to express needs, capabilities, resources, and aspirations, is shortsighted. A country needs the momentum and confidence gained through its own efforts. The shift to capital markets and the resulting market discipline can set the stage for that event. International standards for accounting and banking supervision, transparency, and financial self-testing will accomplish more than international financial institutions, monolithic banks, and complicated crisis management techniques. Continued economic aid, information, and technical assistance to emerging nations should be part of the agenda.

Chapter 12

Megamicroeconomics and Global Federalism

There are many ways in which the world is shared. This chapter is concerned with fundamental economic, political, and social issues that confront individuals and institutions of the nearly 200 nations which inhabit the world. Major issues are: the need for government intervention to assure the provision of public goods, and the correction of externalities. Economic growth, methods of voting to reveal the preferences of individuals and countries, the dissemination of information, and the methods of communication are other topics discussed. The form and extent of government intervention and how it is paid for are briefly outlined. Larger emphasis is placed on the advantages of international trade to all nations and the growing significance of supragovernmental coordination, cooperation, and guidance.

THE CASE FOR GOVERNMENT INTERVENTION: PUBLIC GOODS

The proper grounds for government actions were all-important to John Stuart Mill. He was a firm believer in laissez-faire and is quoted in Ekelund and Hébert's *A History of Economic Thought and Method* as remarking that any move toward government intervention "unless required by some great good, is a certain evil" (1990: 189).

Adam Smith, in his enumeration of the duties of government, or the sovereign, included three necessary expenditures: (1) that of defending society from invasion and violence from other societies, (2) that of affording protection to each individual in the society from others who might be unjust or try to oppress them, and (3) that of erecting and maintaining those public institutions and public works which are vital to a society but will never repay the expense incurred by a few individuals providing it. There are two kinds of expenses involved in the last duty Smith mentions: providing for the facilitation of commerce, and the promotion of instruction for people of all ages. These matters are explained in Book V, "Of the Revenue of the Sovereign or Commonwealth."

Other remarks made in Chapter 1 of Book V refer to abuses at the local level as often appearing enormous; but they are small in comparison to those which take place in the central government's administration. It is easier to correct such difficulties at the lower level of government (Smith 1776/1976: Book V, 249–253).

Two hundred years later, Aaron Wildavsky (1975) made the distinction between urban and central government in terms of their budgets. He found that in cities, where budgets are constrained to expenditures equaling revenues, or a balanced budget, revenue controls expenditures. There is little concern for varying resource allocation because of the limited resources available at the outset. Budgeting is a matter of maintaining past policies while keeping within the limits of revenue raised. If there is additional revenue, increases are usually made proportionally in all directions. The city, however, is usually working in a "constant sum game" as the total pie is fixed. An increase in one agency's expenditures necessarily means a decrease for one or more other agencies.

The federal government did not have tight revenue constraints at the time of Aaron Wildavsky's writing in the 1970s. An increase in one agency's spending did not reduce funds available to others. Because the whole central budget is considerably larger than that of the lower level of government, small changes in expenditures or revenues had a lesser impact on budget processes. Another difference between the two levels of government, at the time, was that many county services were not under the control of the city, such as the Board of Education and the Housing Authority, and therefore did not appear in the city budget. Most expenditures for the federal government include all its activities, claimed Wildavsky. Also, there are differences in the purposes of federal as opposed to municipal spending. Federal spending involves a good deal of income redistribution in the form of welfare or health expenditures, and so forth. City governments tend to provide salaries such as for fire, police, and sanitation. Salaries may take up to 80 percent of city expenditures. The city manager is preoccupied with meeting the payroll rather than allocating the city's resources among competing uses. The municipal government is supply-oriented as result, while the federal government, with its elastic source of revenue, tends to be more demand-concentrated.

The Congress can manipulate the federal debt but the municipality has no such option. The executive predominates at the local level because he is responsible for maintaining the balanced budget. At the national level, the legislature has the opportunity to reshape the budget because federal revenue and expenditures can vary independently of one another. Wildavsky explains that in the city's search for additional revenue, it will frequently participate in programs that have no reason for existence except to generate income. The relative poverty of cities, argues Wildavsky, will lead cities to behave as developing countries do when costs rise and/or revenues decline. He likens the situation of municipal government to a situation in which (1) Congress passes an amendment to the Constitution requiring a balanced budget, (2) the United Nations receives and spends revenue from income taxes, (3) the U.S. government is permitted to levy taxes on property and sales only, and (4) congressional salaries and staff are eliminated. The result of this hypothetical scenario would be to place the federal government in the same constrained condition as city governments. In these surroundings, the federal government or any other central government would budget in the same way as the low-income countries (Wildavsky 1975: 131–135).

Adam Smith continues in Book V by saying that payment for defense and justice is defrayed from general revenues, as all of society benefits. Justice, where the benefit is local, should have expenses paid by that segment of society. Education benefits all of society and/or some of it. A case can be made for the expenses to be paid at either level (Smith 1776/1976: Book V, 241–244). Araine-Jules-Emile-Juvenal Dupuit, an award-winning engineer in the French Department of Sarthe who received the Legion of Honor in 1843, was concerned with measuring the benefits of the public goods which Adam Smith described. He directed his problem-solving mentality toward the measurement of public utility, or the social welfare, contributed by public goods and services. Dupuit discussed and constructed diagrams expressing the concepts of marginal utility, consumer surplus, price discrimination, and profit maximization as they related to individuals and firms, including monopolies and the public sector. The marginal utility function was used to develop a general rule for the provision of public goods. The provision of public goods should be provided by government if the total annual cost of the goods could be met while producing some "net utility." Alternatively, marginal yearly receipts should cover marginal costs, including capital costs, amortized for a specific number of years.

Dupuit expected that government would want to maximize consumers' surplus under a full cost constraint. As an allocative criterion, a single price could achieve an efficient outcome, but there were instances when a government-operated monopoly might use a policy of price discrimination.

Alfred Marshall explained consumer's surplus as the extra amount over what a person pays that he/she would be willing to pay rather than go without it (Ekelund and Hébert 1990: 298–310, 395). The concept may work on an individual basis, but trying to generate a social welfare function by the addition of consumer's surplus when they are not equivalent in utility terms is, at best, frustrating.

The question of who should pay for the public goods that Adam Smith enumerates is closely related to determining value in the private and public sectors of the economy. Friedrich Von Wieser, an Austrian economist, tried to explain the differences in his work *Natural Value*, originally published in 1893. He argued that value in the national economy tends to be subjective because of its far-reaching aspects and its considerations of the general interests. Because of the concern with public interests, it will be politicians who decide the value attached to a public good, not economists. Nevertheless, the estimates by economists are important as a measuring rod of the divergence between economic costs and the subjective valuations made in the public sector (Meyer 1969: 75). Friedrich Von Wieser's welfare theory recognized the need for labor unions as a defensive instrument against large monopoly and monopsony structures long before John Kenneth Galbraith spoke of "countervailing power." Wieser suggested that government could increase economic welfare through regulations and/or control of firms with market power. Social goods or public goods, such as railroads and canals, should be undertaken by government and Wieser described a cost-benefit analysis that included the utility generated by externalities in the private sector. In these cases, he argued, the market can give false signals so that the state should look for projects yielding high total utility to either subsidize or operate them.

With respect to taxation, a rationale for the progressive type on income could be made on the basis of the concept of diminishing marginal utility. However, all income and property inequalities should not be eliminated through government taxation. "To go beyond a progressive tax on income—say, progressive wealth or property taxes—would violate the private spirit of Wieser's social economy" (Ekelund and Hébert 1990: 340).

GOVERNMENT INTERVENTION AND EXTERNALITIES

One of the most important grounds for government intervention is that of externalities. The concern over global warming, acid rain, clean air, and clean water are some of the more recent examples of the concept. An externality means a benefit or a cost to someone or a group who was not part of the original transaction. It is outside or external to the market. An externality is negative when a person or group who is hurt, loses utility or profit, or incurs a cost through no actions of his/her own. A positive externality affects a person or group by raising utility, profit, or lowering costs. The negative externality is frequently illustrated by the example of a factory, located on a river, which dumps refuse into the water and the polluted water prevents the community downstream from swimming or depletes the fish catch that otherwise would be available. Often, such problems arise because of nonassignment of property rights. The factory does not pay for its use of the water. The event is described analytically as a divergence between social marginal costs and private marginal costs. In the 1930s, A. C. Pigou, a British economist, proposed the solution: to impose a tax on the firm so that private marginal costs rise with the additional levy to equal social marginal costs.

The case of a positive externality, such as education of one or a few individuals, not only offers personal benefits but results in a social benefit to the community as a more educated community leads to an improved neighborhood environment and more enlightened citizens. The positive externality represents the divergence between social marginal benefits and private marginal benefits. Arthur C. Pigou and Alfred Marshall's method of correcting this situation would be to grant a subsidy to the private party. Government actions, whether through the tax or the subsidy method, change the allocation of society's resources by reducing output under the tax provision or increasing output in the case of the subsidy. An alternative solution, originated by Ronald Coase and named the "Coase theorem," states that certain expenditures can be corrected by bargaining between the parties involved. If this is possible, government actions may not be required (Coase 1960: 1–44).

Environmental issues are probably the most outstanding examples of the problems which arise in dealing with externalities. The EPA has estimated that the cost of complying with U.S. environmental policies is higher as a fraction of GNP than in any other area of the world, with the possible exception of West Germany. The United States is estimated to spend over $24 billion in FY 2001 to protect environment, conserve resources, provide recreational opportunities, manage federal land, and construct and operate water projects. Of these monies, the EPA will receive $7.3 billion in discretionary funds. According to Frances Cairncross, it is not clear that the environmental benefits achieved will exceed their cost. After a 10-year study on acid rain, it was found that it did less damage than was previously estimated. Similarly, the benefits of the Clean Air Act appear to be exaggerated in comparison with their costs (Cairncross 1992: 60–61).

The problems of measurement are serious ones in environmental issues because of the need: (1) to value human life, (2) to value the damage done by pollution, (3) to value the benefits derived from reducing pollution, and (4) to value the costs of regulation or other corrective method, and many other related issues equally difficult to compute. Cairncross suggests that public perceptions of environmental risk could be altered by greater accessibility to more and better educational materials. He states that "People have to understand that some environmental goals must come before others" (Cairncross 1992: 61).

Kenneth Arrow has raised doubts about the way economists calculate environmental impacts ("Three Nobel Laureates" 2000). He was disappointed in large econometric models. It was not possible to deal with detailed models of an interactive system satisfactorily. Economic planning in nonsocialist countries in Western Europe and developing nations was not successful overall, but it was useful for specific projects. Projects for climate change and environmental problems using cost-benefit analysis did have value for planning purposes. However, public policy recommendations often do not take full account of the size of potential errors.

ECONOMIC GROWTH AND SOCIAL AND POLITICAL INSTITUTIONS

In the same article, Robert M. Solow expresses his dismay at the snail's pace with which economists are expanding knowledge about economic growth. According to Solow, Nobel Memorial Prize recipient in 1987, we have not learned much in the last 20 to 25 years concerning what makes countries grow. Encouraging innovation and developing human capital are the recommendations to make, and they could have been made almost 30 years ago. There are disappointments with some new techniques such as game theory and large econometric models, neither of which have lived up to expectations ("Three Nobel Laureates" 2000: 6–31).

Another viewpoint on the success of game theory as a technique for economic analysis has been presented by Roger B. Myerson in the *Journal of Economic Literature* (1999). He mentions that the early game theorists included Cournot, Edgeworth, Bohm-Bawerk, and Zeuthen. In more recent times, the work of John Von Neumann, the mathematician, and Oskar Morgenstern, the economist, in the *Theory of Games and Economic Behavior* (published by Princeton University Press in 1943), actually laid the groundwork for the significant contribution of John F. Nash. Noncooperative game theory became an alternative to price theory as an analytical method of economic analysis.

Roger B. Myerson's essay attests that Nash's theory of noncooperative games should be recognized as one of the outstanding achievements of the twentieth century. In a paper, "Equilibrium Points in n-Person Games," part of the *Proceedings of the National Academy of Science USA* (1950) which was originally a two-page note received from Nash on 16 November 1949, he explains equilibrium in a noncooperative game as a function of each player's strategy. Given this strategy, each perfectly rational player attempts to maximize his expected utility payoff against the given strategy of each of the others in the game. A Nash equilibrium is reached when it is possible to predict the behavior of all the players. In the event that the conditions of Nash equilibrium are not fulfilled by the predicted behavioral patterns, then the welfare of at least one player can be increased. One or more players can be retrained to better follow his/her self-interest without resort to other social change. In this way, Nash opened the door to the use of game theory for critical analysis of the incentives in problems of cooperation and conflict for most types of social institutions (Myerson 1999: 1067–1082).

Concerning economic growth, the poor performance of transition economies is an example of the boundaries of present knowledge. The transition economies are 75 countries in eastern and central Europe, the Baltics, Russia, and the other countries of the former Soviet Union ranging alphabetically from Albania to Uzbekistan. Initially, output fell in all the countries by more than 40 percent on average from the beginning of the reforms in 1990 throughout the decade. However, by 1999, output was growing again. At the outset, all the countries suffered or were threatened by inflation. At the start of 1993, every country, except Turkministan, was utilizing stabilization policies. They were successful in that inflation, which had been raging in double-digit numbers or worse, dropped to single digits in about a dozen of the countries. Choice of exchange rate played an important part in the stabilization strategies chosen. Russia and the other countries in the former Soviet Union selected fixed exchange rates, while the balance of the former republics linked their currencies to the Deutsche mark or the U.S. dollar. As inflation rates dropped in the 25 countries by the year 2000, 21 of them have adopted flexible exchange rates.

Fiscal balances declined sharply at the beginning of the transitions with large revenue declines and some expenditure cuts made. In 2000, every one of the countries was heavily in debt. Each of them will have difficulty in living with large deficits if reforms and growth do not rapidly proceed (Fischer and Sahay 2000: 2–6).

Amartya Sen, Nobel Memorial Prize winner in 1998, addressed the concerns of emerging countries and growth from a microeconomic viewpoint. In his studies of famines and his experiences as a boy in Bengal at a time when 2 million to 3 million people died of famine, he has learned that the food supply had not been reduced much; the problem was unemployment and loss of income. The political problem was that the leaders of the country did nothing about it because they were not affected. Famine has not occurred in a democratic country, whether rich or poor, because there are too many to criticize the government and the danger of losing elections is too strong.

Sen argues that a democracy advances development by providing economic security and protection for the vulnerable, providing political incentives, which means defining needs in terms of what is feasible and, lastly, providing free exchange of political and social viewpoints among individuals ("Three Nobel Laureates" 2000: 6–31). János Kornai (2000b), in an article in the *Journal of Economic Perspectives*, stresses the importance of democratic conditions, even though it may come with the advantages and disadvantages of the capitalist system. He argues that a necessary condition of democracy is capitalism. Democracy is desirable because it promotes material welfare and economic growth as well as its major value of securing political freedom and preventing dictatorship. A workable democracy is one in which government can be dismissed in an orderly fashion; there are electoral procedures confirmed by laws and conventions to implement the process; the political power is free of monopoly or coercive force, and political freedoms are guaranteed in law and practice.

Vladimir Ilyich Lenin declared how the decision between capitalism and socialism would be made in 1918. According to Kornai, Lenin said it would be decided upon the basis of which system could acquire higher productivity. The collapse of the Soviet Union, which began in 1989–1990, the comparisons of East and West Germany and South and North Korea among others, all demonstrated that the socialist system had not been able to achieve the performance levels of the capitalist countries.

Now, the former socialist countries are faced with the problems of the transition to capitalism. The major ones are the low efficiency and backwardness of their initial conditions, acquisition of capitalism's shortcomings such as unemployment and inequality of income distribution, the weakness of the existing supply structure, and the mistakes and misdemeanors of all government officials in any economic or political system (Kornai 2000b: 27–42). Other nations in transition, like Estonia, are working very hard to be eligible for admission to the European Union and to participate in the EMU. Estonia has been privatizing and restructuring the business sector along with liberalizing prices and deregulating where necessary. However, before Estonia can become a member of the European Union (EU), it will be necessary to fulfill some conditions set by the European Council at its summit meeting in Copenhagen in 1993.

The Copenhagen criteria are meant to determine a country's progress toward the economic and political standards of the European Union. They consist of (1) demonstrating the presence of stable institutions such as democratic government, human rights, rule of law, and protection of minorities; (2) demonstrating an existing market economy strong enough to vie with market forces within the European Union, and (3) the capability of accepting the obligations of membership which entail recognition of the goals of economic, political, and monetary union (Weber and Taube 2000: 28–31).

Nilesh Dattani, in a book chapter entitled "Economic and Monetary Union," has noted that the primary objective of the European System of Central Banks and the European Central Bank, according to the Treaty of Maastricht, is price stability. In order to qualify for the EMU, the Maastricht treaty provides for five convergence conditions to be exhibited by a country to be eligible for admission to the final stage:

1. A country's inflation rate should not exceed 1.5 percent of the average of the inflation rates prevailing in the three best performing EU countries.

2. A country's interest rates on long-term government securities should not be more than 3.0 percent above the average of interest rates on similar securities in the three EU countries with the lowest inflation rates.

3. Three percent of GDP is the maximum allowable national budget deficit.
4. Sixty percent of GDP is the maximum allowable public debt.
5. A country's currency should have remained within the normal band of the Exchange Rate Mechanism (ERM) of the European Monetary System (EMS) for two years without an attempt to devalue its currency.

Dattani reports that these criteria have been supplemented in the years following by other "real" convergence conditions with respect to such items as the unemployment rate, output and growth, and current account balances. No matter what the economic prescriptions may be, Dattani points out that monetary unions have usually followed political integration of states, not the reverse. Besides, this is the first time that a major currency has been created without an issuing state behind it (Dattani 1997: 201–223).

Within twentieth-century capitalism in the United States, other pressures have led to new perceptions and actions with respect to the role of individuals and economic growth. Richard A. Easterlin sees a revolution in the human condition that is "sweeping the world." Besides enjoying longer lives, being healthier and better educated, human beings are changing their careers and political democracy has become more important to women. There is no doubt that women's roles have changed enormously, claims Easterlin. There have been increases in life expectancy at birth, in literacy, and continuous growth in the standard of living. However, there are large differences in rates of growth and the dimensions of improvements across countries. It is not possible to rely on mechanical extrapolation of past trends to predict the future pattern of economic growth. Economics needs to return to the study of history to gain more knowledge concerning how the world of the twenty-first century came to be (Easterlin 2000: 7–26).

PUBLIC CHOICE AND VOTING TECHNIQUES

There have been several other economists who recognized the need for government intervention for certain goods and activities but constituted their inquiries more formally. The theory of public choice is a study of the supply and demand for public goods. Its foundations were laid in the early years of classical economic theory when the field was known as "political economy." Its more recent U.S. revival began in the 1930s and owes a great deal to the works of Knut Wicksell, a Swedish economist. He explained the dual nature of the public economy by tying the expenditures for public goods and the taxpayers' costs together in the decision-making process. Wicksell's essay on "A New Principle of Just Taxation" (1896) reminded economists that public sector decisions are made through the political process. Erik Lindahl, in 1919, offered an analytical solution to the problem of the distribution of tax shares for a given public good in his book *Die Gerechtigkeit der Besteuerung*. The section called "Just Taxation—A Positive Solution" resolved the tax price of the collective good as being equal to the marginal utility or valuation placed on that good by the voter. However, Lindahl recognized that the tax shares would be influenced by the relative political power of the participants.

It was Knut Wicksell who provided the impetus for further investigations in the field of public choice when he insisted that the only way to satisfy the conditions of efficiency and justice in a fiscal system was to require unanimity among all participants concerned in public sector decisions (Ekelund and Hébert 1990: 637–639).

In 1951, Kenneth Arrow, 1972 Nobel Memorial Prize recipient, wrote *Social Choice and Individual Values*, in which he scrutinized voting systems to find one that would fulfill his minimal conditions for social choices. He sought an approach that would accurately reflect the preferences of individual voters. Arrow found that no majority voting scheme could fulfill all the conditions at the same time. The finding, which became known as the "impossibility theorem," has been illustrated by a community of three voters with three issues to be decided. It is demonstrated, through voting for two policies at a time, that the outcome will vary depending on the order in which the policies are voted. In 1962, James Buchanan and Gordon Tullock developed the method of determining decision rules for collective action in the presence of uncertainty about an individual's future preferences in the *Calculus of Consent* (Musgrave and Musgrave 1989: 50–51; Oser and Brue 1988: 405–407).

A voting system, currently in use, illustrates the difficulties in attaining the goals of each participant. The present U.S. method of voting for the president is referred to as the electoral college system. It was chosen by the Constitutional Convention in the closing days of its operations in 1787. The method entitles each state to electors equal to its total number of representatives and senators in Congress. The electors are chosen by the state political parties based on their loyalty to their respective parties. They are, generally, legislators, governors, or party officials. Voters are casting ballots for the slates of electors, not the presidential or vice presidential nominees. Whichever slate wins the most popular votes is elected for that state. Once the popular vote system was established, after 1828 and after the Civil War for South Carolina, the practice of the states voting as a unit was introduced. Some states passed laws requiring their electors to vote as a bloc. Prior to that time, the state legislatures had selected the electors. It is customary in all states for the state's electors to vote for the candidate receiving a plurality or the candidate who receives the largest number of popular votes; 48 states require the entire electoral vote to go to that candidate. Voters in the presidential elections are voting for electors even though the only names which appear on the voting machine are the names of presidential candidates. A candidate must receive 270 out of a total number of electoral votes of 538 to be elected president by the electoral college. If no candidate receives a majority of the electoral votes for president, he is chosen by the House of Representatives using a procedure described in the Twelfth Amendment.

The advantages of the system are (1) it maintains the role of the states in an important decision-making process, and (2) it maintains the stability of the two-party system in view of the winner-take-all procedures in 48 states. Direct popular election, an alternative, would foster the growth of minority parties by making it more difficult for the major parties to win the necessary 40 percent of the popular vote. It would eliminate the role of the states in selecting the president (Volkomer 1997: 34, 138; Wright 1999: 125–126). For example, the existing system revealed that the winning presidential candidate in the 2000 election lost the popular vote but received a plurality in 30 of the 50 states in the Union.

Economists who looked at the supply side of the public choice problem studied the intricacies of government bureaucracy. Among them were Ludwig Von Mises, Gordon Tullock, and William A. Niskanen, Jr. Niskanen discussed the determination of bureaucratic output in *Bureaucracy and Representative Government* in 1971. In his interpretation on the supply side of public goods, the bureaucrat acts as budget maximizer (Meyer 1989a: 8; Musgrave and Musgrave 1989: 101–102; Rosen 1999: 136).

The outstanding model for some form of government intervention in the modern age is the introduction of the "New Economy" and the attendant surge of enormous growth in the amount of information made possible by, literally, lightning-speed communications. There is a vast potential, according to the *Economic Report of the President February 2000* (Council of Economic Advisers [CEA] 2000b), to raise the productivity and to increase the efficiency of firms with the new communications technologies such as the Internet. Among the things that the new information technology affects are the internal organization of firms, the way firms conduct their business, and the initiation of new distribution channels for wholesale transactions. These developments of information technology raise questions about the future structure of firms. Will firms expand to take advantage of economies of scope by selling many different products, or will it be more profitable for them to specialize to achieve economies of scale? Although the report does not say so, either choice would appear to lead to larger-size firms. The change in firm behavior directs attention to the need for a standard communications protocol so that networks can speak to one another. The CEA suggests that the following actions are needed: a commitment to policies that foster innovation; rules to protect property rights, especially intellectual property rights, by the development of international standards; increased support for research and development with emphasis on both technological and nontechnological advancements, in coordination with the private sector firms and research centers.

The *report* views government policy, generally, to be necessary to assure competition is maintained as a stimulus to economic growth. The section entitled "How Information Technology is Changing the Economy" closes with the comment that all members of society benefit from the new technologies. By wiring schools and public libraries, all members of society can have access to the new information technology and have the opportunities they need to develop skills and be a part of a vast information-based economy (CEA 2000b: 112–128).

In the private sector, Bill Gates (with Collins Hemingway) has explained the remarkable features of the Internet as an aspect of "friction-free capitalism." The concept relates to digital processes that can eliminate most of the friction in business transactions by removing middlemen. The Internet enables buyers and sellers to find one another more quickly. It offers buyers more information about products and services, and it provides sellers with more information about certain preferences and shopping patterns. Gates used the term "friction-free" capitalism to describe how the Internet had helped to create Adam Smith's ideal marketplace in which buyers and sellers locate each other easily without wasting much time or spending more money. The problems of markets are (1) finding an interested party, and (2) knowing the nature and quality of goods and services offered for sale. According to Gates, Internet markets change some basic trading practices. The Internet drives down the cost of transactions. Middlemen will be eliminated or must create new value. Few businesses will be able to have a low enough price to compete on that basis; therefore, emphasis will turn to customer service (Gates 1999: 444). What would David Ricardo or Karl Marx say in response to Gates' predictions?

However, Kenneth Arrow agrees that the most significant concept in economics in the last 30 years is the development of the importance of information and its dispersion. The economists' work in this area is called "asymmetric information theory," which deals with economic relationships such as contracts, price distortions, and small, personal interactions rather than markets ("Three Nobel Laureates" 2000: 6–31).

Not all economists maintain the viewpoint that increasing amounts of information and its speed of transmission have the potential of the great inventions of the past. Robert Gordon, in the *Journal of Economic Perspectives* (2000), states the "New Economy" is a huge success as well as a deep disappointment. His definition of the New Economy refers to the increasing rate of technical change in information technology and the introduction of the Internet after 1995. Productivity growth has been impressive in the durable manufacturing sector, which has had favorable repercussions in the rate of productivity growth in the economy and in the creation of great wealth in the stock market. Inflationary pressures have been held in check by these events while the unemployment rate declined over the past few years. Outside of durable manufacturing, trend growth in productivity has decelerated in 88 percent of the economy, claims Robert Gordon. He explains that the reason concerns the fixed endowment of human time as compared to the exponential growth of computer speed and memory. In other words, mainframe and personal computers have reached the point of diminishing returns.

The test that Gordon applied in evaluating the New Economy and the Internet was that they should add at least equal increments to the standard of living that previous great inventions had, such as the electric light, the automobile, or the airplane. But, says Gordon, the New Economy and the Internet added a much smaller increment than the former inventions achieved (Gordon 2000: 63–72). Five or six years does not appear to be sufficient time to permit all the ramifications of the new "inventions" to have worked their ways through the U.S. economy, much less that of the world.

TYPES OF GOVERNMENT INTERVENTION

Another aspect of the rationale for government intervention is the extent of that intervention, the level of government to undertake it, and the manner in which it is presented. For instance, the provision of social services is often said to require some government involvement. For those who prefer a minimum of public intrusion, regulation, subsidy, or a voucher system is recommended. When greater government control is preferred, ownership and/or management is the prescription. R. M. Blank (2000) describes the framework in which the decision is frequently made. Decisions will reflect the individual's opinion on such topics as (1) the recipient's capacity to make effective decisions and the government's ability to improve on individual choices, (2) the degree to which quality of the service is measurable in the private market, (3) the emphasis placed on universal standards of service, and (4) the degree of trust in the effectiveness and efficiency of the public sector (Blank 2000: C48–C49).

The federal government has been aware of the necessity for private and public sector contributions to the issues concerning the provision of goods and services with public interest features. A GAO glossary speaks to the role of government in managing its buildings and properties. The topic has been reviewed in an effort to reduce costs while maintaining the appropriate level of services. To place the task on a more businesslike basis, the formation of partnerships between the federal government and the private sector were examined. The GAO wrote the booklet to explain commonly used terms and practices employed by the private economy and the government asset management community. The involvement of the private sector may extend in many directions for the public purpose facility. Some of these are designing, constructing, financing, operation, maintenance, management and/or ownership. The 1999 booklet was devised mainly from six glossaries published over the period from 1991 to 1999 by private and public sources (GAO 1999e: 1–2).

Regulation is another method of government oversight when the private sector is furnishing goods or services with public characteristics. Much of recent antitrust policy is directed toward these occurrences. William E. Kovacic and Carl Shapiro write that the Sherman Act in 1890 and later statutes which laid the groundwork for dealing with monopoly, cartels, and illegal collusion, have gained considerable attention in recent years. There has been a move toward the use of analytical techniques and away from the "rule of reason" that dominated the earlier periods' consideration of cooperation or collusion. In addition, antitrust enforcement has focused on innovation elements as it did in the 1995 federal guidelines for licensing intellectual property. Joseph Schumpeter had discussed the importance of innovation as a major condition for economic performance and growth as early as 1942. However, today's economists have stressed the role of technology, patents, and licensing. The Microsoft litigation, as presented by the government, relies on game theory strategies to explain its position. Economists have inspired a modification of former government policies with respect to antitrust issues. At one time, these policies required much government intrusion including controls over entry and prices. Now, the emphasis is on the relative merits of competition as the better mechanism for a healthy economy. Moreover, there are now closer ties between the law and economics (Kovacic and Shapiro 2000: 58–60).

TAXATION AND REFORM

At the beginning of the twenty-first century, one-third of all economic activity in the United States involves the public sector. More than half of the revenues of all levels of government are collected by the federal government and it spends slightly less than half of all government expenditures (Wallis 2000: 82).

In a study of the tax systems of France, the United Kingdom, and the United States done by the author in 1991 and presented at the Eastern Economic Association meetings in Pittsburgh in March of that year, some similarities were noted in the philosophy behind tax reforms in the three countries. The first was the frequent mention of the desire for greater fiscal neutrality or least interference with private economic decisions. This concept was met for each case by lowering tax rates, broadening the tax base, and moving away from a combined income and expenditure base. A second implication of the study was the recognition that high marginal tax rates are distortionary and should be avoided. Interestingly, the observation appeared to mean that the French devotion to indirect taxation was likely to diminish, while in the United Kingdom it meant the opposite (Meyer 1991b: 23–25).

More recently, the German Parliament passed a radical tax program, effective in 2005, that slashes tax rates on individuals and corporations by $24 billion annually. The top tax rates for individuals will be 42 percent instead of 51 percent, and the corporate tax is scheduled to be 40 percent instead of 50 percent. The most radical part of the legislation calls for a change in the way that Germans do business. It is a provision that allows corporations to sell shares of subsidiaries without paying a tax on their profits. Big banks and insurance companies will be able to sell better than $100 billion worth of shares in large industrial companies such as Daimler-Chrysler and Siemens. Formerly, a sale of this size could have meant a 50 percent tax on profits. Several economists including Norbert Walter, Chief Economist for Deutsche Bank, forecast economic growth greater than 3 percent next year as opposed to the previous prediction of 2.6 percent.

Within the United States, public opinion has been that taxes are too high. That perception together with the recent evidence of slowdown in the economy and the administration's success in instituting a large tax cut, suggests that the possibility of some form of consumption or wealth-based taxation is less likely. Edward D. Wolff, in a Twentieth Century Fund Report, states that wealth inequality had been increasing and was particularly steep in its rise during the period 1983 to 1989. Practically all the gains in real wealth went to the top 20 percent of wealth holders. There was a slight drop in this inequality between 1989 and 1992. The composition of household wealth in 1992 included of owner-occupied housing, 28.7 percent; and business equity, 20 percent. Another quarter of the total was in other real estate, 14.9 percent; and total deposits consisting of checking, savings, time, money market funds, and certificates of deposit, 10 percent. The balance was in pension accounts, 7.0 percent; corporate stock and mutual funds, 7.8 percent; and miscellaneous assets, 11.6 percent.

The only wealth tax existing in the United States at the federal level is the estate tax. At the local level, there is the unpopular property tax. Wealth is taxed at the federal level, in addition, by the levy on capital gains included as an income tax provision. OECD countries use taxes on wealth. There are 11 OECD countries using wealth taxes but none of them employ the tax as a major revenue source and tax rates are low. Nevertheless, if a wealth tax similar to that of Switzerland were adopted in the United States, with its $100,000 exclusion and a top rate of 0.3 percent, an estimated $40 billion could be collected (Wolff 1996: 3–72).

The rationale for wealth taxation rests on the original Haig-Simons definition of income—all capital gains, realized or not belong in the tax base—is part of that definition. Currently, realized capital gains, alone, are taxed. A person's ability to pay includes income and wealth. From an egalitarian point of view, taxation of wealth reduces its concentration, which may be desirable. Wealth taxation may be looked upon as a benefit payment, alternatively. Individuals who accumulate wealth do so under the protection of the legal, the defense, the political, and economic systems of the United States. In short, the case for wealth taxation can be built upon either the ability-to-pay or benefit doctrine (Rosen 1999: 459–461).

Current law exempts estates up to $675,000 in year 2000 and the figure rises to $1 million in 2006. The exemption for family-owned businesses and farms is $1.3 million. Taxable estates pay from 37 percent to a top rate of 55 percent. In 1998, there were 6 percent of these who had assets of $5 million or more and they accounted for 51 percent of all estate taxes paid (Rosen 1999: 460–466). In 2001, the OMB released a document, *A Blueprint for New Beginnings*, which announced that the elimination of the death tax is a presidential commitment. It is argued that the death tax is unfair because it taxes the same income that had been taxed when it was earned. If the tax is removed, the document continues, it will serve as an incentive to risk taking and wealth creation (OMB 2001: 35).

WORLD TRADE

In the *Economic Report of the President Transmitted to Congress February 2000*, the Council of Economic Advisers (CEA 2000b) writes that the benefits of specialization in production and greater access to markets is achieved through international trade. Whatever one country can produce at relatively less cost than another country, it should export. It should import those items which it produces relatively more expensively. Resources are freed in this manner to shift to areas where their economic value is the greatest, and therefore income rises. Simultaneously, access to more and larger markets can reduce costs and spur innovation. The consumer benefits by having a wider variety of goods available at lower costs. International capital mobility permits similar advantages by enabling investment to take place where it provides the highest returns. Both sides of the transaction benefit as the lender receives a higher return than at home and the borrower is able to put to productive use the capital not available or available at higher cost domestically.

The financial and trade activities are mutually reinforcing and together contribute to raise the incomes, the growth, and the productivity of the participating countries. It is foreign competition which offers incentive to domestic firms to raise productivity if they are directly and/or indirectly related to export industries. Foreign direct investment can play a significant role in the development of emerging nations. Not the least of the benefits accruing to all participating nations is that "Both trade and investment contribute to the flow of knowledge and transfer of technology" (CEA 2000b: 217).

These concepts are some of the fundamental reasons why the United States has been working to extend the benefits of trade and investment through bilateral and multilateral negotiations of the WTO. Among the areas where the United States has been seeking additional market access are agriculture, services, and some industrial products. The United States would prefer to see nations eliminate export subsidies and lower tariffs and domestic supports in agriculture. For services, a commitment to more openness is encouraged for the sectors of finance, construction, telecommunications, and agricultural biotechnology products.

The WTO has attempted to strike a balance between the needs of the trading system and those of sovereign nations. In no way do the actions of the WTO prevent any nation from setting its own standards in any field, or effectively enforcing, establishing, and maintaining its own laws. Consensus among WTO members is its method of operation. Disputes are resolved within the framework of the multilateral system. The framework continues to be improved in order to shorten the process, to allow greater public access and participation, and to clarify the issues. Economic growth is encouraged through the multilateral trading system.

There are 135 members of the WTO, a great many of which are developing nations. The developing countries have been increasing their share of world trade, which was 29.1 percent in 1989 and rose to 34.7 percent in 1997. The rate of growth of emerging nations' total trade or exports plus imports, from 1989 to 1997, was 9.9 percent. For developing nations belonging to the WTO, the rate of growth was 10.5 percent. The 48 least-developed countries, many of which belong to the WTO, grew at an annual rate of 6.1 percent through 1996. U.S. trade in goods with developing countries, excluding Eastern Europe, has been increasing also. In 1996, U.S. trade in goods with these countries in Asia, Africa, and Latin America totaled $241.9 billion and rose to $277.3 billion in 1999, a growth rate of 11 percent (CEA 2000a: 395).

The United States has proposed measures in the WTO addressed to the questions of the relationship between core labor standards, environmental objectives, and the benefits of trade. Sovereign nations have the responsibility of adopting appropriate domestic policies. The United States, through the auspices of the WTO, can offer technical assistance to foster sound institutions domestically and to guide the implementation of trade policy (CEA 2000a: 219–225; GAO 2000e: 3–5).

It was the Uruguay Round of International Trade Negotiations that resulted in the establishment of the WTO on 1 January 1995. It is responsible for the rules of international trade; it provides the framework for settling disputes, and the forum for negotiating trade agreements. The specific details are listed in the 1994 Marrakesh Agreement Establishing the World Trade Organization. The relations between the WTO, China, and the United States were discussed in the GAO report of 17 March 2000 directed to W. F Roth, Jr. and D. P. Moynihan, Chairman and Ranking Minority Member, respectively, of the Committee on Finance of the Senate; and B. Archer and C. B. Rangel, Chairman and Ranking Minority Member, respectively, of the Committee on Ways and Means of the House of Representatives; and signed by S. S. Westin, Associate Director, International Relations and Trade Issues of the General Accounting Office. The WTO is the successor to the organization formerly known as the General Agreement on Tariffs and Trade (GATT). China has been negotiating for a relationship with the WTO since 1986. The United States has been actively involved in the negotiations. WTO agreements require granting member nations equal trade privileges called "most favored nation" status or, more recently, "normal trade relations." China has had normal trade relations with the United States on an annual basis since 1980. If China becomes a member of the WTO, Congress may have to consider giving China permanent normal trade status. Currently, the United States and China have a tentative agreement on eight areas of trade practices: tariffs, nontariff barriers, intellectual property rights, trade framework, services, agriculture, standards and regulatory practices, and monitoring and compliance mechanisms. Areas of minor differences remain for these categories. Areas of major differences exist but they are not revealed because they are deemed national security information (GAO 2000e: 3–6).

SUPRAGOVERNMENT INTERVENTION

As of October 1999, there were 188 members of the United Nations, ranging alphabetically from Afghanistan, which became a member in 1946, to Zimbabwe, which attained membership in 1980. At the time, the following countries did not belong: China (Taiwan), Switzerland, Tuvalu, and Vatican City (Holy See). Switzerland and the Vatican City are permanent observers. In 2000, Tuvalu became the 189th member of the United Nations (McGevran 2001: 887).

The preamble to the charter of the United Nations, which was agreed to by 50 initial members at a meeting in San Francisco in the spring of 1945, was based on proposals drawn up by representatives from China, the Soviet Union, the United Kingdom, and the United States, at Dumbarton Oaks in 1944. The United Nations officially came into existence on 24 October 1945 and United Nations Day is celebrated annually on that day.

The United Nations system includes the IMF, the World Bank group, and a dozen other independent groups that are linked to the United Nations through cooperative agreements. Each has its own governing body, budgets, and secretariat. Even though the groups have their own programs and interests, they have become increasingly coordinated in their activities. The total budget of the biennium, 1998–1999, for the United Nations was

$2.53 billion as approved by the General Assembly, the main decision-making organ (Famighetti 1999: 884; United Nations 1999: 7).

According to *Basic Facts about the United Nations* (1998), the financial situation of the United Nations has been weak over the past several years because of nonpayment of assessed contributions of member states. Voluntary contributions, borrowing from its Working Capital fund, and peace-keeping operations have managed to keep its programs afloat. As of 15 June 1998, unpaid contributions to the regular budget by member states totaled almost $1 billion (United Nations 1999: 20).

In testimony before the Joint Economic Committee of Congress in 1999, Harold J. Johnson and Gary T. Engels, representing the GAO, reported on the current financial situation of the IMF. The IMF holdings of gold represented about 9 percent of the world's official gold holdings in 1999, which amounts to 103 million fine ounces of gold. With an 85 percent majority vote of the voting members of the Executive Board, the IMF may sell the gold or may accept gold at market prices in payment of a member's obligations. Gold had been acquired by the IMF before 1974 when members' quota subscription included a gold requirement. IMF values its gold at $30 billion as of 30 April 1999, which is computed at a valuation of approximately $47 per ounce. A new quota level was approved by the highest decision-making body of the IMF, the IMF Board of Governors, in January 1998. The new level was $288 billion, or special drawing rights of $212 billion. The amount was approved by the required majority of members and became effective January 1999. The quota resources of the IMF are used to aid members with credit demands. When demand of funds is high, the IMF will borrow from member countries. In 1978, the IMF borrowed from members for up to 62 percent of its credit outstanding. The borrowing is usually from central banks, although the IMF does have the right, according to its Articles of Agreement, to borrow in private capital markets, a procedure which it has never followed. As of 30 April 1999, the IMF had $287 billion in its General Resources Account. Only about $195 billion of these resources from members' quota was usable because the balance consisted of members' weak currencies and gold which is not considered a liquid resource. The IMF may borrow, also, from member countries through two standing arrangements: (1) general arrangements to borrow, and (2) new arrangements to borrow, up to a combined total of $46 billion. It financed lending to Russia and Brazil in 1998 by borrowing $6 billion under these arrangements. The obligations were repaid in March 1999.

As might be expected, on 30 April 1999, the United States had the highest reserve tranche position at $23.05 billion, which represents 46 percent of its quota of $50.2 billion. Japan is next with $8.26 billion, representing 46 percent of its quota of $17.99 billion. Germany is third with a reserve tranche position of $7.72 billion, or 44 percent of its quota of $17.58

billion. The three largest borrower countries as of 30 April 1999 were India, Venezuela, and Korea. The market value of the IMF's holdings of gold in July 1999 were approximately $26 billion. Ownership rights to the gold are held by the IMF and it uses the gold for contingency purposes including selling it to raise funds for a variety of purposes. Members may have residual rights to the gold if the fund agrees to give a member that privilege or if the IMF is liquidated (GAO/Johnson and Engel 1999: 2–6).

At the United Nations headquarters in New York City, virtually all the world's nations held a three-day summit which ended 8 September 2000. Kishore Mahubani, United Nations Representative from Singapore, remarked that the meeting was "the mother of all summits." The United Nations Millennium Declaration from the General Assembly announced the need for globalization to be a positive force in the world. Efforts must be made to establish a shared future founded on the diversity of humanity. The fundamental values essential to international associations in the twenty-first century are concerned with six broad areas: freedom, equality, solidarity, tolerance, respect for nature, and shared responsibility. There were eight pages of resolutions on these matters. However, the emphasis for all countries appeared to be that the United Nations is the most universal and most representative organization in the world. Given its position, the United Nations should be the central organ for expressing the policies and measures to attain the goals and values agreed upon by the active participation of the world of sovereign nations.

CONCLUDING COMMENTS

Public goods and externalities continue to be difficult to measure, difficult to provide in one case or to correct in the other, and difficult to explain to the voters who pay for the government actions. Economists have not been able to identify the stimulus to economic growth accurately enough to impart workable advice to emerging nations or to transition economies. Perhaps the vast amounts of information and the speed of its transmission will be a welcome boon to economists along with the rest of the world. Tax reform remains a major challenge to politicians and economists alike. Whatever the final outcome, tax rate reduction proportionately across the income brackets or not, less paperwork and time expended by the taxpayer would be, undoubtedly, greatly appreciated. International trade relations are more significant than most individuals realize. Trade is a major key to harmony among nations while, at the same time, improving the welfare of nations and their citizens. The major forum for economic, social, and political negotiations among nations has been the United Nations. Whether it can continue to perform this enormous task to the satisfaction of its participants depends on the individual and combined efforts of all.

Epilogue: Mega-economics and the Federal Budget

21 February 2001

To the Congress

To the President of the
United States of America

This final statement is meant to reaffirm the comments of each of the previous chapters. The overall proposal for the existing budget is that it become briefer, more informal, and be contained within an international framework. Other comments would expand its coverage in less quantifiable matters but as important as those which have been measured:

1. All forms of regulation, whether in the form of congressional legislation or executive edict, if they impinge on the conduct or behavior of the private or public economy, should be included.

2. Any type of private, private/public, or public enterprise or activity undertaken in the public interest, in whole or in part, should be mentioned and briefly described in the budget.

3. Every participation in agreements, treaties, international organizations, or other associations by the United States government, for whatever purpose, should be officially recognized within the budget.

The federal budget should be the place to find any and all the programs and actions of the central government as a single entity or in concert with others.

Sincerely,

Annette E. Meyer

References

Aaron, Henry J., William Gale, and James Sly. (1999). "The Rocky Road to Tax Reform." In Henry J. Aaron and Robert D. Reischauer, eds., *Setting National Priorities: The 2000 Election and Beyond*. Washington, D.C.: Brookings Institution Press, pp. 211–266.

Alm, James. (1996). "What Is an 'Optimal' Tax System?" *National Tax Journal* 49 (March): 117–133.

Analytical Perspectives. Budget of the United States Government FY 2000. (1999). Washington, D.C.: U.S. GPO, 1999.

Analytical Perspectives. Budget of the United States Government FY 2001. (2000). Washington, D.C.: U.S. GPO.

Analytical Perspectives. Budget of the United States Government FY 2002. (2001). Washington, D.C.: U.S. GPO.

Appendix. Budget of the United States Government FY 2001. (2000). Washington, D.C.: U.S. GPO.

Auerbach, Alan J. (1993). "Public Finance in Theory and Practice." *National Tax Journal* 46 (December): 519–526.

———. (1999). "On the Performance and Use of Government Revenue Forecasts." *National Tax Journal* 52 (December): 433–438.

———. (2000). "Formation of Fiscal Policy: The Experience of the Past Twenty-Five Years." *Economic Policy Review* 6 (April): 9–23. Fiscal Policy in a Era of Surpluses: Economic and Financial Implications. Proceedings of a Conference Sponsored by the Federal Reserve Bank of New York.

Bane, Mary Jo. (1992). "Overview: Social Security." In Mark Green, ed., with Wade Green, John Siegel, Olivier Sultan, and Michael Waldman, *Changing America: Blueprints for the New Administration: The Citizens Transition Project*. New York: Newmarket Press, pp. 375–397.

Barro, R. (1974). "Are Government Bonds Net Wealth?" *Journal of Political Economy* 82: 1095–1175.

Barth, James R., R. Dan Brumbaugh, Jr., and James A. Wilcox. (2000). "The Repeal of Glass-Steagall and the Advent of Broad Banking." *Journal of Economic Perspectives* 14 (Spring): 191–204.

Bazelon, Coleman, and Kent Smetters. (1999). "Discounting Inside the Washington, D.C. Beltway." *Journal of Economic Perspectives* 13 (Fall): 213–228.

Bernanke, Ben S., and Fred S. Mishkin. (1997). "Inflation Targeting: A New Framework for Monetary Policy." NBER Working Paper No. 5893 (January).

Blanchard, Oliver. (2000). "Commentary" on Darrel Cohen and Glenn Follette's "The Automatic Fiscal Stabilizers: Quietly Doing Their Thing." *Economic Policy Review* 6 (April): 69–74.

Blank, R. M. (2000). "When Can Public Policy Makers Rely on Private Markets? The Effective Provision of Social Services." *The Economic Journal* (March): C34–C49.

Blinder, Alan S. (1991). "Is the National Debt Really—I Mean Really—a Burden?" In J. M. Rock, ed., *Debt and the Twin Deficits Debate*. Mountain View, Calif.: Mayfield Publishing Company, pp. 206–226.

———. (1997). "What Central Bankers Learn from Academics—and Vice Versa." *Journal of Economic* Perspectives 11 (Spring): 3–19.

Board of Governors of the Federal Reserve System (FRS). (1999). *86th Annual Report 1999*. Washington, D.C.: Board of Governors of the FRS Publications Services.

———. (2000). *87th Annual Report 2000*. Washington, D.C.: Board of Governors of the FRS Publications Services.

Boards of Trustees. (1999). *Status of the Social Security and Medicare Programs: A Summary of the 1999 Annual Reports*. Social Security and Medicare Boards of Trustees. Washington, D.C.: Social Security and Medicare, March.

Bordo, Michael D., and David C. Wheelock. (1998). "Price Stability and Financial Stability: The Historical Record." Federal Reserve Bank of St. Louis *Review* (September/October): 41–52.

Boskin, Michael J. (2000). "Getting the 21st Century GDP Right: Economic Measurement: Progress and Challenges." *American Economic Association Papers and Proceedings* 90 (May): 248–252.

Bosworth, Barry. (2000). "Commentary" on Alan J. Auerbach's "Formation of Fiscal Policy: The Experience of the Past Twenty-Five Years." *Economic Policy Review* 6 (April): 25–27.

Bowsher, Charles A. (1997). *General Accounting Office Report on the Federal Reserve System*. Hearing before the Committee on Banking, Housing and Urban Affairs, Senate. Comptroller General of the United States. Washington, D.C.: U.S. GPO, U.S. GAO.

Brunner, Karl. (1997). *The Selected Essays of Karl Brunner, Vol. 2: Monetary Theory and Monetary Policy*. Edited by Thomas Lys. Cheltenham, England and Brookfield, Vt.: Edward Elgar.

Budget of the United States Government FY 1992. (1991). Washington, D.C.: U.S. GPO.

Budget of the United States Government FY 1999. (1998). Washington, D.C.: U.S. GPO.

Budget of the United States Government FY 2001. (2000). Washington, D.C.: U.S. GPO.

Bullard, James M., and Alvin L. Marty. (1998). "What Has Become of the

'Stability-Through-Inflation' Argument?" Federal Reserve Bank of St. Louis *Review* (January/February): 37–45.

Burkhead, Jesse. (1956). *Government Budgeting.* New York: John Wiley and Sons.

Cairncross, Frances. (1992). *Costing the Earth: The Challenge for Governments, the Opportunities for Business.* Boston: Harvard Business School Press.

Capital Budgeting. (1995). Hearing before the Subcommittee on Government Management, Information, and Technology, Committee on Government Reform and Oversight, House of Representatives, March 6. Washington, D.C.: U.S. GPO.

Caves, Richard E., Jeffrey A. Frankel, and Ronald W. Jones. (1990). *World Trade and Payments: An Introduction.* 5th ed. Glenview, Ill.: Scott, Foresman and Company.

Cecchetti, Stephen G. (1998). "Policy Rules and Targets: Framing the Central Banker's Problems." Federal Reserve Bank of New York *Economic Policy Review* (June): 1–14.

A Citizen's Guide to the Federal Budget: Budget of the United States Government FY 2001. (2000). Washington, D.C.: U.S. GPO.

Clayton, James L. (2000). *The Global Debt Bomb.* Armonk, N.Y.: M. E. Sharpe.

Coase, Ronald. (1960). "The Problem of Social Cost." *The Journal of Law and Economics* (October): 1–44.

Cogan, John F., Timothy J. Muris, and Allen Schick, eds. (1994). *The Budget Puzzle: Understanding Federal Spending.* Stanford, Calif.: Stanford University Press.

Cohen, Darrel, and Glenn Follette. (2000). "The Automatic Fiscal Stabilizers: Quietly Doing Their Thing." *Economic Policy Review* 6 (April): 35–67. Fiscal Policy in an Era of Surpluses: Economic and Financial Implications. Proceedings of a Conference Sponsored by the Federal Reserve Bank of New York.

Congress of the United States. Congressional Budget Office (CBO). (1997). *The Economic Effects of Comprehensive Tax Reform* (July 1997). Washington, D.C.: U.S. GPO.

Congressional Budget Office (CBO). (1985). *The Budgetary Status of the Federal Reserve System.* Washington, D.C.: CBO.

———. (1991). *Controlling the Risks of Government-Sponsored Enterprises.* Washington, D.C.: U.S. GPO, April.

———. (1996). *Assessing the Public Costs and Benefits of Fannie Mae and Freddie Mac.* Washington, D.C.: U.S. GPO.

Constitution of the United States of America. (1974). Presented by Mr. Rodino. As Amended through July 1971 (7 February 1974). House Document no. 93–215. Washington, D.C.: U.S. GPO.

Corder, J. Kevin. (1998). *Central Bank Autonomy: The Federal Reserve System in American Politics.* New York and London: Garland Publishing.

Cordes, Joseph J. (1996). "How Yesterday's Decisions Affect Today's Budget and Fiscal Options." In C. Eugene Steuerle and Masakiro Kawai, eds., *The New World Fiscal Order: Implications for Industrialized Nations.* Washington, D.C.: The Urban Institute Press, pp. 95–116.

Coughlin, Cletus C. (2000). Editor's Introduction. "Multilateral Trade Negotiations: Issues for the Millennium Round." Federal Reserve Bank of St. Louis *Review* 82 (July/August): 5–10.

Council of Economic Advisers (CEA). (1999). *Economic Report of the President Transmitted to Congress February 1999*. Together with the Annual Report of the Council of Economic Advisers. Washington, D.C.: U.S. GPO.

———. (2000a). *Economic Report of the President Transmitted to Congress January 2000*. Together with the Annual Report of the Council of Economic Advisers. Washington, D.C.: U.S. GPO.

———. (2000b). *Economic Report of the President Transmitted to Congress February 2000*. Together with the Annual Report of the Council of Economic Advisers. Washington, D.C.: U.S. GPO.

Dattani, Nilesh. (1997). "Economic and Monetary Union." In S. Stavridis, E. Mossialos, R. Morgan, and H. Machin, eds., *New Challenges to the European Union: Policies and Policy-Making*. Brookfield, Vt.: Dartmouth Publishing Company, pp. 201–223.

Davie, Bruce F. (1999). "Addressing Tax Expenditures in the Budgetary Process." In Roy T. Meyers, ed., *Handbook of Government Budgeting*. San Francisco: Jossey-Bass, pp. 277–307.

Dawson, John E., and Peter J. E. Stan. (1995). *Public Expenditures in the United States 1952–1993*. Santa Monica, Calif.: RAND.

DiIulio, John J., Jr. (1995). "Works Better and Costs Less? Sweet and Sour Perspectives on the NPR." In Donald F. Kettl and John J. DiIulio, Jr., eds., *Inside the Reinvention Machine: Appraising Governmental Reform*. Washington, D.C.: Brookings Institution, pp. 1–6.

Dornbusch, Rudi. (1998). "Debt and Monetary Policy: The Policy Issues." In G. Calvo and M. King, eds., *The Debt Burden and Its Consequences for Monetary Policy*. Proceedings of a Conference held by the International Economic Association at the Deutsche Bundesbank, Frankfurt, Germany. New York: St. Martin's Press, pp. 3–22.

Easterlin, Richard A. (2000). "The Worldwide Standard of Living Since 1800." *Journal of Economic Perspectives* 14 (Winter): 7–26.

Ekelund, Robert B., Jr., and Robert F. Hébert. (1990). *A History of Economic Theory and Method*. 3rd ed. New York: McGraw-Hill.

Famighetti, Robert, Editorial Director. (1999). *The World Almanac and Book of Facts 2000*. Mahwah, N.J.: Primedia Reference.

Federal Reserve Bank of Atlanta. (2000). *Financial Update* (January–March).

Federal Reserve Bulletin (March 2000): 217. Announcements. Modification to the Disclosure Procedures of the Federal Open Market Committee.

———. (August 2001a). Minutes of the Meeting of the Federal Open Market Committee, May 15: 1–5.

———. (September 2001b). Minutes of the Meeting of the Federal Open Market Committee, June 26–27: 1–9.

Fischer, Stanley, and Patma Sahay. (2000). "Taking Stock." *Finance and Development* (September): 2–6.

Fisher, Louis. (1997). *Constitutional Conflicts between Congress and the President*. 4th ed., rev. Lawrence: University Press of Kansas.

Friedman, Benjamin M. (1992). "Learning from the Reagan Deficits." *AEA Papers and Proceedings* 82 (May): 299–310.

Friedman, Milton, and Anna Schwartz. (1963). *A Monetary History of the United States, 1967–1960*. Princeton, N.J.: Princeton University Press.

Galbraith, John Kenneth. (1958). *The Affluent Society*. Boston: Houghton Mifflin.

Gates, Bill, with Collins Hemingway. (1999). *Business @ the Speed of Thought: Using a Digital Nervous System*. New York: Warner Books.

General Accounting Office (GAO). (1993a). *Budget Issues: Incorporating an Investment Component in the Budget*. Washington, D.C.: U.S. GPO.

———. (1993b). *A Glossary of Terms Used in the Federal Budget Process: Exposure Draft*. Washington, D.C.: U.S. GAO, revised January.

———. (1994). *Government Auditing Standards 1994 Edition*. Comptroller General of the United States. Washington, D.C.: U.S. GAO.

———. (1996). *Federal Reserve System: Current and Future Challenges Require Systemwide Attention*. Report to Congressional Requesters. Washington, D.C.: U.S. GAO.

———. (1999a). *Budget Issues: Budget Enforcement Compliance Report*. Report to the Chairman, Committee on the Budget, House of Representatives. Washington, D.C.: U.S. GAO, April.

———. (1999b). *Federal Debt: Answers to Frequently Asked Questions—An Update* (May). Washington, D.C.: U.S. GAO.

———. (1999c). *Federal Debt: Debt Management in a Period of Budget Surpluses*. Report to Congressional Requesters (September). Washington, D.C.: U.S. GAO.

———. (1999d). *Performance Budgeting*. "Initial Experiences Under the Results Act in Linking Plans with Budgets." Report to the Chairman, Committee on Governmental Affairs, Senate. Washington, D.C.: U.S. GAO.

———. (1999e). *Public-Private Partnerships: Terms Related to Building and Facility Partnerships*. Washington, D.C.: U.S. GAO.

———. (1999f). *Social Security Capital Markets and Educational Issues Associated with Individual Accounts*. Report to the Chairman, Committee on Ways and Means, House of Representatives. Washington, D.C.: U.S. GAO, June.

———. (1999g). *Social Security Reform Implementation Issues for Individual Accounts*. Report to the Chairman, Committee on Ways and Means, House of Representatives. Washington, D.C.: U.S. GAO, June.

———. (2000a). "Budget Issues: Treasury's Interest Rate Charges." Letter to Honorable Bill Archer, Chairman, Committee on Ways and Means, House of Representatives, p. 2. Washington, D.C.: U.S. GAO.

———. (2000b). *Financial Audit*. "Bureau of the Public Debt's Fiscal Years 1999 and 1998 Schedules of Federal Debt." GAO Report to the Secretary of the Treasury. Washington, D.C.: U.S. GAO.

———. (2000c). *Financial Audit*. "Financial Report of the United States Government." Report to the Congress. Washington, D.C.: U.S. GAO.

———. (2000d). *Financial Audit: 1999 Financial Report of the United States Government Fiscal Year 1999* (March): 88–90. Washington, D.C.: U.S. GAO.

———. (2000e). *World Trade Organization: Chinese Membership Status and Normal Trade Relations Issues*. Washington, D.C.: U.S. GAO, March.

General Accounting Office/Johnson, Jarold J., and Gary T. Engel. (1999). *International Monetary Fund Current Financial Situation*. Testimony before the Joint Economic Committee of Congress, for release July 21.

General Accounting Office/McCool, Thomas J. (1999). Letter of 8/31/99 addressed to R. H. Baker, Chairman and P. E. Kanjorski, Ranking Minority Member, Subcommittee on Capital Markets, Securities, and GSEs, Committee on Banking and Financial Services, House of Representatives.

General Accounting Office/Posner, Paul L., and Christopher J. Mihm. (1998). *GAO Budget Issues: Budgeting for Capital.* Testimony before the President's Commission to Study Capital Budgeting. Washington, D.C.: U.S. GAO, March 6.

———. (1999). Testimony, "Performance Budgeting: Initial Agency Experiences Provide a Foundation to Assess Future Directions." Statements of Paul L. Posner and Christopher M. Mihm, both representing the General Accounting Office before the Subcommittee on Government Management, Information and Technology, Committee on Government Reform, House of Representatives. Washington, D.C.: U.S. GAO.

General Accounting Office/White, James R. (1999). *IRS Management Formidable Challenges Confront IRS as It Attempts to Modernize.* Testimony for the Government Accounting Office before the Subcommittee on Oversight, Committee on Ways and Means, House of Representatives. Washington, D.C.: U.S. GAO.

Gensler, Gary. (2000). "Fiscal Policy in an Era of Surpluses." *Economic Policy Review* 6 (April): 83–85. Proceedings of a Conference Sponsored by the Federal Reserve Bank of New York.

Geyer, Herbert. (1985). "Changes in Budget Policy Goals and Instruments: Five Decades of Development in the United States of America." In *Budgetpolitik im Wandel.* Herausgegeben von Karl Haüser. Vereins fur Social Politik, Gesellschaft fur Wirtschafts-und-Sozialwissenschaften. Neue Folge Bank 149. Berlin: Duncher and Humblot, pp. 33–58.

Giannini, Curzo. (1999). "The IMF and the Lender of Last Resort Function: An External View." *Finance and Development* (September): 24–27.

Gordon, Robert J. (2000). "Does the 'New Economy' Measure Up to the Great Inventions of the Past?" *Journal of Economic Perspectives* 24 (Fall): 49–74.

Greenspan, Alan. (2000). "Statement" before the Special Committee on Aging, Senate, 3/27/00. *Federal Reserve Bulletin* (May): 318–320.

Hanweck, Gerald A., and Bernard Shull. (1996). *Interest Rate Volatility: Understanding, Analyzing, and Managing Interest Rate Risk and Risk-Based Capital.* Chicago: Irwin.

Hillery, Paul V., and Stephen E. Thompson. (2000). "Bank Operations and Payment Systems." *Federal Reserve Bulletin* 86 (April): 251–259.

Hines, James R., Jr. (1999). "Lessons from Behavioral Responses to International Taxation." *National Tax Journal* 52: 305–322.

Historical Tables. Budget of the United States Government FY 2001. (2000). Washington, D.C.: U.S. GPO.

Historical Tables. Budget of the United States Government FY 2002. (2001). Washington, D.C.: U.S. GPO.

Horowitz, John K. (2000). Review of P. R. Portney and J. P. Weyant, eds., *Discounting and Intergenerational Equity* (1999). *Journal of Economic Perspectives* 38 (June): 424–425.

International Financial Institution Advisory Commission (IFIAC). (2000). *Report.* Allen H. Meltzer, Chairman. Washington, D.C.: U.S. GPO, March.

Investing in America: Proposed Changes in the Federal Budget Process. (1993). Hearing before the Legislation and National Security Subcommittee, Committee on Government Operations, House of Representatives, July 28, 1992. Washington, D.C.: U.S. GPO.

Irving, Susan J. (1999). *Budget Issues Cap Structure and Guaranteed Funding.* GAO Testimony before the Committee on Rules, House of Representatives. Washington, D.C.: U.S. GAO, July 21.

Jones, L. R., and Jerry McCaffery. (1999). "Financial Reform in the Federal Government." In Roy T. Meyers, ed., *Handbook of Government Budgeting.* San Francisco: Jossey-Bass, pp. 53–81.

Joyce, Philip G. (1999). "Performance-Based Budgeting." In Roy T. Meyers, ed., *Handbook of Government Budgeting.* San Francisco: Jossey-Bass, pp. 597–619.

Karacadag, Cem, and Michael W. Taylor. (2000). "Toward a New Global Banking Standard: The Basel Committee's Proposals." *Finance and Development* (December): 50–53.

Kasten, Richard A., David J. Weiner, and G. Thomas Woodward. (1999). "What Made Receipts Boom and When Will They Go Bust?" *National Tax Journal* 52: 339–347.

Kaufman, Henry. (2000). *On Money and Markets: A Wall Street Memoir.* New York: McGraw-Hill.

Kay, J. A. (1990). "Tax Policy: A Survey." *The Economic Journal* 100 (March): 18–75.

Kepplinger, George L. (1999). *Impoundment Control Act. Use and Impact of Rescission Procedures.* Testimony before the Subcommittee on Legislation and Budget Process, Committee on Rules, House of Representatives. Washington, D.C.: U.S. GAO.

Kettl, Donald F. (1995). "Building Lasting Reform: Enduring Questions, Missing Answers." In Donald F. Kettl and John J. DiIulio, Jr., eds., *Inside the Reinvention Machine: Appraising Governmental Reform.* Washington, D.C.: Brookings Institution, pp. 9–83.

———. (1999). "The Three Faces of Reinvention." In Henry J. Aaron and Robert D. Reischauer, eds., *Setting National Priorities: The 2000 Election and Beyond.* Washington, D.C.: Brookings Institution Press, pp. 421–448.

Keynes, John Maynard. (1936/1964). *The General Theory of Employment, Interest and Money.* New York: Harcourt, Brace and World.

Keyserling, L. H. (1979a). *"Liberal" and "Conservative" National Economic Policies and Their Consequences, 1919–1979.* A Study to Help Implement Promptly the Humphrey Hawkins Full Employment and Balanced Growth Act of 1978. Washington, D.C.: Conference on Economic Progress.

———. (1979b). *1979 Economic Report and Budget vs. Fulfilling the Humphrey Hawkins Act of 1978.* Washington, D.C.: Full Employment Action Council.

Kho, Bong-Chan, Ding Lee, and Rene M. Stulz. (2000). "U.S. Banks, Crises, and Bailouts: From Mexico to LTCM." *American Economic Review Proceedings* (May): 28–31.

Kornai, János. (2000a). "Making the Transition to Private Ownership." *Finance and Development* 37 (September): 2–6.

Kornai, János. (2000b). "What the Change of System from Socialism to Capitalism Does and Does Not Mean." *Journal of Economic Perspectives* 14 (Fall): 27–42.

Kovacic, William E., and Carl Shapiro. (2000). "Antitrust Policy: A Century of Economic and Legal Thinking." *Journal of Economic Perspectives* 14 (Winter): 43–60.

Lane, Timothy. (1999). "The Asian Financial Crisis: What Have We Learned?" *Finance and Development* 36 (September): 44–47.

LeLoup, Lance T. (1998). "Budget Policy Transformations." In S. A. Shull, ed., *Presidential Policymaking: An End-of-Century Assessment*. Armonk, N.Y.: M. E. Sharpe, pp. 210–221.

Light, Paul C. (1999a). "Changing the Shape of Government." In Henry J. Aaron and Robert D. Reischauer, eds., *Setting National Priorities: The 2000 Election and Beyond*. Washington, D.C.: Brookings Institution Press, pp. 393–419.

———. (1999b). *The True Size of Government*. Washington, D.C.: Brookings Institution Press.

Mayer, Martin. (1999). "Risk Reduction and the New Financial Architecture." Public Policy Brief No. 56. Annandale-on-Hudson, N.Y.: The Jerome Levy Economics Institute of Bard College.

McGevran, William A., Jr., Editorial Director. (2001). *The World Almanac and Book of Facts 2001*. Mahwah, N.J.: World Almanac Books.

McLure, C. E., Jr. (1985). "Rationale Underlying the Treasury Proposals." *Economic Consequences of Tax Simplification* (October): 1–3. Conference Proceedings at Melvin Village, New Hampshire. Federal Reserve Bank of Boston.

Melton, William C. (1985). *Inside the Fed: Making Monetary Policy*. Homewood, Ill.: Dow Jones–Irwin.

Meulendyke, Ann-Marie. Federal Reserve Bank of New York. (1989). *U.S. Monetary Policy and Financial Markets*. New York: Federal Reserve Bank of New York.

———. (1998). *U.S. Monetary Policy and Financial Markets*. New York: Federal Reserve Bank of New York.

Meyer, Annette E. (1969). *Five Non-Marxian Views on the Form and Function of the Socialist Public Economy: From Proudhon to Pareto*. M.A. Thesis, Hunter College of City University of New York.

———. (1978). *A Comparative Study of Changes in the Budgetary Process of France and the United States: 1921–1971*. Ph.D. diss., City University of New York. Ann Arbor, Mich.: UMI Dissertation Services.

———. (1986). "Financing the Federal Budget: Sources and Structure." *Public Budgeting and Finance* 6 (Winter): 56–68.

———. (1989a). *Evolution of United States Budgeting: Changing Fiscal and Financial Concepts*. Westport, Conn.: Greenwood Press.

———. (1989b). "From Budget Authority to Deficit: The Federal Budget Maze." Paper presented at the Eastern Economic Association Conference, Baltimore, Maryland, March.

———. (1991a). "Tax Policy and the Federal Budget." *The American Economist* 35 (Fall): 32–40.

————. (1991b). *Tax Policy in France, the United Kingdom, and the United States.* Paper presented at the Eastern Economic Association Conference in Pittsburgh, Pennsylvania, March.

Meyers, Roy T. (1999). "Legislatures and Budgeting." In Roy T. Meyers, ed., *Handbook of Government Budgeting.* San Francisco: Jossey-Bass, pp. 485–501.

Mundell, R. A. (2000). "A Reconsideration of the Twentieth Century." *American Economic Review* 90 (June): 327–340.

Musgrave, Richard A. (1959). *The Theory of Public Finance: A Study in Public Economy.* New York: McGraw-Hill.

————. (1997). "Reconsidering the Fiscal Role of Government." *American Economic Review* 87 (May): 156–159.

————, and Peggy B. Musgrave. (1989). *Public Finance in Theory and Practice.* 5th ed. New York: McGraw-Hill.

Myerson, Roger B. (1999). "Nash Equilibrium and the History of Economic Theory." *Journal of Economic Literature* 37 (September): 1067–1082.

Nas, Tavfik F. (1996). *Cost-Benefit Analysis: Theory and Applications.* Thousand Oaks, Calif.: Sage Publications.

Niskanen, William A. (1971). *Bureaucracy and Representative Government.* Chicago: Aldine.

Oates, Wallace C. (1999). "An Essay on Federalism." *Journal of Economic Literature* 37 (September): 1120–1149.

Office of Management and Budget (OMB). (1999). *Federal Financial Management Status Report and Five Year Plan.* Washington, D.C.: OMB.

————. (2000). Circular A-129 Revised. *Policies for Federal Credit Programs and Non-Tax Receivables.* Washington, D.C.: OMB.

————. (2001). *A Blueprint for New Beginnings: A Responsible Budget for America's Priorities.* Washington, D.C.: U.S. GPO.

————. (n.d.). *The President's Management Agenda FY 2002.* Washington, D.C.: U.S. GPO.

Office of the Federal Register. (1999). National Archives and Records Administration. *United States Government Manual 1999/2000.* Washington, D.C.: U.S. GPO.

————. (2000). National Archives and Records Administration. *United States Government Manual 2000/2001.* Washington, D.C.: U.S. GPO.

————. (2001). National Archives and Records Administration. *United States Government Manual 2001/2002.* Washington, D.C.: U.S. GPO.

Office of the Secretary of the Treasury. (2000). *Treasury Bulletin.* Washington, D.C.: U.S. Treasury, September.

Oser, Jacob, and Stanley L. Brue. (1988). *The Evolution of Economic Thought.* 4th ed. New York: Harcourt Brace Jovanovich.

Parcell, Ann D. (1999). "Challenges and Uncertainties in Forecasting Federal Income Individual Income Tax Receipts." *National Tax Journal* 52: 325–338.

Pechman, J. A. (1987). *Federal Tax Policy.* 5th ed. Washington, D.C.: Brookings Institution.

Penner, Rudolph G. (2000). "The Near-Term Outlook for Fiscal Policy." *Economic Policy Review* 6 (April): 77–80. Fiscal Policy in an Era of Surpluses. Proceedings of a Conference Sponsored by the Federal Reserve Bank of New York.

Phaup, Marvin, and David F. Torregrosa. (1999). "Budgeting for Contingent Losses." In Roy T. Meyers, ed., *Handbook of Government Budgeting*. San Francisco: Jossey-Bass, pp. 699–719.

Poole, William. (1999). "Monetary Policy Rules?" Federal Reserve Bank of St. Louis *Review* (March/April): 3–12.

Popkin, Joel. (2000). "The U.S. National Income and Product Accounts." *Journal of Economic Perspectives* 14 (Spring): 215–224.

Potter, Barry H., and Jack Diamond. (2000). "Building Treasury Systems." *Finance and Development* 37 (September): 36–39.

Premchand, A. (1999). "Budgetary Management in the United States and in Australia, New Zealand, and the United Kingdom." In Roy T. Meyers, ed., *Handbook of Government Budgeting*. San Francisco: Jossey-Bass, pp. 82–103.

Public Law (P.L.) 63–43. Federal Reserve Act of 1913.

Public Law (P.L.) 93–344. Congressional Budget and Impoundment Control Act of 1974.

Public Law (P.L.) 95–188. Federal Reserve Reform Act of 1977.

Public Law (P.L.) 95–326. Federal Banking Agency Audit Act of 1978.

Public Law (P.L.) 95–523. Full Employment and Balanced Growth Act of 1978, known as the Humphrey-Hawkins Act.

Public Law (P.L.) 99–177. Balanced Budget and Emergency Deficit Control Act of 1985, known as the Gramm-Rudman-Hollings Act.

Public Law (P.L.) 101–58. Federal Credit Reform Act of 1990 and Budget Enforcement Act of 1990. Formerly known as the Omnibus Budget Reconciliation Act of 1990.

Public Law (P.L.) 103–62. Government Performance and Results Act of 1993.

Public Law (P.L.) 103–66. Omnibus Reconciliation Act of 1993.

Public Law (P.L.) 104–68. Internal Revenue Code of 1986, pp. 1452–1455.

Public Law (P.L.) 105–33. Budget Enforcement Act of 1997.

Public Law (P.L.) 106–102. Financial Modernization Act of 1999, known as the Gramm-Leach-Bliley Act.

Quinlan, Joseph P. (2000). *Global Engagement: How American Companies Really Compete in the Global Economy*. Chicago: Contemporary Books.

Reischauer, Robert D. (1999). "The Dawning of a New Era." In Henry J. Aaron and Robert D. Reischauer, eds., *Setting National Priorities: The 2000 Election and Beyond*. Washington, D.C.: Brookings Institution Press, pp. 1–14.

Report of the President's Commission on Budget Concepts. (1967). Washington, D.C.: U.S. GPO, October.

Report of the President's Commission to Study Capital Budgeting. (1999). Washington, D.C.: U.S. GPO, February.

Rice, Stephen J. (1992). *Introduction to Taxation*. New York: HarperCollins.

Rich, Robert W., and Donald Rissmiller. (2000). "Understanding the Recent Behavior of U.S. Inflation." *Current Issues in Economics and Finance* (Federal Reserve Bank of New York) 6 (July): 1–5.

Rosen, Harvey S. (1999). *Public Finance*. 5th ed. New York: Irwin McGraw-Hill.

Rutherford, Donald. (1992). *Routledge Dictionary of Economics*. London and New York: Routledge.

Samuelson, Paul A. (1948). *Economics: An Introductory Analysis*. New York: McGraw-Hill.

———. (1957). "The Pure Theory of Public Expenditures." *Review of Economics and Statistics* 36 (November): 387–389.

Schick, Allen. (1987). *The Whole and the Parts: Piecemeal and Integrated Approaches to Congressional Budgeting*. Report prepared for the Task Force on the Budget Process of the House Committee on the Budget. Washington, D.C.: U.S. GPO.

———. (1994a). *The Federal Budget: Politics, Policy, Process*. Washington, D.C.: The Brookings Institution.

———. (1994b). "The Study of Microbudgeting." In John F. Cogan, Timothy J. Muris, and Allen Schick, eds., *The Budget Puzzle: Understanding Federal Spending*. Stanford, Calif.: Stanford University Press, pp. 105–157.

Schott, Jeffrey J. (2000). "Toward WTO 2000: A Seattle Odyssey." Federal Reserve Bank of St. Louis *Review* 82 (July/ August): 11–23.

Schwartz, Anna. (1988). "Financial Stability and the Federal Safety Net." In William S. Haraf and Rose Marie Kushmeider, eds., *Restructuring Banking and Financial Services in America*. Washington, D.C.: American Enterprise Institute, pp. 34–62.

———. (1997). "Comment on 'Debt Inflation and Financial Instability: Two Historical Explanations' by Barry Eichengreen and Richard L. Grossman." In Forrest Capie and Geoffrey E. Wood, eds., *Asset Prices and the Real Economy*. New York: St. Martin's Press, pp. 100–105.

Simons, Henry. (1988). *Personal Income Taxation*. Chicago: University of Chicago Press.

Slemrod, Joel. (1996). "Which Is the Simplest Tax System of Them All?" In H. J. Aaron and W. J. Gale, eds., *Economic Effects of Fundamental Tax Reform*. Washington, D.C.: Brookings Institution, pp. 355–391.

———, and Jon Bakija. (1996). *Taxing Ourselves: A Citizen's Guide to the Great Debate over Tax Reform*. Cambridge, Mass.: The MIT Press.

Smith, Adam. (1776/1976). *An Inquiry into the Nature and Causes of the Wealth of Nations*. Edited by Edwin Cannan. Chicago: University of Chicago Press.

Social Security Administration. Office of Research, Evaluation and Statistics. (1998). *Fast Facts and Figures about Social Security*. Washington, D.C.: U.S. GPO.

Stein, Herbert. (1994). *Presidential Economics: The Making of Economic Policy from Roosevelt to Clinton*. 3rd rev. ed. Washington, D.C.: American Enterprise Institute for Public Policy Research.

———, ed. (1997). *Tax Policy in the Twenty-First Century*. New York: John Wiley & Sons.

Steuerle, C. Eugene. (2000). "Commentary" on Alan J. Auerbach's "Formation of Fiscal Policy." *Economic Policy Review* 6 (April): 29–32.

Stevens, L. Nye. (1999). *Federalism Implementation of Executive Order 12612 in the Rulemaking Process*. Testimony for the Government Accounting Office before the Committee on Governmental Affairs, Senate. Washington, D.C.: U.S. GAO.

Stewart, Jamie B., Jr. (2000). "Changing Technology and the Payment System." *Current Issues in Economics and Finance* 6 (October): 1–5.

Summers, Lawrence H. (1999). "Reflections on Managing Global Integration." *Journal of Economic Perspectives* 13 (Spring): 1–18.

———. (2000). "International Financial Crises: Causes, Prevention and Cures." *American Economic Review Proceedings* (May): 1–16.

Summers/Treasury. (1996). *Government Sponsorship of the Federal National Mortgage Association and the Federal Home Loan Mortgage Corporation. Department of Treasury.* Washington, D.C.: U.S. GPO, July 11.

Svensson, Lars E. O. (2000). "Inflation Targeting The First Year of the Eurosystem: Inflation Targeting or Not?" *Finance and Development* (September): 95–98.

Swoboda, Alexander. (1999). "Reforming the International Financial Architecture." *Finance and Development* (September): 2–4.

Taylor, John B., ed. (1999). *Monetary Policy Rules.* National Bureau of Economic Research Conference Report. Chicago: University of Chicago Press.

Thornton, Daniel L. (2000a). "Lifting the Veil of Money from Monetary Policy: Evidence from the Fed's Early Discount Rate Policy." *Journal of Money, Credit and Banking* 32 (May): 155–167.

———. (2000b). "Money in a Theory of Exchange." Federal Reserve Bank of St. Louis *Review* (January/February): 35–62.

"Three Nobel Laureates on the State of Economics, with Robert Solow, Kenneth Arrow and Amartya Sen." (2000). *Challenge* 43 (January/February): 6–31.

Tietmeyer, Hans. (1999). "Evolving Cooperation and Coordination in Financial Market Surveillance." *Finance and Development* (September): 20–23.

Tomkin, S. Lynne. (1998). *Inside OMB Politics and Process in the President's Budget Office.* Armonk, N.Y.: M. E. Sharpe.

Trustees Report. (1999). *The 1999 Annual Report.* Communication from the Board of Trustees, the Federal Old-Age and Survivors Insurance and Disability Insurance Trust Funds. Washington, D.C.: U.S. GPO, April 12.

United Nations. Department of Public Information. (1999). *Basic Facts about the United Nations.* New York: United Nations.

United States Government Annual Report FY 1999. Appendix. (n.d.). Washington, D.C.: Department of the Treasury, Financial Management Service.

U.S. Treasury. (1997). *Consolidated Financial Statements of the United States Government Fiscal Year 1997.* Washington, D.C.: U.S. Treasury.

———. (2001). *U.S. Treasury Launches Online Option for Paying Federal Taxes: Press Release.* Washington, D.C.: Financial Management Services Public Affairs, September 6.

———. (n.d.). *United States Government Annual Report Fiscal Year 1999.* Financial Management Service of Treasury. Washington, D.C.: U.S. GPO.

Various Proposals to Regulate GSEs and to Examine the Risk These Entities Pose to U.S. Taxpayers. (1991). Hearing before the Subcommittee on Government Information and Regulation, Committee on Governmental Affairs, Senate. Washington, D.C.: U.S. GPO, July 18.

Veblen, Thorstein. (1899/1934). *The Theory of the Leisure Class.* New York: Modern Library.

Volkomer, Walter E., with the editorial assistance of Carolyn D. Smith. (1997). *American Government.* 8th ed. Upper Saddle River, N.J.: Prentice Hall.

Von Neumann, John, and Oskar Morgenstern. (1943). *Theory of Games and Economic Behavior*. Princeton, N.J.: Princeton University Press.

Walker, David M. (1999). *Social Security Criteria for Estimating Social Security Reform Proposals*. Testimony before the Subcommittee on Social Security, Committee on Ways and Means, House of Representatives. Washington, D.C.: U.S. GAO, March 25.

———. (2000). *Auditing the Nation's Finances*. "Fiscal Year 1999 Results Continue to Highlight Major Issues Needing Resolution." Statement and Testimony before the Subcommittee of Government Management, Information and Technology, Committee on Government Reform, House of Representatives. Comptroller General of the United States. Washington, D.C.: U.S. GAO.

Wallis, John Joseph. (2000). "American Government Finance in the Long Run: 1790 to 1990." *Journal of Economic Perspectives* 14 (Winter): 61–82.

Weber, René, and Günther Taube. (2000). "Estonia Moves Toward EU Accession." *Finance and Development* (September): 28–31.

White, Joseph. (1999). "Budgeting for Entitlements." In Roy T. Meyers, ed., *Handbook of Government Budgeting*. San Francisco: Jossey-Bass, pp. 678–697.

Wicksell, Knut. (1896/1967). "A New Principle of Just Taxation." Trans. J. M. Buchanan. In Richard A. Musgrave and Alan T. Peacock, eds., *Classics in the Theory of Public Finance*. New York: St. Martin's Press, pp. 72–118.

Wieser, Friedrich von. (1893/1956). *Natural Value*. Ed. William Smart, trans. Christian A. Malloch. New York: Kelley and Millman.

Wildavsky, Aaron. (1975). *Budgeting: A Comparative Theory of Budgeting Processes*. Boston: Little, Brown and Company.

Wolff, Edward D. (1996). *Top Heavy: The Increasing Inequality of Wealth in America and What Can Be Done about It*. An expanded edition of a Twentieth Century Fund Report. New York: The New Press.

Woodford, Michael. (2000). "Pitfalls of Forward-Looking Monetary Policy." *American Economic Review Proceedings* (May): 100–104.

World Bank. (1998). *Public Expenditure Management Handbook*. Washington, D.C.: The World Bank, p. 63.

Wright, John W. ed., with editors and reporters of the Times. (1999). *The New York Times 2000 Almanac*. New York: Penguin Reference.

Index

Saving: balance of payments, 206–7; debt, 39, 40, 208; fiscal policy, 8; income tax, 20, 23, 24; international financial crises, 216; Ricardian equivalence, 11; Social Security, 187, 202

Savings bonds, 97, 156

Schick, Allen, 55, 81–82, 177, 195, 196, 197

Schumpeter, Joseph, 236

Schwartz, Anna J., 5, 31, 36

Scorecard, 80, 200, 201

Secretary of the Treasury, 42, 47

Securities and Exchange Commission, 28, 30, 193

Securitization, 33

Seignorage, 148, 214

Sen, Amartya, 228

Sequestration, 57, 76–79, 180

Service exports, 205–6, 239, 240

Setting National Priorities: The 2000 Election and Beyond (Aaron, Gale and Sly), 22–23

Shapiro, Carl, 236

Shull, Bernard, 41

Shuster, Bud, 172

Simons, Henry, 18–19

Slemrod, Joel, 20, 21–22

Sly, James, 22–23

Smetters, Kent, 66–67

Smith, Adam, 3, 223–24, 225, 226, 234

Social Choice and Individual Values (Arrow), 232

Social good, 126. *See also* Public good

Social imbalance, 5

Social investment, 170, 183

Socialism, 230

Social marginal benefits, 227

Social marginal costs, 227

Social policy, 183

Social rate of return, 67

Social Security, 183–88; Budget Summary FY 2001, 144; debt, 157; discounting, 66–67; electronic payments, 96; entitlements, 7, 63; financial audit, 103–5; fiscal policy, 201–3; growth, 113, 117, 129, 133, 139; interest, 42, 155; off-budget, 77, 182, 198; PAYGO exemption, 78; permanent laws, 76, 167; Social Security Act, 79; surplus, 9, 12, 13, 156, 194, 200, 207; trust funds, 196, 208. *See also* Entitlements; Mandatory spending

Social Security estimates, 185–86, 187, 188

Social Security reform proposals, 184, 186, 201

Social Security taxes, 129, 165, 185, 186–88, 203. *See also* Payroll taxes

Social services, 235

Social welfare, 225

Solow, Robert M., 228

Special drawing rights, 241

Spending: appropriations, 76, 90, 164; budget authority, 75, 165–66; budget resolution, 74; capital budgeting, 170–74; credit, 80; discretionary, 81–82, 180; entitlements, 94, 196–97; environmental, 227; fiscal policy, 5, 200–202; outlays, 98, 111–12, 131, 142; *Report of the President's Commission to Study Capital Budgeting*, 174–77; total government, 113, 117; Wildavsky, 224. *See also* Discretionary spending; Mandatory spending; Outlays

Spending caps, 12, 13, 63, 78, 200, 201

Spending limits, 8, 12–13, 77, 78, 87, 92, 166–68

Stability-through-inflation argument, 36

Stagflation, 7

Stan, Peter J. E., 112

Statutory debt limitation, 46

Stein, Herbert, 4–6, 23–24

Steuerle, C. Eugene, 8

Stevens, L. Nye, 68

Stewart, Jamie B., Jr., 87

Stone, Richard, 58

Strategic plans, 42, 81, 89, 94, 174

Structural deficit, 198

About the Author

ANNETTE E. MEYER retired as Associate Professor of Economics at The College of New Jersey (Trenton State College) in 1992 and more recently has been Adjunct Assistant Professor of Economics at Hunter College. In addition to the earlier edition of this book, she is the author of numerous articles.